1,000,000 Books

are available to read at

Forgotten Books

www.ForgottenBooks.com

Read online
Download PDF
Purchase in print

ISBN 978-1-5282-1004-1
PIBN 10911588

This book is a reproduction of an important historical work. Forgotten Books uses state-of-the-art technology to digitally reconstruct the work, preserving the original format whilst repairing imperfections present in the aged copy. In rare cases, an imperfection in the original, such as a blemish or missing page, may be replicated in our edition. We do, however, repair the vast majority of imperfections successfully; any imperfections that remain are intentionally left to preserve the state of such historical works.

Forgotten Books is a registered trademark of FB &c Ltd.
Copyright © 2018 FB &c Ltd.
FB &c Ltd, Dalton House, 60 Windsor Avenue, London, SW19 2RR.
Company number 08720141. Registered in England and Wales.

For support please visit www.forgottenbooks.com

1 MONTH OF FREE READING

at

www.ForgottenBooks.com

By purchasing this book you are eligible for one month membership to ForgottenBooks.com, giving you unlimited access to our entire collection of over 1,000,000 titles via our web site and mobile apps.

To claim your free month visit:

www.forgottenbooks.com/free911588

* Offer is valid for 45 days from date of purchase. Terms and conditions apply.

English
Français
Deutsche
Italiano
Español
Português

www.forgottenbooks.com

Mythology Photography **Fiction**
Fishing Christianity **Art** Cooking
Essays **Buddhism** Freemasonry
Medicine **Biology** Music **Ancient Egypt** Evolution Carpentry Physics
Dance Geology **Mathematics** Fitness
Shakespeare **Folklore** Yoga Marketing
Confidence Immortality Biographies
Poetry **Psychology** Witchcraft
Electronics Chemistry History **Law**
Accounting **Philosophy** Anthropology
Alchemy Drama Quantum Mechanics
Atheism Sexual Health **Ancient History**
Entrepreneurship Languages Sport
Paleontology Needlework Islam
Metaphysics Investment Archaeology
Parenting Statistics Criminology
Motivational

THE RECORD SOCIETY

FOR THE

Publication of Original Documents

RELATING TO

LANCASHIRE AND CHESHIRE.

VOLUME LI.

1906.

COUNCIL, 1904-5.

Sir GEORGE J. ARMYTAGE, Bart., F.S.A., Kirklees Park, Brighouse, *President*.

G. E. COKAYNE, M.A., F.S.A., Clarenceux King of Arms, Heralds' College, London, E.C., *Vice-President*.

Lieut.-Col. HENRY FISHWICK, F.S.A., The Heights, Rochdale, *Vice-President*.

JOHN PAUL RYLANDS, F.S.A., 2 Charlesville, Birkenhead, *Vice-President*.

HENRY BRIERLEY, Mab's Cross, Wigan.

THOMAS H. DAVIES-COLLEY, M.A., Newbold, near Chester.

WILLIAM FARRER, Hall Garth, Carnforth.

Colonel PARKER, Browsholme, Clitheroe.

R. D. RADCLIFFE, M.A., F.S.A., Old Swan, Liverpool.

The Rev. Canon STANNING, M.A., The Vicarage, Leigh, Lancashire.

CHARLES W. SUTTON, M.A., Free Reference Library, Manchester.

WM. ASHETON TONGE, Staneclyffe, Disley.

HONORARY TREASURER.

JOHN PAUL RYLANDS, F.S.A., 2 Charlesville, Birkenhead.

HONORARY SECRETARY.

WM. FERGUSSON IRVINE, F.S.A., 56 Park Road South, Birkenhead.

The Rolls of the Freemen
OF THE
City of Chester.

PART I.

1392–1700.

TRANSCRIBED AND EDITED BY

J. H. E. BENNETT.

PRINTED FOR

THE RECORD SOCIETY.

1906.

**STANFORD UNIVERSITY
LIBRARIES**

STACKS

INTRODUCTION

THE extensive rights and privileges enjoyed in the past by the Freemen of Chester have been so fully treated in Canon Morris's "Chester in the Plantagenet and Tudor Reigns," that it is unnecessary to dwell on them here, and the following notes deal chiefly with the manuscripts from which this register of the Chester Freemen has been compiled. While it is a matter for regret that a complete record is not to be obtained, there is cause for congratulation that so much has been preserved, taking into consideration the vicissitudes through which the Corporation MSS. have passed.

In the Muniment Room of the Town Hall is a veritable gold mine of information respecting the city's past, contained in numerous series of manuscripts, and among these are:—

1. Mayors' Year-Books.
2. Rolls of the Freemen.

The first mentioned of these consist of an imposing number of dark, stained, parchment-covered volumes, measuring 13 inches by 8 inches, and of varying thickness. Each contains references to matters presided over by the Mayor of the year, and the following list may be taken as an indication of the information to be found in each:—

1. List of city officers.
2. List of aldermen.
3. List of common councillors, &c.
4. Oath of leave-lookers.
5. List of butchers.
6. Oath of butchers.
7. List of bakers.
8. Oath of bakers.
9. Portmote Court cases.
10. Crownmote Court cases.
11. Sessions Court cases.
12. Admissions of freemen.

This, however, must not be taken as an invariable rule, as frequently some of these sections are not to be found in the books, and sometimes additional matter is included, such as:—

INTRODUCTION

1. Particulars of the distribution of the city charities, special prominence being given to that founded by Valentine Broughton.
2. Copies of various petitions, &c.
3. List of packets of letters passing to and from Ireland, &c.

It was the custom for the Mayor of Chester to enter upon his office on the Friday following the Feast of S. Denis, and the mayoral year began and ended on that day [Chester Corporation MSS. 8th Rep. Hist. Com., p. 367], so that, generally speaking, the dates of the entries in these books commence and terminate with the mayoral years, but there are a number of exceptions in which earlier and later dates are included. The pages are of the rough paper known as "pott," with various water-marks, and are, with the covers, in all stages of preservation; some being practically perfect, while others are represented by a few thin strips of paper with the edges rotted away, for although these manuscripts, with the other contents of the Muniment Room, are well and safely housed now, they have passed through many dangers of fire, of water, with its insidious attendant damp, and of the ravages of vermin, &c. In the seventeenth century they were examined by the second Randle Holme, and in the Harleian Collection [MS. 2056, fol. 1 b] are his remarks on their very unsatisfactory condition. In his day they would doubtless be stored at the Old Pentice Hall, situated in front of S. Peter's Church, and facing Bridge Street. On the erection of the Exchange in the present Market Square they were probably removed to that building, and remained there until its destruction by fire on the 30th December 1865, when they sustained considerable damage. The collections were then stored for a number of years in the old City Gaol, and while in this place were seriously injured by damp. Subsequently, in 1878, the manuscripts were transferred to a strong-room in the Town Hall; but their wanderings were not yet finished, as sundry alterations being made after the fire of a few years ago, a fresh strong-room was built, into which they were finally transferred, and are now preserved.

Near to the volumes of Mayors' Books are a number of paper-covered parcels, which contain fragments of Mayors' and Sheriffs' Books, in too fragile or dilapidated a condition to be placed with those previously mentioned.

The handwriting in the books varies from a beautiful Court style to a debased and abbreviated scribble. The best examples are to be found up to the year 1600, or thereabout, thanks to the careful and beautiful hand taught in the monastery cloisters. Afterwards there is a great falling off, due to the death of the priestly taught scribes, and to their places being filled by men who had picked up the art as best they could. About 1700 there is a marked improvement, and a very neat round chancery style fills the volumes for a number of years, until finally replaced by a sloping and cursive style similar to that now in use.

The ink used in the early books, and, indeed, as far as late in the eighteenth century, is, in most instances, still clear where the volume has met with average treatment. It forcibly contrasts with the fluid in use about 1800 and later, as the entries about this period have become very much faded wherever there has been any suspicion of damp, and consequently portions of some of them are illegible.

In the Eighth Report made by the Commissioners on Historical MSS., p. 366, a list is given of Mayors' Books said to be existing at the time of the making of the report, but this is inaccurate, as not only are a number of existing books not included in it, but also a number said to be existing are not now to be found.

From these Mayors' Books most valuable information concerning the parentage of the Freeman, the date of his admission, the name and trade of his master in cases where the admission was based on apprenticeship, the amount paid by the Freeman for the privileges attached to the enfranchisement, the place of the father's residence, whether the parent or master was dead, and other particulars are to be obtained. The details, however, vary very much, and, in some cases, as much information is obtainable from the Rolls of the Freemen hereafter described.

The oath at the present time taken by candidates for admission runs as follows :—

FREEMEN'S OATH.

" I do declare that I will be faithful, profitable, and
" true to the King of Great Britain, and to the Common-
" alty of the City of Chester, and truly the franchises of
" Chester maintain, and be not assenting nor abetting to
" any confederacy nor conspiracy against the City nor my
" neighbours."

This has probably been the form used for a long period.

The following are examples of the headings of the sections devoted to the admissions of freemen, and also of admissions themselves :—

HEADINGS.

" Isti quorum Noia subleguntur Intrauerunt
" ffraunchesias et libertates Civitatis Cestr. hoc Anno."

"Nomina eorum qui admissi fuerunt in
"ffraunchess' et libtat. Civitatis Cestr.
"tempore Maioralitatis Philippi Phillipps
"maioris eiusdem Civitatis incept.
"decimo die mensis Octobris Anno Dñi 1606
"et continuat. in Anū Dñi 1607."

ADMISSIONS.

"HENRICUS CHALNER.

"Memorand qd. decimo octavo die Novembris Anno regni
"Regis Henrici Septimi post conquestū Anglie decimo
"septimo Henricus Chalner weĺ p Radum Davenporte
"maiorem civitat. Cestr. admissus fuit ad libtat. et fraun-
"chesias Civitat. Cestr. ħend. et optinend. Et dat de fine
"xxvj^s viij^d videlt p^{i}mam vj^s viij^d Et residuum infra tres
"annos tūc px. sequent. videlt ad festā Sc̄i Michis Archi
"quolibet anno vj^s viij^d p ptm Nichi" ["Henrici" crossed
out] "ffraunces merc̄ Nichi Newhouse gloĺ David. Robyn-
"son Sherman et Robti Heghfeld pvis. semp qd. si contingat
"p̄d Henricus moram seu residentiam suam ex't Cite.
"Cestr. et fraunchēs ejusd face^9 qd. tūc p̄sens admissio
"p nullo ħeat."

"M. qd xxviij die Januarij" [anno regni reginae Elizabethae
&c. vicesimo quinto] "Willm̄s Lea shomaker filius Wiħmi
"Lea de Cits. Cestr. shomaker admissus et jurat. est
"in franch et libtatẹ de pd." [Civitatis &c.] "ħend et
"gaudend. &c."

"RIC̄US PEMBERTON, shoomaker.
"Memorandum qd. vicesimo sexto die mensis Januarij Anno
"Regni Dñi nr̄i Jacobi dei gr̄a regis nunc Anglie ffrauncie
"et Hibnie quarto et Scocie quadragesimo Ricardus Pem-
"berton nup apprenticius Ricardo Lingley nup de Civitate
"Cestr. shoomaker defunct. sup visum Indentur. sue admiss's
"et Jurat. fuit p Philippum Phillipps Maiorem Civitatis Cestr.
"p'dce in fraunches's et libtat. eiusdem Civītis Ħend sibi
"sub Condicone p^{o}dc̄a Et dedit p ingr̄u suo xx^s fecitque
"Solucōem inde thesaurar. Civītis p̄dce Protulitque falcem
"et galeam que Jur̄ esse sua ppria semp futuro parat.
"Serviendum p Civile quoties opus et usus postulent aut
"alia &c."

In the later years the forms are much abbreviated. From 1694 to 1805 and after, the left-hand margin of a number of pages in the books are embossed with stamps of values ranging from 1s. in 1694 to 20s. in 1805, and against each of these is the entry of a Freeman's admission.

INTRODUCTION

The earliest of the Mayors' Books existing is a fragment of one for 1392 containing a few Freemen admissions. Frequently, although a Mayor's Book is extant, no Freemen enrolments are to be found in it, due in some instances to the last portion of the book, in which place these admissions were almost invariably entered, being lost. In other cases the book is complete, and therefore the only conclusion to be arrived at is that the entries were made elsewhere.

With these Mayors' Books are two rough note-books; they are long and narrow, and contain similar information for a number of years between 1600 and 1625. These books are in fair condition, but require very careful examination as Portmote, Crown-mote, Freemen admissions, &c., are not entered in separate portions of the book, evidently each case having been noted as it arose. To add to the difficulty the handwriting is generally bad, and, as many of the entries are very brief, it is rather doubtful sometimes to what section they belong. A check has, however, been possible in a number of the early years for which there are also Mayors' Books.

The second source of information respecting the Freemen is contained in a small paper parcel in which are thirteen rolls of parchment, averaging from 4 to $5\frac{1}{2}$ inches in width, and extending to a great length. In one of the rolls are particulars of certain disbursements, &c., and this is not of any particular interest here; but the remaining twelve, which are the Rolls of the Freemen, are of great importance, and are in very good condition, although the ends of one or two are torn and a few of the entries missing. These spaces have, however, been filled in by comparison with the admissions in the Mayors' Books. The following shows the periods covered by the twelve Rolls:—

1. 1538–1612.
2. 1636–1658.
3. 1658–1679.
4. 1679–1704.
5. 1704–1717.
6. 1717–1721.
7. 1721–1732.
8. 1732–1741.
9. 1741–1755.
10. 1755–1774.
11. 1774–1787.
12. 1787–1805.

A later roll exists which carries the admissions forward to 1884. There is now, unfortunately, no roll to cover the period from 1612 to 1635, and this was probably lost in the confusion which followed the Civil War. At the commencement of the last century there existed a roll which carried the list of Freemen back for a considerable period prior to 1538, but this valuable

INTRODUCTION

manuscript is not now to be found, and is supposed to have been lost or destroyed when the Old Exchange was burnt down.[1]

The Rolls, which are divided up into the mayoral years of office, give the name and, in most cases, the occupation of the Freemen. The latter information, however, is not always to be relied upon, as in frequent cases, where freedom has been taken up by right of birth, it has been found, on comparing the entry on the roll with that in the Mayor's Book, that the father's occupation has been placed against the Freeman's name, although there is no proof that the latter followed it. In a few isolated cases the Freeman's father is given on the roll, and, from 24th December 1685 until 4th November 1693, the date of admission is given.

The following are two examples of the headings of the various years:—

"Thomas Harv'
"Mayor Civitatis Cestriae
"Anno Regni Regis Jacobi
"Angliae nunc &c. octavo
"Scocie quadragesimo [quarto].

and:—

"In the tyme of Thomas
"Hand Esquire Maior
"of the Cittie of
"Chester 1658-9.

On the first Roll the numerical year dates have been inserted from 1574 to 1611 at a date subsequent to that on which the admissions themselves were inscribed, but they are inaccurate up to 1600, being in each case a year out. Against the year of office of Sir John Savage, the date 1573 has been placed, evidently with the intention of intimating that his year of office commenced in that year, although he was actually elected mayor in 1574, and from this the error runs until the mayoralty of John Ratcliffe, which is correctly shown as commencing in 1601. It has been brought about by the mayoralties of Robert Brerewood and Richard Bavand being shown as two complete years, although both held office in the same year:—October 1600 to October 1601—the former having died in his term, and being succeeded by the latter for the unexpired portion.

A third source of information has been the list of Freemen admissions for 1505-6 preserved among the Harleian MSS.[2]

From these manuscripts it has been possible to compile a most

---

[1] Cheshire Sheaf, 1st series, i. p. 341.
[2] 2105, fol. 262 *b*, *et seq.*

valuable record of Chester citizens. The record, as stated, commences in 1392, 150 years before the Act was passed requiring incumbents to keep parish registers, and nearly 200 years before the majority of them paid any serious attention to carrying out the regulation. Unfortunately, from 1392 to 1550 records are only extant for sixty years, the total number of admissions in these years being 972.

Further information might have been obtained of those Freemen who were admitted by Order of Assembly, from an examination of the Assembly books, but time has prevented the necessary search being made.[1]

With the exception of the entries in a few Mayors' Books, which it was not found practicable to go through a second time, the whole of the admissions on the Rolls and in the Mayors' Books have been checked. The books which have not been checked are as under:—

1628–9
1676–7
1784–6.

Admission to the freedom of the city was, and still is, obtained in the three following ways, viz.:—

1. Birth. The father must, in this case, have been a freeman of the city. It was not therefore necessary for the candidate to have served as apprentice either here or elsewhere. This is now somewhat modified, as direct male descent from a freeman who was admitted prior to the passing of the Municipal Act in 1835 (at which time the privileges were much curtailed) has now to be proved.
2. Indenture of apprenticeship.
3. Order of Assembly. This method was resorted to when it was considered that the prosperity of the city would be increased by admitting a tradesman who was eligible neither by birth nor by apprenticeship, but who had perhaps better or more up-to-date methods of following his calling than those at the time in use in the city. This means was also adopted when honorary admissions were granted.

There are numerous instances in which single entries are not to be found in the Mayors' Books, and others again are not to be

[1] Since this volume has been set up in type, but before going to press, Mr. Fergusson Irvine has discovered that information, somewhat similar to what is contained in the Mayors' Books, is to be found in the incomplete series of Treasurers' Accounts.

INTRODUCTION

found in the Rolls, but attention is called to these as they occur. In many cases where the Rolls are missing, and where the Mayors' Books consist of a few loose sheets, although no remark is made, it is quite possible that the record is incomplete, additional sheets having been lost.

The appended table shows the number of existing enrolments in each mayoral year from A.D. 1392 to 1805 and also the periods for which no such information has been obtainable. The figures are shown in three columns:—

Column 1. Number of entries for which there are both Rolls and Mayors' Books.
    ,,   2. Number of entries for which there are Mayors' Books only.
    ,,   3. Number of entries for which there are Rolls only.

Year	1	2	3	Year	1	2	3
1392–1393	–	3	–	1426–1427	–	–	–
3– 4	–	–	–	7– 8	–	–	–
4– 5	–	–	–	8– 9	–	–	–
5– 6	–	–	–	9– 30	–	–	–
6– 7	–	–	–	30– 1	–	–	–
7– 8	–	9	–	1– 2	–	–	–
8– 9	–	–	–	2– 3	–	5 §	–
9–1400	–	–	–	3– 4	–	–	–
1400– 1	–	–	–	4– 5	–	–	–
1– 2	–	21 §	–	5– 6	–	–	–
2– 3	–	–	–	6– 7	–	–	–
3– 4	–	–	–	7– 8	–	–	–
4– 5	–	6 §	–	8– 9	–	–	–
5– 6	–	–	–	9– 40	–	–	–
6– 7	–	–	–	40– 1	–	–	–
7– 8	–	–	–	1– 2	–	–	–
8– 9	–	–	–	2– 3	–	–	–
9– 10	–	4	–	3– 4	–	–	–
10– 1	–	–	–	4– 5	–	–	–
1– 2	–	–	–	5– 6	–	–	–
2– 3	–	–	–	6– 7	–	–	–
3– 4	–	–	–	7– 8	–	–	–
4– 5	–	8 §	–	8– 9	–	–	–
5– 6	–	–	–	9– 50	–	–	–
6– 7	–	–	–	50– 1	–	–	–
7– 8	–	–	–	1– 2	–	–	–
8– 9	–	19 §	–	2– 3	–	9	–
9– 20	–	13	–	3– 4	–	–	–
20– 1	–	–	–	4– 5	–	14	–
1– 2	–	–	–	5– 6	–	–	–
2– 3	–	–	–	6– 7	–	–	–
3– 4	–	–	–	7– 8	–	–	–
4– 5	–	–	–	8– 9	–	12	–
5– 6	–	–	–	9– 60	–	13	–

INTRODUCTION

	1	2	3		1	2
1460–1461	–	–	–	1515–1516	–	–
1– 2	–	–	–	6– 7	–	–
2– 3	–	11	–	7– 8	–	–
3– 4	–	8	–	8– 9	–	–
4– 5	–	–	–	9– 20	–	–
5– 6	–	–	–	20– 1	–	15
6– 7	–	8	–	1– 2	–	–
7– 8	–	–	–	2– 3	–	20
8– 9	–	–	–	3– 4	–	–
9– 70	–	5	–	4– 5	–	–
70– 1	..	10	–	5– 6	–	–
1– 2	–	–	–	6– 7	–	18
2– 3	–	–	–	7– 8	–	25
3– 4	–	–	–	8– 9	–	–
4– 5	–	46	–	9– 30	–	–
5– 6	–	–	..	30– 1	–	26
6– 7	–	7	–	1– 2	–	20
7– 8	–	–	–	2– 3	–	29
8– 9	–	–	–	3– 4	–	24
9– 80	–	–	–	4– 5	–	–
80– 1	–	–	–	5– 6	–	–
1– 2	–	–	–	6– 7	–	27
2– 3	–	–	–	7– 8	–	21
3– 4	–	16	–	8– 9	20	–
4– 5	–	22	–	9– 40	–	–
5– 6	–	–	–	40– 1	13	–
6– 7	–	–	–	1– 2	19	–
7– 8	–	22	–	2– 3	15	–
8– 9	–	8	–	3– 4	21	–
9– 90	–	–	–	4– 5	7	–
90– 1	–	2	–	5– 6	–	–	1
1– 2	–	–	–	6– 7	32	–
2– 3	–	9	–	7– 8	31	–
3– 4	–	11	–	8– 9	–	–
4– 5	–	–	–	9– 50	23 §	–
5– 6	–	16	–	50– 1	18	–
6– 7	–	18	–	1– 2	35	–
7– 8	–	–	–	2– 3	19	–
8– 9	–	1	–	3– 4	–	–	1
9–1500	–	9	–	4– 5	33	–
1500– 1	–	21	–	5– 6	56	–
1– 2	–	4	–	6– 7	–	–	2
2– 3	–	–	–	7– 8	–	–	4
3– 4	–	–	–	8– 9	35	–
4– 5	–	19	–	9– 60	–	–	2
5– 6	–	23	–	60– 1	–	–	3
6– 7	–	25	–	1– 2	–	–	2
7– 8	–	20	–	2– 3	–	–	1
8– 9	–	–	–	3– 4	16	–
9– 10	–	–	–	4– 5	–	–	1
10– 1	–	35	–	5– 6	–	–	2
1– 2	–	–	–	6– 7	–	–	2
2– 3	–	–	–	7– 8	31	–
3– 4	–	–	–	8– 9	–	–	2
4– 5	–	–	–	9– 70	33	–

xiv INTRODUCTION

Year	1	2	3	Year	1	2	3
1570–1571	26	–	–	1623–1624	–	28	–
1– 2	23	–	–	4– 5	–	53	–
2– 3	–	–	28	5– 6	–	61	–
3– 4	86	–	–	6– 7	–	–	–
4– 5	–	–	11	7– 8	–	44	–
5– 6	32	–	–	8– 9	–	46	–
6– 7	–	–	21	9– 30	–	–	–
7– 8	–	–	44	30– 1	–	–	–
8– 9	–	–	33	1– 2	–	–	–
9– 80	28	–	–	2– 3	–	–	–
80– 1	–	–	38	3– 4	–	–	–
1– 2	–	–	66	4– 5	–	47	–
2– 3	34	–	–	5– 6	–	–	46 ¶
3– 4	35	–	–	6– 7	47	–	–
4– 5	53	–	–	7– 8	–	–	39
5– 6	–	–	34	8– 9	–	–	51
6– 7	–	–	34	9– 40	–	–	48
7– 8	38	–	–	40– 1	–	–	44
8– 9	32	–	–	1– 2	–	–	39
9– 90	27	–	–	2– 3	–	–	28
90– 1	28	–	–	3– 4	–	–	29
1– 2	43	–	–	4– 5	–	–	12
2– 3	34	–	–	5– 6 [1]	–	–	–
3– 4	–	–	29	6– 7	–	–	55
4– 5	31 §	–	–	7– 8	67	–	–
5– 6	56	–	–	8– 9	–	–	27
6– 7	39	–	–	9– 50	23	–	–
7– 8	44	–	–	50– 1	–	–	52
8– 9	41	–	–	1– 2	49	–	–
9–1600	39	–	–	2– 3	–	–	37
1600– 1	–	–	46	3– 4	41	–	–
1– 2	–	–	73	4– 5	–	–	54
2– 3	–	–	31	5– 6	–	–	27
3– 4	–	–	21	6– 7	–	–	45
4– 5	52	–	–	7– 8	–	–	43
5– 6	65	–	–	8– 9	–	–	40
6– 7	40	–	–	9– 60	–	–	48
7– 8	36	–	–	60– 1	45	–	–
8– 9	30 §	–	–	1– 2	47	–	–
9– 10	–	–	38	2– 3	–	–	48
10– 1	37 §	–	–	3– 4	42	–	–
1– 2	–	–	37	4– 5	–	–	43
2– 3	–	31	–	5– 6	36	–	–
3– 4	–	40	–	6– 7	31	–	–
4– 5	–	51	–	7– 8	56 §	–	–
5– 6	–	45	–	8– 9	–	–	42
6– 7	–	–	–	9– 70	–	–	27
7– 8	–	–	–	70– 1	46	–	–
8– 9	–	–	–	1– 2	40	–	–
9– 20	–	29	–	2– 3	71	–	–
20– 1	–	23	–	3– 4	–	–	32
1– 2	–	34	–	4– 5	–	–	55
2– 3	–	40	–	5– 6	–	–	29

[1] No election of city officers in this year.

INTRODUCTION

			1	**2**	**3**				**1**	**2**	**3**
1676–1677		. .	40	–	–	1731–1732		. .	648 §	–	–
7–	8	. .	47	–	–	2–	3	. .	113	–	–
8–	9	. .	–	–	125	3–	4	. .	44 §	–	–
9–	80	. .	28	–	–	4–	5	. .	14 §	–	–
80–	1	. .	–	–	56	5–	6	. .	25	–	–
1–	2	. .	–	–	27	6–	7	. .	39 §	–	–
2–	3	. .	–	–	33	7–	8	. .	41 §	–	–
3–	4	. .	–	–	8	8–	9	. .	15	–	–
4–	5	. .	–	–	40	9–	40	. .	23	–	–
5–	6	. .	–	–	45	40–	1	. .	21 §	–	–
6–	7	. .	–	–	41	1–	2	. .	35 §	–	–
7–	8	. .	–	–	53	2–	3	. .	24	–	–
8–	9	. .	85	–	–	3–	4	. .	63	–	–
9–	90	. .	152	–	–	4–	5	. .	30	–	–
90–	1	. .	30	–	–	5–	6	. .	28	–	–
1–	2	. .	12	–	–	6–	7	. .	412	–	–
2–	3	. .	41	–	–	7–	8	. .	20	–	–
3–	4	. .	37	–	–	8–	9	. .	15	–	–
4–	5	. .	42	–	–	9–	50	. .	19	–	–
5–	6	. .	49	–	–	50–	1	. .	15	–	–
6–	7	. .	144	–	–	1–	2	. .	31	–	–
7–	8	. .	49	–	–	2–	3	. .	30	–	–
8–	9	. .	27	–	–	3–	4	. .	26	–	–
9–	1700	. .	28	–	–	4–	5	. .	85	–	–
1700–	1	. .	38	–	–	5–	6	. .	32	–	–
1–	2	. .	52	–	–	6–	7	. .	32	–	–
2–	3	. .	65	–	–	7–	8	. .	26	–	–
3–	4	. .	28	–	–	8–	9	. .	54	–	–
4–	5	. .	86 §	–	–	9–	60	. .	17	–	–
5–	6	. .	57	–	–	60–	1	. .	19	–	–
6–	7	. .	35	–	–	1–	2	. .	45	–	–
7–	8	. .	120	–	–	2–	3	. .	22	–	–
8–	9	. .	42	–	–	3–	4	. .	13	–	–
9–	10	. .	35	–	–	4–	5	. .	18	–	–
10–	1	. .	51	–	–	5–	6	. .	27	–	–
1–	2	. .	33	–	–	6–	7	. .	15	–	–
2–	3	. .	31	–	–	7–	8	. .	188	–	–
3–	4	. .	46	–	–	8–	9	. .	38	–	–
4–	5	. .	69	–	–	9–	70	. .	53	–	–
5–	6	. .	35	–	–	70–	1	. .	16	–	–
6–	7	. .	32	–	–	1–	2	. .	61	–	–
7–	8	. .	28 §	–	–	2–	3	. .	27	–	–
8–	9	. .	33	–	–	3–	4	. .	12	–	–
9–	20	. .	68 §	–	–	4–	5	. .	51	–	–
20–	1	. .	515 §	–	–	5–	6	. .	37	–	–
1–	2	. .	95	–	–	6–	7	. .	68	–	–
2–	3	. .	17	–	–	7–	8	. .	32	–	–
3–	4	. .	28	–	–	8–	9	. .	35	–	–
4–	5	. .	32	–	–	9–	80	. .	19	–	–
5–	6	. .	37	–	–	80–	1	. .	27	–	–
6–	7	. .	47 §	–	–	1–	2	. .	22	–	–
7–	8	. .	30 §	–	–	2–	3	. .	29	–	–
8–	9	. .	16	–	–	3–	4	. .	462	–	–
9–	30	. .	34	–	–	4–	5	. .	7	–	–
30–	1	. .	35	–	–	5–	6	. .	17	–	–

		1	2	3			1	2	3
1786–1787	. .	27	–	–	1797–1798	. .	21	–	–
7– 8	. .	21	–	–	8– 9	. .	52	–	–
8– 9	. .	21	–	–	9–1800	. .	31	–	–
9– 90	. .	26	–	–	1800– 1	. .	29	–	–
90– 1	. .	31	–	–	1– 2	. .	91	–	–
1– 2	. .	36	–	–	2– 3	. .	20	–	–
2– 3	. .	29	–	–	3– 4	. .	19	–.	–
3– 4	. .	24	–	–	4– 5	. .	14	–	–
4– 5	. .	53	–	–			8743	1309	2374
5– 6	. .	20	–	–					
6– 7	. .	33	–	–					

The grand total of the admissions is therefore 12,426 for 305 years, although the period covered from the earliest admission to the latest is 413. This gives 108 years as the period for which records do not exist. The average yearly admissions, based on the existing entries, are given hereunder:—

Period.	No. of Years for which Records exist.	Number of Admissions.	Average Annual Number of Admissions.
1392–1400	2	12	6
1400–1450	7	76	10.8
1450–1500	22	277	12.5
1500–1550	29	607	20.9
1550–1600	50	1651	33.0
1600–1650	40	1633	40.8
1650–1700	50	2365	47.3
1700–1750	50	3499	69.9
1750–1800	50	2133	42.6
1800–1805	5	173	34.6

The rise and fall in the number of admissions is clearly shown, although the fact that so many of the early Records are missing must be taken into account. It is very noticeable that from the latter end of the seventeenth century there is periodically a year in which the number of admissions is far above the normal number, and in one year, 1731–2, the great total of 648 is reached. Probably strongly contested elections took place in these heavy years, and efforts were made to enrol every man eligible for admission, many from distant parts of the country being included.

The transcription of the Records of the Freemen of Chester was commenced more than four years ago, and my intention at the time was simply to make copies of the Rolls. This work was not one of very great magnitude, and as it approached completion the result seemed of such small value, when compared with the information lying dormant in the Mayors' Books, that I decided to collate the entries in those volumes with my transcripts of the

Rolls, and include the additional details. A start was made at the earliest moment, but progress has been slow, as the work could only be continued in the daytime, and the time at my disposal has been limited.

I am greatly indebted to the Mayor and Corporation of Chester, the Town Clerk, and other officials with whom I have come in contact, especially Mr. Peers, and his assistants, Messrs. Davies and Johnson, for the facilities granted, and for the unvarying courtesy which I received at the Town Hall. I am also indebted to Mr. G. P. Gamon for kindly copying a manuscript in the Harleian Collection, as well as for other assistance, and to those who have given me their services in what was, I am afraid, the rather tedious work of checking. Lastly, my thanks are tendered to Mr. W. Fergusson Irvine for the most valuable help he has given me whenever appealed to, and, I may say, it is to him that the elucidation of many a puzzling and faintly visible contraction is due.

J. H. E. BENNETT.

CHESTER,
January 1906.

NOTES

The entries after 1600 have been condensed as far as possible; the surname of the freeman has been omitted wherever practicable when the father's has been given, and the trade of the freeman has also been omitted when this has corresponded with the master's.

Most of the various Records are written in Latin, but the names, &c., have been Anglicised for the sake of convenience and uniformity. As, however, some of the names bear two translations, a list is given below of a few Latin names, &c., together with the translation adopted.

Agricola	husbandman.
Xpoferus	Christopher.
Egidius	Giles.
Eliceus	Ellis.
Forensicus	foreigner.
Fulcus	Foulk.
Galfridus	Geoffrey.
Jacobus	James.
Josua or Joshua	Joshua.
Lodovicus	Lewis.
Radulphus	Ralph.
Ranulphus	Randle.
Riceus	Rice.
Silvanus	Silvan..

ABBREVIATIONS, ETC.

s.	son.
ss.	sons.
s. and h.	son and heir.
p.	apprentice.
pp.	apprentices.
B	Freedom taken up by right of birth.
I	Freedom taken up by right of indenture.
M.B.	Mayor's Book.
*	Freedom granted by Order of Assembly.
†	No Mayor's Book entry found. [Used only in single instances.]
‡	No Roll entry found. [Used only in single instances.]
§	Mayor's Book incomplete.
¶	Roll incomplete.

The Rolls of the Freemen of the City of Chester.

1392-3 [16-17 R. ii.] GILBERT TRUSSELL, Mayor.

—— — John Tayte.
— — Hugh de Prestecote [Prescot], flechier.
— — William de Laghok, late of Speek [Speke].

1397-8 [21-22 R. ii.] JOHN DE CAPENHURST, Mayor.

Oct. 18 John de Wilberfoce, spycer.
Dec. 3 Edward Halkyn, tailor.
 „ 3 John Syme, tailor.
 „ 4 Maurice s. of Stephen the Clerk.
— — William Mody, tailor.
— — John Blound, " portor de ——"
— — John Derlington.
—— ———
— — —— Barton, glover.

*1401-2 [3-4 H. iv.] JOHN DE BEBINGTON [died, JOHN MARESCHAL succ.], Mayor[s].

Nov. 20 John s. of John Bolde, sherman.
Dec. 5 Roger de Penwortham, mercer.
—— — John s. of Henry de Byrchenshagh.
—— — Robert the Heuster, shipmon.
—— — Nicholas Hunt, tailor.
—— — Walter de Radford, goldsmith.
—— — John de Heley of Flynt.
—— — William s. of Robert de Croxton, flesher.

* Ten entries at the commencement of this year, and three at the end of it are undecipherable.

2   THE ROLLS OF THE FREEMEN OF   [1404–19

*1404–5 [6–7 H. iv.] JOHN DE PRESTON, Mayor.

——— —   ——— Wyrvyn of Wyco Malby [Nantwich]. [Nicholas de Wyrvyn, a guarantor.]
—   ———   ——— of S. Johns Lone [Lane].

* One entry at the commencement of this year, and three at the end of it are undecipherable.

1409–10 [11–12 H. iv.] [JOHN DE EWLOWE, removed, JOHN DE PRESTON, locum tenens, Mayors, succ. by] WILLIAM DE BRERTON, Governor.

——— —   ——— ———
—   Thomas s. of [Adam ?] Hunte of Rudheath.
——— —   ——— ———
—   ———   ——— of co. Lanc., fletcher.

*1414–5 [2–3 H. v.] JOHN WHYTEMORE, Mayor.

——— —   ——— s. of William de Derby of Salop, and Elizabeth his wife.
—   Roger s. of Roger de Draycote.
—   Robert s. of William de Wesshynton, saddler.

* First four and sixth entries undecipherable.

1418–9 [6–7 H. v.] WILLIAM DE HAWARDEN, Mayor.

——— —   ——— s. of Richard Hyklyng of Couyntrie [Coventry], mercer.
—   ——— ———, skinner, brother of David the Skinner.
—   Robert s. of William Wodward of Honston.
—   Richard [Hull ?], weaver.
—   John [Walsh ?] the stringer.
—   ——— Jonson, corviser.
Mar. 26   John Gyne, glover.
„   26   John Minor.
Aug.   8   Richard Culmer, cooper.
——— —   John s. of Henry the [portor ?].
—   William Preston of Droghda.
—   ——— ———, furbur.
—   ———   ——— — of John del Hey of Chester.
—   Henry s. of Richard Gaunt of Willaston, husbandman.
—   ——— s. of Nicholas Fyton of Chester, butcher.

1419-53] THE CITY OF CHESTER 3

— —— [Gyddinges?] of Chester.
— John s. of Henry de Bebynton.
— Ellis del Wade.
— William s. of John Rogerson of Hawardyn.

1419-20 [7-8 H. v.] JOHN HOPE, Mayor.

— — —— s. of Thomas Pylkynton of Haleton.
— —— s. of John Percyvale of Frodesham.
— Henry s. of Thomas Botyler, baker.
— William Lyalton of Chester, baker.
Feb. 25 William s. of Robert s. of Hugh de Prestaton of Chester, shipman.
„ 25 Robert de Wenseley of York, bowier.
Mar. 22 David Dewe of Nantwich, co. Ches.
Apr. 1 Robert [Vrane?] of Ireland.
—— —— Roger Gill, baker.
— —— ——, ——.
— —— Gregory of Chester, barber, late "mañ oñ" [servant of] John de Chambre.
— John the barber, s. of Geoffrey of Welley.
— John s. of Roger [Shermon?] of Chester.

*1432-3 [11-12 H. vi.] RICHARD MASSEY, Mayor.

May 15 Robert Stansfeld.
—— — Nicholas Stoke.
— Walter Okborne, draper, of Havyndon.
Sep. — William Meller of Chester, weaver.
—— — —— s. of Richard [Haye?] of Podyngton.

* A number of other entries undecipherable.

1452-3 [31-32 H. vi.] WILLIAM STANMERE, Mayor.

Christmas Eve . . . { Richard Caerlyle s. of Hugh Carlyle.
{ Randle Bolde s. of Richard Bolde.
M. after Feast of S. George, M. . John Barowe s. of John Barowe of Great Trogh [ford].
Tu. after F. of S. Barnabas { John Wotton s. of Thomas Wotton of Chester.
{ William Clerc s. of Thomas Clerc, vintner.

Tu. before F. of Nat. of Virg.	Thomas Marshall.
W. after F. of S. Denis	{ Thomas Bernard, mercer. { John Fregret s. of William Fregret.
F. after F. of S. Denis	Richard Sharpe, draper.

1454-5 [33-34 H. vi.] NICHOLAS DANYELL, Mayor.

F. after F. of S. Denis	Peter s. and h. of Edmund Minshull.
S. before F. of SS. Simon and Jude	Roger s. of David Hylton.
Tu. after F. of S. Martin	John Warner.
W. after F. of S. Martin	Robert Berdeshyll.
F. before F. of Epiphany	John Harper otherwise called John Hicson.
——	Ken Dye s. of Richard Dye.
M. in F. of S. Patrick	Hugh Thomasson, hardwareman.
M. before F. of Ascension	Henry Rauthwell of Chester, hewster.
M. in F. of S. Dunstan	John Newton of Chester, sherman.
W. before F. of S. Mich. Arch.	Thomas Dye s. of John Dye of Chester.
Tu. before F. of S. Denis	{ Nicholas Abbot. { Geoffrey Dunham. { John Richardson, wright.
Th. in F. of S. Denis	John Hope

1458-9 [37-38 H. vi.] NICHOLAS DANYELL, Mayor.

F. after F. of S. Denis	William Redich.
Tu. after F. of S. Leonard	Nicholas Hudde.
F. after F. of S. Martin	William Rav[en]son.
M. in F. of S. Edmund	Lawrence William, wright.
M. after F. of S. Andrew the Apostle	Robert Lyth.
W. after F. of S. Peter	Thomas Fox.
Th. after F. of S. Edith V.	{ Peter Holynshede. { John Lancaster.
Th. after F. of S. Teol [? Olave].	Henry Port.
Oct. 10	Henry Ellom.
11	Hugh Frer.
F. after F. of S. Denis	William Lee.

1459–60 [38–39 H. vi.] JOHN SOUTHWORTH, Mayor.

F. after F. of S. Denis .	John Hegynson.
Tu. before F. of All Saints.	Peter Mykelhalgh.
———.	Henry Dyke.
Concep. of Virgin . .	John Benet, [joiner ?].
Sa. before F. of Cir. of our Lord	William Morgan, capper.
F. after F. of Epiph. .	Robert Falyngbron.
W. before F. of S. Peter *in cathedra*	John Carrok s. of John Carrok.
Th. after F. of S. George	William Sylk, merchant.
M. after F. of Ascension .	David Smyth.
W. after F. of Assumption of the Virgin . .	Nicholas Ravenscroft.
W. after F. of S. Bart. .	William Rycchemond of Chester, dyer.
M. after F. of S. Denis .	Robert Neturfeld, mercer.
M. before F. of S. Denis	John Pady, barker.

1462–3 [2–3 E. iv.] ROBERT BRYNE, Mayor.

F. after F. of S. Denis .	William Snede.
M. after F. of S. Romaric	{ Robert Waley. Richard Ball. Hugh Fenton. }
M. after F. of S. Leonard	John Hog.
Tu. in F. of S. David .	John Wynsley.
W. after F. of S. Chad .	Henry Bekenshawe.
F. in F. Annunc. Virg. .	John Dycon, baxter.
M. before F. of S. Bart.	Peter Croft.
M. before F. of Exalt. of Holy Cross	Nicholas Pensell.
F. after F. of Exalt. of Holy Cross	William Godeman, "did not pay."

1463–4 [3–4 E. iv.] ROBERT ROGERSON, Mayor.

—— —	John Carlyle of Chester, ——.
Apr. 7	John Clyff.
„ 7	Richard Smyth.
„ 20	Jevan ap Gryff ap Jevan.
Oct. 10	Thomas P——, hewster.
„ 21	Roger Hurleton.
—	Ralph Froddesham.
Nov. 18	William s. of Christopher Marshall.

1466-7 [6-7 E. iv.] WILLIAM LILLY, MAYOR.

Nov. 4 Robert s. of Thomas Munkesfeld.
„ 15 Nicholas Swetnam.
Jan. 12 William Frauncys, fishmonger.
Feb. 14 John Lokley.
June 16 Richard Holynshed, glover.
Oct. 12 Roger Burgeye, carpenter.
Th. after F. of S. Denis ⎰ William Stanley of Hoton, esquire, s. and h. of William Stanley, late of Hoton, esquire.
— . . . . . ⎱ Henry Wermyncham s. of Roger Wermyncham.

1469-70 [9-10 E. iv.] THOMAS KENT, MAYOR.

—— 13 Walter ap Ythell, ——.
Oct. 26 Thomas Calye.
Dec. 21 Nicholas Hopkynson, fishmonger.
Mar. 1 John Botiler s. of John Botiler, defunct.
„ 14 Richard Pole, butcher.

1470-1 [10-11 E. iv.] THOMAS COTYNGHAM, MAYOR.

— Mathew Jonson.
Aug. 26 John s. of Thomas Her ——.
— —— Ellom.
Oct. 18 Lewis Smith, mercer.
Dec. 3 John Cholle of Chester, corviser.
„ 3 Robert Whitley, corviser.
„ 3 Henry Sexten, baker.
„ 24 Thomas ⎱
„ 24 Henry ⎰ ss. of John Fenton the elder.
May 11 Nicholas Dykyn of Chester, baker.

1474-5 [14-15 E. iv.] JOHN SOTHEWORTHE, MAYOR.

Oct. 15 David Talbot of Chester, weaver.
„ 17 Richard Hokenhull, baxter.
„ 17 Patrick Neileson, baxter.
„ 18 Richard Wilkynson, baxter.
„ 18 Richard Wright s. of John Wright.
Nov. 2 Henry Mycalhalgh.
„ 2 Thomas Wikstad.

1476–7] THE CITY OF CHESTER

Nov.	3	Richard Clyve.
,,	3	George Bulkeley.
,,	7	John Baguley, bowier.
,,	16	William ap John, tailor.
,,	16	John Hert s. of John Hert.
,,	17	Nicholas Spicer, mason.
,,	17	Edward Faryngton, saddler.
,,	17	Henry Wiksted, draper.
,,	21	John Davyson, weaver.
,,	21	John s. of Robert, bower.
,,	21	William Smyth, sailor.
,,	26	Hugh Hyne.
,,	28	Nicholas Wilkynson, sherman, *alias* Nicholas Shermon.
,,	28	Thomas Maccane, fisher.
Jan.	16	Ralph Davenport, macebearer.
,,	16	Thomas Wynstanley, barker.
,,	31	Ralph Eton s. of Robert Eton.
,,	31	Stephen Warmynsham ⎱ ss. of Roger
,,	31	James Warmynsham ⎰ Warmynsham.
,,	31	John Bithell, weaver. [Richard Bithell, a guarantor.]
Feb.	21	George Assheton.
,,	28	Thomas Barowe, mercer, s. of John Barowe the elder.
,,	28	Richard Donne, draper.
,,	28	John Barker, tailor.
Apr.	18	John Bellyn, barker.
,,	18	William Humfrey.
,,	18	William Bowell, butcher.
,,	18	Thomas Sirard, tailor.
July	10	John Merssh of Chester, corviser.
,,	10	Randle Sparowe.
,,	10	John Lowe, smith.
,,	10	John Hicok, draper.
,,	11	Thomas Hurlton s. of James Hurlton.
,,	11	Thomas Bunbury.
Aug.	1	Richard Forneby, skinner.
,,	1	William Spele, fletcher.
,,	1	Christopher Whitill, corviser.
,,	1	Richard Williams, *alias* Richard Barker, butcher.
,,	10	William Norman, pewterer.

1476–7 [16–17 E. iv.] HUGH MASSY, Mayor.

Mar.	3	John Downald.
Apr.	28	Nicholas Newhouse, glover.
,,	28	Richard Hellesby, glover.

8 THE ROLLS OF THE FREEMEN OF [1483-5

May 6 John Waley. [Robert Waley, a guarantor.]
„ 6 John Bowell, baker.
„ 13 Thomas Fichet of Chester.
Sep. 11 William Anyon, baxter.

1483-4 [1-2 R. iii.] JOHN DEDWODDE, Gentleman, Mayor.

Nov. 17 Hugh Werburton, bowier.
„ 17 Lawrence David, fletcher.
„ 17 Thomas Harrisone, baker.
„ 17 Ralph Pole.
„ 17 John Mascy s. of Richard Mascy of Chester, vintner.
Jan. 27 Edward Hoghton, draper.
„ 27 William Okeley, merchant.
„ 27 William Crew, barber.
June 13 John Tildesley } ss. of Henry Tildesley.
„ 13 William Tildesley, mercer,
„ 13 Richard Walton, mercer.
July 13 William Harresone, baker.
„ 13 George [Wombe?], baker.
„ 13 Thomas Brigges, baker.
Aug. 3 Gervase de Vuldre, *alias* Gervase de Vuldur.
„ 3 John David, fletcher, *alias* John David s. of Lawrence David, fletcher.

1484-5 [2-3 R. iii. & 1 H. vii.] Sir JOHN SAVAGE, Mayor.

Feb. 9 Nicholas Staynor, *alias* Nicholas Robicoite, " staynor."
„ 9 Thomas David, weaver.
„ 9 John Pantre.
Mar. 14 James Savage s. of Sir John Savage the elder, knight.
„ 14 Lawrence Savage s. of Sir John Savage, knight.
„ 14 William Tatton.
— Edward Savage } ss. of Sir John Savage the elder, knight.
„ 14 Christopher Savage
„ 14 Robert Wilcocke.
— George Savage }
„ 14 William Savage } ss. of Sir John Savage the elder, knight.
„ 14 Richard Savage
— Thomas Feror s. of David Feror of Chester, gentleman, and formerly mayor of the city.
— Humphrey Savage s. of Sir John Savage, knight.
— Richard Hokenhull, " ceriant " [? sergeant].
July 5 James Holynworth.

[1487–9] THE CITY OF CHESTER

July 5 James Byrome, mercer.
 ,,   5 Gitten Calnor, *alias* Gitten ——
 —   Sir John Savage the younger, knight, "p corpore dni
         Regis," s. and h. apparent of Sir John Savage
         the elder, knight, "p corpore dni Regis."
 ,, 11 Richard Oldome.
 ,, 11 John Jankynsone, weaver.
 ,, 11 John Wodwerde, *alias* John Webster, hewster.

1487–8 [3–4 H. vii.] HUGH HURLTON, Mayor.

Jan. 3 William Pantre. [John Pantre, a guarantor.]
 ,,   3 John Walshe, plymñ [? plumber].
 ,,   3 Robert Glidall.
 ,,   3 Peter Ravenscroft s. of Nicholas Ravenscroft.
 ,,   3 Patrick Raynald.
 ,, 18 Thomas Bekenshaw, tailor.
 ,, 18 Jenkin Croke. [Shown as "John Croke" in margin.]
 ,, 18 Robert Bradsha.
 ,, 18 Richard Runcorne s. of William Runcorne.
 ,, 27 Robert Knowseley.
 ,, 27 Walter Waynwrighte, *alias* Walter Anderton.
 ,, 27 John Moscrop, corviser.
 ,, 27 Thomas Robinsone, barker.
Apr. 20 Ralph Birkenhed.
 ,, 20 James Manley s. of John Manley of Pulton.
June 12 Thomas Carden s. of Richard Carden.
 ,, 12 Randle Wyrehall, baker.
Aug. 28 Thomas Bellet s. of John Bellet.
 ,, 28 Thomas Thorneton, barker.
 ,, 28 John Brodfeld, barker.
 ,, 28 Thomas Jankynson, barker.
 ,, 28 William Donald, milner, s. of Donald Walsh, baker.

1488–9 [4–5 H. vii.] GEORGE BULKELEY, Mayor.

—— — William Davy, shoemaker.
Oct. 1 William Balle, draper, s. of Henry Balle.
 ,,   1 William Swetenham, mercer, s. of Nicholas Sweten-
         ham.
 ,,   1 William Rogerson, ironmonger.
 ,,   1 William Rothe, pewterer.
 ,, 14 Roger Walton, mercer.
 ,, 14 Robert Cauncefeld, draper.
 ,, 14 John Barry, patynmaker.

1490–1 [6–7 H. vii.] JOHN BAROWE, Mayor.

Nov. 19 Richard Godeman, mercer.
„ 25 Richard Yonge, saddler, s. of John Yonge, saddler.

1492–3 [8–9 H. vii.] ROGER HURLTON, Mayor.

Nov. 8 Richard Ledesham, hewster.
„ 8 Richard Lymme, baker.
„ 8 William Hanley, sherman.
Apr. 18 Robert Bellerby, fletcher.
„ 18 Robert Cona, saddler.
„ 18 John s. of Richard Walley of Chester, fishmonger.
June 13 Robert Wright, draper, s. of John Richardson [sic], wright.
„ 13 Thomas Stretton, walker, s. of Thomas Stretton.
„ 13 Ralph Maccally, weaver. [Shown in margin as "M^cally."]

1493–4 [9–10 H. vii.] RALPH DAVENPORT, Mayor.

Jan. 14 Roger Barbor, sherman.
„ 14 Robert Wilkynson, corviser.
„ 14 Robert Cragge.
„ 14 Thomas Torbok, hewster.
„ 14 William Chaumber, glover.
„ 14 Richard Marshall, sherman, s. of John Marshall.
„ 28 John Robynson, saddler.
„ 28 John Gleive, milner.
„ 28 Peter Assheton, goldsmith.
„ 28 James Busshell, glover.
„ 28 John Smyth, "gurdeler."

1495–6 [11–12 H. vii.] RICHARD WYREHALL, Mayor.

May 10 Thomas Walton, singuler.
„ 10 William Morpeth, tailor.
„ 10 Roger Merton, tailor.
„ 10 Richard Hunt, tailor.
„ 10 John Merbury, tailor.
„ 10 Lewis Gruff, tailor.
„ 10 Danald Adamsone, tailor.
„ 10 John Taillior, tailor.
„ 10 Roger Taillior, tailor.
„ 10 Richard Bell, corviser.

May	10	Richard Sawer, cooper.
,,	10	James Bower, barker.
,,	10	William Whitby, dyer.
,,	10	John Harper, mercer, s. of Richard Harper, butcher.
,,	10	Thomas Hoghton, bowier.
,,	10	Thomas Adams, tailor.

1496–7 [12–13 H. vii.] THOMAS BARROW, Mayor.

Jan.	19	Robert Barowe s. of Thomas Barowe, mercer.
,,	19	William Snede ⎫ ss. of William Snede the elder, draper.
,,	19	Nⁱc^ho^la^s Snede ⎭
,,	19	Thomas Snede s. of William Snede the elder.
,,	19	Richard Carlille s. of John Carlille.
,,	26	Thomas Wyrrehall, glover. [Richard Weyrehall, a guarantor.]
,,	26	Nicholas Lyghtefote, barber, s. of James Lyghtefote.
,,	26	Thomas Hale, butcher, s. of Richard Hale, butcher.
,,	26	Robert Lace, baker.
,,	26	William Clerke, pewterer.
,,	26	John Carter, baker.
May	30	Charles Eton, ironmonger.
,,	30	Richard Plumpton, butcher.
,,	30	William Davyson, barber.
,,	30	Richard Brewster, barker.
,,	30	John Poghton, corviser.
,,	30	Richard Gronno, corviser.
,,	30	John Horton, smith.

1498–9 [14–15 H. vii.] RICHARD GODEMON, Esquire, Mayor.

Oct.	1	Thomas Smyth, mercer, s. of Peter Smyth, mercer.

1499–1500 [15–16 H. vii.] JOHN CLYFFE, Mayor.

Nov.	14	Thomas Newton of Chester, weaver.
,,	14	John ap Lle——, goldsmith.
,,	14	Robert Cornell, *alias* Robert Ster, s. of Danald Ster.
,,	14	John Wryght, butcher.
,,	14	Gilbert Morys, slater.
,,	14	Nicholas Fraunces, mercer.
Feb.	14	Thomas Ball, corviser.
,,	14	John Holond, glover.
,,	14	Henry Ashton, draper.

12   THE ROLLS OF THE FREEMEN OF   [1500-5

1500-1 [16-17 H. vii.] THOMAS FERROUR, Mayor.

Dec.	1	Donald Macwyn, *alias* Donald Saer.
„	1	Roger Criscilton, barker.
„	1	John ap Ithell, butcher, s. of Walter Ithell.
„	4	Thomas Cany, pewterer.
July	29	Christopher Wermynsham, goldsmith. [Stephen Wermynsham, a guarantor.]
„	29	John Henrison, cooper.
„	29	Nicholas Ketell, walker.
„	29	Thomas Forbour, barber.
„	29	Richard Pate, skinner.
„	29	Ralph Norley, glasier.
„	29	Hugh Clerke, draper, s. of Thomas Clerke.
Sep.	28	Nicholas Davy, ironmonger.
„	28	Roger Whithed, barker.
„	28	Robert Mercer, capper.
„	28	Richard Pole, skinner.
„	28	Richard Johnson, glover.
„	28	Robert Medelton, fletcher } ss. of Robert Medelton.
„	28	Ralph Medelton, baker
„	20	John Tatton, gentleman.
„	20	Nicholas Johnson.
„	20	William Cause, hewster.

1501-2 [17-18 H. vii.] RALPH DAVENPORT, Mayor.

Nov.	18	Henry Chalner, weaver.
„	18	Thomas Jankynson, weaver.
„	18	Robert Shermon s. of Nicholas Shermon.
„	18	John Twisse, butcher.

1504-5 [20-21 H. vii.] THOMAS SMITH, Mayor.

Nov.	26	Roger Rydley, butcher.
„	26	Ralph Monkesfilde [baker?].
„	26	William Gyle, butcher.
„	26	John Fenton, butcher, s. of Henry Fenton.
Dec.	19	Thomas Sharpe of Chester, merchant, s. of Richard Sharpe.
„	19	Thomas Adamson, mercer.
„	19	Robert Rathbone, barker. [John Rathbone, draper, a guarantor.]
„	19	James [Gatgley?], barker.

Oct.	8	Roger Abbot, shoemaker.
,,	8	William Richardeson, butcher.
,,	8	Thomas Harpur, butcher.
,,	8	Richard Pemberton, cook.
Aug.	26	Thomas Sandeson of Chester, bowier.
,,	26	Thomas Ince, ironmonger, s. of William Ince.
	—	Richard Hale, glover, s. of Richard Hale, butcher.
	—	William ap Ithell s. of John ap Ithell, weaver.
	—	Edward Astbrock, glover.
	—	William Thomasson, pewterer.
	—	William [Brech ?], brickman.

1505-6 [21-22 H. vii.] [THOMAS THORNTON, Mayor.]

May	19	Henry Anneon, barker.
,,	19	Robert Pety, tailor.
,,	19	Randle Palmer, tailor.
,,	19	Robert Guilliam, tailor.
,,	19	Roger Gray [sherman ?].
,,	19	William Leche, tailor.
,,	19	Thomas Wynchester, tailor.
,,	19	Laurence Wyche, tailor.
July	24	Charles Bostock.
,,	24	John Cartwright, butcher.
,,	24	George Lightfot, butcher.
,,	24	Hugh Fisher, salter.
,,	24	Robert Ithel, *alias* Robert Harwarden.
,,	24	John Bruyn, butcher.
Sep.	16	Thomas Ball, weaver.
,,	16	John Wyrhall the younger, weaver.
,,	16	Thomas Huet, corvisor.
,,	16	Robert Walshe, sherman.
,,	16	Robert Wryght, corvisor.
,,	16	John Sharp, sherman.
,,	16	Richard Tyrell, sherman.
,,	16	Robert Broue, weaver.
Oct.	15	Thomas Danne, merchant.

1506-7 [22-23 H. vii.] THOMAS BARROW, Mayor.

— Hugh ap Ithell s. of John ap Ithell.
— Richard Newhouse, glover.
— Richard Couper, baker.
— John Bent, smith, *alias* Wastenburye.
— Richard Short, smith.

		Henry [Lucas?], cooper.
	—	Robert Godeman, hewster, s. of William Godeman.
	—	Thomas Shekelach, smith.
	—	Robert Percivall, cardmaker.
	—	Peter Cowper, glover.
	—	Thomas Spragge, smith.
	—	Thomas Shirrewod, pinner.
	—	Nicholas Gerarde, glover.
Oct.	5	Roger Leye, merchant.
,,	5	Ralph Smith, sherman, s. of Randle Smith.
,,	5	Richard Barker the younger s. of Richard Barker the elder.
,,	5	Richard Finchett, sherman.
,,	5	William Whityngham, baker.
,,	5	William Shurlache, barker.
,,	26	Henry Gruff, sherman.
,,	26	William Pessaunt, tailor.
,,	26	Thomas Deane, cooke.
,,	26	Robert Brerewod, glover. [John Brerewood, a guarantor.]
,,	26	William Richardson, ironmonger.
,,	26	John Grono, sherman.

1507–8 [23–24 H. vii.] RICHARD WYRALL, Mayor.

Feb.	22	Richard Erdeley, carpenter.
,,	22	William Wright, glover. [Thomas Wright, baker, a guarantor.]
,,	22	William Catell, barker.
,,	22	William Haywart, fletcher.
,,	22	Richard Ryding, weaver.
,,	22	Thomas Chaloner, weaver.
,,	22	Geoffrey Grono, weaver.
,,	22	William Hamnet, furbur.
,,	ult	John Mason, barber.
,,	ult	Thomas Meire, corviser.
,,	ult	Henry Fox, sherman.
,,	ult	Christopher Rogerson, parish clerke.
,,	ult	Hugh Pekkell, butcher.
,,	ult	Thomas Pekkell, butcher.
,,	ult	Roger Chaloner, merchant.
Aug.	21	Thomas Golborn, merchant.
,,	22	William Godeman s. of Hamon Godeman.
Sep.	26	John Radclive, carpenter.
,,	26	Hugh Ellomes, saddler.
,,	26	Peter Gerard, sherman.

1510-11 [2-3 H. viii.] WILLIAM ROGERSON, Mayor.

	—	Adam Agar, draper.
	—	Hugh Aldersey, draper.
	—	Thomas Hertford s. of Richard.
Jan.	28	Hugh Hurlton, merchant, s. of Hugh.
,,	28	Edward Davenport s. of Ralph Davenport.
,,	28	Edward Lokker, smith, s. of Richard.
,,	28	William Dio, baker.
,,	28	David ap Med [Meredith], hewster.
Feb.	18	George Henrison, weaver.
,,	18	Robert Hatton, weaver.
,,	18	Geoffrey Richardson, barker. [William Richardson, a guarantor.]
,,	18	Thomas Fletcher s. of William Fletcher, baker.
,,	18	William Pulton, weaver.
,,	18	Peter Richardson, weaver.
Apr.	2	John Yong of Chester, merchant.
,,	2	James Fletcher, merchant.
,,	2	Thomas Boman, merchant.
,,	2	Thomas Martyn, merchant.
,,	2	William Radley, fletcher.
,,	2	William Caldwall, butcher.
July	8	David ap Gruff of Handbrige, drover.
,,	8	Richard Jynkynson, sherman.
,,	8	Richard Barker, saddler, *alias* [ ], s. of John Barker.
,,	8	Robert Hoton, butcher.
,,	8	Thomas Nicholasson, butcher.
Oct.	6	Peter Dutton of Hatton, esquire.
,,	6	Thomas ["Richard" crossed out] Horton, walker.
,,	6	Richard Crosse, draper.
,,	6	Robert Rosingreve.
,,	6	Thomas Hargreve.
,,	6	John Henrison.
,,	6	Thomas Chipyngdale.
,,	6	Robert Crosse, glover.
,,	6	Richard Dayner.
,,	6	Hugh Bolde.

1520-1 [12-13 H. viii.] THOMAS SMITH the Elder, Mayor.

Sep.	11	Humphrey Aldersey, merchant.
,,	11	Thomas Richardson, furber [s. of Richard Lokker?].
,,	11	John Cotgreve, draper.

16   THE ROLLS OF THE FREEMEN OF   [1522-7

Sep. 11   Thomas Robynson, glover.
„   11   William Pert, hewster.
„   11   Richard Harker, mason.
„   11   Richard Momford, founder.
„   26   Nicholas Ithell, sherman.
„   26   William Hervy, sherman.
„   26   Phillip Walker, sherman.
„   26   John Sudlowe.
„   26   John Rosingreve.
„   26   John Byngley.
„   26   William Fletcher, baker.
„   26   Richard Orton.

1522-3 [14-15 H. viii.] WILLIAM DAVIDSON, Mayor.

Oct. 26   William Wethynse.
„   26   Hamon Smith, carpenter.
„   26   Roger Whithed ["Whitehed," MB], sherman.
Nov. 10   William Brassy, draper.
„   10   Foulk Dutton, draper.
„   10   John White, merchant.
„   10   Thomas ap Edward, barber.
Jan. 31   Richard Myddelton, skinner.
Feb. 6   Henry Heyton, mercer.
„   6   John Taillior.
—— 30   John Tirell, barber.
May 18   Edmund Hamnet, saddler, s. of Robert Hamnet, saddler.
July 10   James Shawe s. of William Shawe.
„   10   Richard Leche, barker, s. of ——.
„   10   John Framway, barker. [William Framway, barker, a guarantor.]
June 1   William Dunderdale, tailor, s. of Thomas Dunderdale.
Oct. 3   John Leche, barker.
„   3   Richard Godeman the younger, merchant, s. of Richard Godeman, esquire.
„   6   Richard James, barker.
„   12   Geoffrey Woode, corviser.

1526-7 [18-19 H. viii.] ROBERT BARROWE, Mayor.

Feb. 5   John Anyon, corviser.
„   5   William Stockton, ironmonger.
„   5   Randle Ashton, tailor.
„   5   Thomas Bayledonne, ironmonger, s. of Robert Bayledonne, mason.

Feb.	5	Nicholas Perisson, glover.
,,	5	Richard Parlowe, cooper.
May	16	Richard Hurlton, gentleman, s. of Hugh Hurlton.
,,	16	Roger Barlowe.
,,	16	Hugh Gregory, corviser.
,,	16	Robert Finch, butcher.
,,	23	Adam Walton, mercer, s. of Richard Walton, mercer.
,,	23	John Barrowe s. of Roger Barrowe.
July	2	Robert Forster.
,,	2	Roger Barlowe. [The name is given in the margin as Henry Barlowe, and this is probably correct, as a Roger Barlowe was admitted on May 16.]
—		John Robynson.
—		John Robynson, baker.
—		John Faircliff, baker.
—		Thomas Kettell s. of Nicholas Kettell.

1527–8 [19–20 H. viii.] THOMAS SMITH THE ELDER, MAYOR.

Oct.	24	Robert Lace, barker, s. of Nicholas Lace.
,,	24	John Hale, butcher, s. of Thomas Hale, butcher.
,,	24	John Kirkes.
,,	24	Edward Birkenhed, baker.
,,	24	Geoffrey Coke, mariner.
,,	24	Peter Strete, butcher.
Feb.	20	John Yong, barber.
,,	20	Thomas Cotgreve, mercer.
,,	20	John Thornton s. of Thomas Thornton, alderman.
,,	20	Thomas Smith, mercer, s. of Edmund Smith, mercer.
,,	20	Roger Spragge, smith, s. of Thomas Spragge.
,,	20	Thomas Richardson [Ricson], butcher, s. of William Richardson, butcher.
Mar.	3	Thomas Agar, glover, s. of —— Agar.
,,	3	William Gleyse, glover.
,,	3	Richard Ledesham, glover, s. of Roger Ledesham.
May	28	Henry ap David, saddler.
,,	28	William Schirwod, pinner, s. of Thomas Schirwod.
,,	28	Thomas ap Ithell, butcher, s. of John ap Ithell, butcher.
,,	28	John Taillior, sherman.
,,	28	John Mayler [or Mailer], founder.
,,	28	Henry Nichollasson, barber.
Aug.	13	William Davy s. of David Robynson, sherman. [In a similar book William Davy is shown as s. of David dd. or David, probably a clerical error.]

18 THE ROLLS OF THE FREEMEN OF [1530-2

Aug. 13 Randle Maynwaryng, draper.
„ 13 Hamon Brassy.
Oct. 9 William Bekyngsam or Bekingsam, corvisor.

1530-1 [22-23 H. viii.] THOMAS SMITH, Mayor.

Feb. 6 Ralph Wright, mercer, s. of John Wright.
„ James Chamblayne, barker.
„ John Weston, butcher.
„ Richard Thomsson, butcher.
„ John Busshell, glover.
„ William Hurst, stringer.
„ Thomas Hasellwall, dyer.
„ William Gryse, glover.
„ 6 John Ellom, tailor.
„ 6 William Abbot, corviser, s. of Roger Abbot, corvisor.
May 25 Roger Cowper, sherman, s. of James Cowper.
„ 25 Thomas Smyth s. of William Smyth, sherman.
„ 25 Thomas Duke, *alias* Thomas Rogerson, corviser.
„ 25 Roger Basford, tailor.
„ 25 Richard Middleton, glover, s. of Ralph Middleton.
„ 25 Thomas Hope, ironmonger.
July 18 Simon Momford, founder.
„ 18 William Bokeley, tailor.
„ 18 Thomas Ley, glover.
„ 18 John Percyvall s. of Robert Percyvall.
„ 18 Richard Percyvall the younger s. of Robert Percyvall.
„ 18 Richard Barow, barker.
Sep. 26 Robert ap John, mercer.
„ 26 Thomas Powell, baker.
„ 26 William Whatton, cooper.
Oct. 10 Thomas Fletcher, baker. [William Fletcher, baker, a guarantor.]

1531-2 [23-24 H. viii.] WILLIAM SNEYD, Mayor.

Nov. 7 John Hokes of Chester, cooper, s. of Stephen Hokes, mercer, freeman of Chester.
„ 7 Ralph Thorneton, barber, s. of Thomas Thorneton, freeman of Chester.
„ 7 Henry Heylyn, baker.
„ 7 William Whitby, fletcher. [Richard Whitby, a guarantor.]
„ 7 Charles Ridyng, cooper.

1532-3] THE CITY OF CHESTER 19

Jan.	11	Richard Pope, shoemaker.
Mar.	27	John Guttyn, mercer.
June	3	Ralph Heyton, ironmonger, s. of Charles Heyton, freeman of Chester.
,,	3	Thomas Smyth s. of Thomas Smyth, freeman of Chester.
,,	3	Peter Smyth s. of Thomas Smyth, freeman of Chester.
,,	3	Thomas Barrowe s. of Thomas Barrowe, glover, freeman of Chester.
Aug.	8	Richard Grymesdiche s. of Richard Grymesdiche, freeman of Chester.
,,	8	Thomas Bradburne s. of John Bradburne.
,,	8	William Hill.
Sep.	24	Peter Brerewode, glover, s. of Robert Brerewode.
,,	24	William Erdeley s. of Richard Erdeley.
,,	24	Thomas Smethers, barber, s. of Richard Smethers.
,,	24	Thomas Crosse, glover, s. of Stephen Crosse.
,,	24	John Brerewode, glover. [Robert Brerewode, sheriff, guarantor.]
,,	24	William Strete, bower.

1532-3 [24-25 H. viii.] WILLIAM GODEMAN, Mayor.

Dec.	12	Thomas Harper, mercer, s. of John Harper.
,,	12	John David, sergeant.
,,	12	Thomas Richardson, shoemaker.
,,	12	John Peccowe, butcher.
,,	12	Thomas Wermyncham, saddler.
Feb.	13	Danald Lucas, hooper.
,,	13	Richard Pole, merchant.
,,	13	Richard Parker, *alias* Hichon, bower.
,,	13	Edward Wodhop, merchant.
,,	13	David ap John, glover.
,,	13	Magnus Mee, cooper.
,,	13	John Tuder. [Described in a cancelled entry as tailor.]
,,	13	William Wright, barker.
,,	13	Thomas Johnson, barker.
,,	13	Thomas Bavant, ironmonger, s. of William Bavant.
,,	13	Thomas Richardson, weaver.
	—	William Glasior. [? a freeman, entry only commenced in M.B.]
,,	13	John Newhall, draper.
,,	13	Peter Conway, goldsmith.
,,	13	George Chorleton, goldsmith.
,,	13	Thomas Denson, baker.

Feb. 13	John Leche the younger. [John Leche the elder, and William Leche, draper, guarantors.]
Sep. 25	Richard Barton, mercer.
,, 25	John Scons, baker.
,, 25	Thomas ap Res, merchant.
,, 25	John Fraunces, butcher.
,, 5	Richard Hoton, butcher.
,, 5	James Weston, butcher.
,, 5	Richard Taillior, baker, s. of Roger Taillior, baker.

1533–4 [25–26 H. viii.] HENRY GEE, Mayor.

Dec. 3	Thomas Pillyn, shoemaker, s. of Henry Pillyn, freeman.
,, 3	Thomas ap William, weaver. [Gruff ap William, a guarantor.]
,, 3	Thomas Dickley, smith.
,, 3	Richard Croughton, sherman.
,, 3	Robert Hilton, shoemaker.
Apr. 21	Thomas Bek, baker.
,, 21	Roger Taillior, sherman. [Ralph Taillior, a guarantor.]
,, 21	Thomas Smyth, organmaker. [Thomas Smith, sherman, a guarantor.]
,, 21	Thomas ap Howell, painter.
June 3	John ap Gruff, baker.
,, 3	Hamon Johnson, draper.
,, 3	Nicholas Wedderley, baker.
,, 3	James Heyton, broderer.
,, 3	John Radford, barker, s. of Henry Radford, alderman.
July 23	John Wau'ton [Waverton].
Oct. 8	John Costerdyne, draper.
,, 8	Ralph Bower, shoemaker.
,, 8	Roger Cottrell, sherman.
,, 8	George Foxcroft, draper.
,, 8	Hugh Hulme, draper.
,, 8	John Kempe, shoemaker.
,, 8	William Sneyde, gentleman, s. of Richard Sneyde, esquire.
,, 8	Richard Bruyn, butcher, s. of Richard Bruyn, bocher, freeman of Chester.
June 20	Robert Chalnor, merchant.

1536–7 [28–29 H. viii.] WILLIAM GOODMAN, Mayor.

Dec. 18	Roger Radford.
,, 18	John Heylyn, baker.
,, 18	William Kery, founder.

| 1537-8] | THE CITY OF CHESTER | 21 |

Dec. 18   Roger Glover, shoemaker.
„   18   Seth Rosingreve, pewterer.
„   18   Michael Hestok, beer-brewer.
Jan. 15   Robert Yorke, shoemaker.
„   15   George More, carpenter.
Apr. 12   Thomas Mascy.
„   12   Adam Goodman, merchant, s. of William Goodman.
„   12   Anthony Hurleton, draper.
„   12   Roger Lynley, shoemaker.
„   12   Gruff Tuder, tailor.
„   12   Richard Irrelle, barber.
„   12   Hugh Heylin, glover.
„   12   Richard Gutten, sherman.
„   12   Hugh Gillam, *alias* Pesaunt, tailor, s. of Gillam Pesaunt.
May 27   Roger Ledsham, goldsmith.
„   27   William Williamson, skinner.
„   27   Roger Ledesham, pewterer.
Sep. 25   Gilbert Arrosmith, sergeant [ceryant].
„   25   Richard Rathbone.
„   25   William Lytherland.
„   25   Robert Lewys, butcher.
„   25   Thomas Gillam s. of Gillam Pesaunt.
„   25   Richard Bewley.
„   25   Thomas Maykyn.

1537-8 [29-30 H. viii.] FOULK DUTTON, Mayor.

Jan. 10   Randle Domvyle, draper.
„   10   Richard Radford.
Feb. 5   John Tylston, shoemaker.
„   5   Richard Brerewode, glover.
Mar. 26   George Vernon, shoemaker, s. of George Vernon.
Apr. —   William Newhall s. of Robert Newhall.
„   2   John Smith, carter, s. of —— Smyth.
„   2   Richard Newhall.
July 16   Thomas White, merchant.
Aug. 1   Lawrence Fox, merchant.
Sep. 20   William Smith, mayor's officer.
„   20   Thomas Taillior, barker.
„   20   Edward Smith.
„   20   Edward Orton, shoemaker.
„   20   Thomas Dobbe, shoemaker.
„   20   William Ball, glover.
„   20   William Bruyn s. of Robert Bruyn.

Sep. 20 Thomas Richardson s. of Geoffrey Richardson.
Oct. 3 Nicholas Pemberton.
 „   7 Lawrence s. of Sir Thomas Smith, knight.
 „   7 William Shawe the younger, sherman, s. of William Shawe, walker.

1538-9 [30-31 H. viii.] DAVID MIDLETON, Mayor.

Dec. 3 John Robinson, smith.
 „   3 Roger [Richard, M.B.] Grey, smith, s. of Roger Grey.
 „   3 Richard Pasmich [Passhemyche, M.B.], tanner.
 „   3 Richard Yonge, glover, s. of Richard Yonge.
Apr. 21 Ralph Gudman s. of Ralph Gudman, alderman.
 „ 21 Robert Birkhened s. of Adam [Ralton ?].
 „ 21 Ralph Aldersey.
 „ 21 Edmund Thomson, tailor.
 „ 29 John Midleton, smith, s. of Ralph Midleton.
 „ 29 George Goz, butcher, s. of Thomas Goz.
July 18 Robert Johns, merchant.
 „ 18 Ralph Pillin, barber, s. of Henry Pyllyn, carpenter.
 „ 18 Henry Jhanion, weaver.
 „ 18 Thomas Gorstilow [Gorstellow, M.B.], merchant.
 „ 18 Robert Hey [Hay, M.B.], glover.
 „ 18 Richard Wildinge, wright.
Sep. 4 William Houghton.
 „   4 Richard Massey, upholsterer.
 „   4 John Hanky, smith.
 „   4 Richard Baunt, baker, s. of Richard Baunt, ropier.

1539-40 [31-32 H. viii.] HENRY GEE, Mayor.

Thomas Greene.

1540-1 [32-33 H. viii.] Sir LAURENCE SMITH, Knight, Mayor.

Mar. 4 Thomas Radley, bower, of Chester, s. of —— Radley of Chester, tailor.
 „   4 William Gitten, butcher, s. of —— Gitten, butcher.
 „   4 Richard Shephard, fishmonger.
 —   John Bird, barker.
 —   William Rogerson s. of Ralph Rogerson, alderman.
 —   Ralph Rogerson, ironmonger.
 —   Peter Rogerson, ironmonger.

1541-3] THE CITY OF CHESTER 23

— Richard Rogerson, merchant.
— Ralph Smith, mercer, s. of Peter Smith, mercer.
— John Webster, mercer.
— Thomas Gruff, ironmonger.
— John Coleor, tailor.
— Thomas Hatton, ship carpenter, s. of Robert Hatton.

1541-2 [33-34 H. viii.] HUGH ALDERSEY, Mayor.

Nov. 17 Peter Hill, tailor.
  „ 12 Gilb. Taillior,
  „ 17 Richard Browster s. of Hugh Broster [or Brewster].
  „ 17 Richard [Randle, M.B.] Kettell s. of Nicholas Kettell.
  „ 17 Richard Loker s. of John Locker.
  „ 17 Thomas Eaton [?Barow] s. of Charles Eaton [?Barow].
  „ 17 Randle Persivall s. of Robert Persivall.
  „ 17 Richard Lyme the younger s. of Richard Lyme.
  „ 17 Richard Cowper s. of John Cowper.
  „ 17 John Cooke [Coke, M.B.].
  „ 17 John Dicus.
         Robert Rathbone.
         William Dodd, sharman.
         Edward Marten.
         William Curmyn.
         Robert Jenyn [?Jevyn].
         Thomas Radcliffe s. of John Radcliffe.
         Ralph Fisher s. of Robert Fisher.
         Richard Lute.

1542-3 [34-35 H. viii.] WILLIAM BEXWICKE, Mayor.

Nov. 22 Richard Badeley.
  — 2   James Brerewood s. of Robert Brerewood.
     2   Richard Whithed s. of Gilbert Whitehed.
     2   William Johnson, glover.
     2   Ralph Midleton s. of Richard Midleton.
     2   Gilbert Quirke.
Jan. 18 William Fletcher, shoemaker.
  „ 18 William Annion, tailor.
  „ 18 Ralph Vernon, shoemaker.
  „ 18 Richard Lute, merchant.
Feb. 22 Christopher Warmingham [Wermyncham, M.B.], goldsmith, s. of Christopher Warmingham.
  „ 22 Ralph Crosse s. of ——— ———.

Mar. 20 William Cawllame [Callame, M.B.], mercer.
Oct. 2 Laurence Smith, goldsmith.
 „   2 Thomas Ellice.

1543-4 [35-36 H. viii.] WILLIAM SNEYDE, Esquire, Mayor.

Oct. 20 Richard Horton, sherman, s. of Roger Horton, sherman.
Nov. 13 William Walton, tallow-chandler,⎫ ss. of William
 „ 13 Robert Walton, baker,   ⎭ Walton.
 „ 23 Robert Yardley [Yerdeley, M.B.], draper.
 „ 23 Peter Nicholas, baker.
 „ 23 George Wade, corvisor.
 „ 23 John Bateman, sherman.
Apr. 21 Richard Sneyd, esquire.
 „ 21 Hugh Goodman, gentleman.
 „ 21 John Wrighte.
June 30 William Meo, *alias* [Bakstove?].
Sep. 26 George Linson, hedmaker.
 „ 26 John Cowper, merchant.
 „ 26 Richard Calley, sklater.
 „ 26 William Looker [Lokker, M.B.].
 „ 26 John Chetam, public notary.
 „ 26 Henry Chetam s. of the aforesaid John Chetam.
Oct. 8 John Lynley, "corier."
 „   8 John ap Howell, corvisor.
 „ 10 Laurence Warmincham, saddler.
 „ 10 Robert Hancoke, smith.

1544-5 [36-37 H. viii.] ROBERT BARTON, Mayor.

Jan. 27 George Persivall, saddler, s. of Robert Persivall, cardmaker.
Aug. 19 Robert Brid, mercer.
 „ 19 William Meoles, ironmonger.
 „ 19 Thomas Ashton, glover.
 „ 19 Urian Ryder, smith.
 „ 19 Roger Bryne, butcher.
 „ 19 Thomas Bebinton, butcher.

1545-6 [37-38 H. viii.] WILLIAM HOLCROFT, Esquire, died, and JOHN WALLEY, succ., Mayors.

Robert Amery.
David ap Edward.
William Jeinus [? Jevins], baker.

Thomas Johnson.
John Litherland, tanner.
Richard Jeynson.
Thomas Steward, ironmonger.
Richard Jein, weaver.
Thomas Fallowes.
Stephen Holenbury.
Ralph Bostock, tanner.
Richard Walley, ironmonger.
Thomas Walley, ironmonger.
Thomas Wederall, ironmonger.
John Annion, glover.
Richard Holland, glover.
Richard Bexwick, goldsmith.
John Birkhened, esquire.
Robert Smith, glover.

1546-7 [38 H. viii.–1 E. vi.] HUGH ALDERSEY, Mayor.

Dec.	16	Edward Adam, shoemaker.
,,	16	Henry Hardware, draper.
,,	16	William Joet, syngyngman.
,,	16	Richard Wright, baker [barker, M.B.].
,,	16	Ralph [Richard, M.B.] Mawdesley, baker.
,,	16	Robert Cowper, baker.
,,	16	Henry Curmyn.
Feb.	6	John Bastwell the younger, bower.
,,	6	Thomas Fisher, cowper.
,,	6	Henry Otie [Ottye, M.B.], baker.
,,	6	Thomas Blith [Blythe, M.B.], shoemaker.
,,	6	Hugh Lymme, baker.
Apr.	5	Henry Hill of Chester, tanner.
,,	5	Peter Anningson, shoemaker.
,,	5	Henry Trafford, baker.

1547 [1 E. vi.] JOHN SMITH, Draper, Mayor.

June	4	Robert Filston of Chester, yeoman.
,,	14	Richard Parry of Chester, merchant.
July	5	Robert Mawdesley of Chester, sherman.
Aug.	8	William Rowlandson, tanner.
,,	8	John Newhall of Chester, yeoman.
,,	8	John Delahey, draper.
,,	8	William Congley, stringer.

Aug. 8 Robert Pova of Chester, yeoman.
„ 8 Richard Tomlinson of Chester, cowper.
„ 8 William Cotgreve of Chester, innholder.
Sep. 27 Ralph Barlowe, linen-draper.
Oct. 6 Thomas Yoken, fishmonger.
„ 6 John Mason, shoemaker.
„ 6 Hugh Rogerson, draper.
„ 6 Ralph Huxley, draper.
„ 6 Richard Boydell, carver.
„ 6 William Lyverpole.

1547-8 [1-2 E. vi.] RALPH GOODMAN THE ELDER, MAYOR.

Nov. 7 John Whithed, baker.
„ 7 Roger Totty, smith.
„ 7 Robert Whithed, baker.
„ 7 Richard Robinson, hewster.
May 10 John Twis, sherman.
„ 10 William Symcock, shoemaker.
„ 10 John Balle, smith.
„ 10 Richard Garrat, baker.
„ 10 Randle ap Robin, sherman.
June 14 William Dymocke, ironmonger.
„ 14 Richard Gruff, tailor.
„ 14 Oliver Smyth, draper.
„ 14 Henry Finchet, sherman.
„ 14 James Johnson, baker.
„ 14 Robert Burges, tailor.
„ 14 Thomas Hamnet, saddler.
„ 14 William Framall, barber.
„ 14 Robert Congley, stringer.
„ 14 John Bingley, sherman.
„ 14 John Henrison, tailor.
„ 14 William Yate, carpenter.
July 9 John Harvy, glover.
„ 9 Robert Harvy, glover.
„ 9 Robert Hatton, glover.
„ 9 James Johnson, glover.
„ 9 John Holland, cowper.
„ 9 John Barton, glover.
„ 9 William Madock, glover.
Sep. 25 Geoffrey Crompton.
„ 25 Richard Richardson, *alias* Locker.
„ 25 Robert Jevan.

[1548–50] THE CITY OF CHESTER 27

1548–9 [2–3 E. vi.] FULKE DUTTON, Mayor.

Hugh Richards, draper.
Edward Tumson, merchant.
Thomas Prees, merchant.
James Banes, barber.
Reginald Hughes, merchant.
William Browne, mercer.
Robert Hill, tailor.
Laurence Sherington, dyer.
Hugh Davy, sherman.
William Sale, baker.
Simon Nugent, tailor.
Reginald Walker, glover.
Richard Caldey, glover.
William Caldey, glover.
Robert Brome, shoemaker.
Nicholas Synot, merchant.
Robert Robinson, tanner.
John Marshe, glover.
John Taylor, tanner.
Thomas Lloyd, weaver.
Richard Birche, weaver.
George Bellen, shoemaker.
Thomas Claver, candle-maker.
Robert ap Thomas, cliderall haberdasher.
William Wighe, sherman.
Richard Twie, sherman.
John Rees, mercer.
John Warton, mariner.
William Preson.
Walter Foxse.
Edward Hey.
Thomas Hancock, baker.
Richard Peny, weaver.
Dannold Stole, mariner.

1549–50 [3–4 E. vi.] THOMAS ALDERSEY, Mayor.

Jan.	27	William Aynsdale.
,,	27	John Birth, butcher.
Mar.	25	John Hill, weaver.
,,	25	Richard Tilston, shoemaker.
,,	25	William Cliffe, pewterer.

Mar. 25 Richard Johnson.
„ 25 Richard Henson.
„ 25 Robert Marten.
„ 25 Gilbert Knowles [Knolles, M.B.], pewterer.
„ 25 Thomas Fletcher.
June — Hugh Stockton, smith.
— Thomas Holbruck [Holbroke, M.B.].
— Richard Dutton, draper.
— Peter Mutton, draper.
— Robert Hughson, glover.
Sep. 23 Henry Annyon, sherman.
„ 23 Thomas Wiswall, glover.
„ 23 Richard Prenton, smith.
„ 23 Richard Cooke [Coke, M.B.], glover.
George Monxfield.
Richard Orton, glover.
John Lucas, cooper.
William Wood, glover.

1550-1 [4-5 E. vi.] EDMUND GEE, DIED, AND WILLIAM GOODMAN, SUCC., MAYORS.

—— — Ingerham ap Robert, weaver.
Dec. — Thomas Lawton, glover.
— John Lovet, hatmaker.
Jan. 7 Richard Wolfe, cowper.
„ 7 Randle Crewe, shoemaker.
„ 21 Thomas Richardson, shoemaker.
„ 21 Henry More, weaver.
Feb. 12 Robert Hinton, capper.
„ 23 Richard Wareton, tanner.
—— — Ralph Johnson, draper.
—— — Robert Fisher, glover.
May 11 Robert Milner, baker.
July 8 Hugh Lingley, butcher.
„ 8 John Bellingham.
„ 28 Richard Grise, glover.
Aug. 2 Hugh Jenson, merchant.
„ 2 Andrew Tayler.
„ 2 Thomas Throp, fletcher.

1551-2 [5-6 E. vi.] WILLIAM GLASEOR, MAYOR.

Nov. 5 Thomas Glaseor.
„ 5 Ralph Thornton.

Nov.	5	William Fletcher, saddler.
,,	5	Thomas Mason, baker.
,,	5	Hugh Hyne, tallow-chandler.
Dec.	4	Thomas Bennet, shoemaker.
,,	4	William Ancocke, shoemaker.
,,	4	William Richardson, shoemaker.
,,	4	Robert Moston, shoemaker.
,,	4	Richard Coldock, shoemaker.
,,	4	William Richards, draper.
,,	4	Henry Leeche, draper.
,,	4	George Leeche, merchant.
,,	4	William Leeche, ironmonger.
,,	8	John Hoper, draper.
,,	8	Edward Hanmer, draper.
,,	8	John Huntington, smith.
,,	8	George Garrot, barber.
,,	8	William Lynaker, shoemaker.
,,	8	Robert Crocket, girdler.
,,	8	Richard Downton, draper.
Feb.	22	Fulke ap Richard Owen, cardmaker.
Mar.	7	Thomas Bostock, merchant.
,,	7	Ralph Foster, merchant.
June	2	Randle Lawton, cardmaker.
,,	2	William Crosse, glover.
July	28	William Child, gentleman.
,,	28	Francis Bamvile, ironmonger.
,,	28	William Kinge, baker.
,,	28	Robert Bildon, chandler.
Aug.	19	Robert Pvall, shoemaker.
,,	19	Richard Wright, butcher.
Oct.	10	Richard Kinge.
,,	10	Robert Phillips, cowper.
,,	10	George Lucas, glover.

1552-3 [6-7 E. vi. & 1 M.] THOMAS SMITH, Mayor.

Nov.	10	Thomas [Roger, M.B.] Aspshowe, merchant.
,,	10	Nicholas Trafford, smith.
,,	10	John Basford, tailor.
,,	22	Phillip Colmashe, cooper.
,,	22	Ralph Calveley, tailor.
,,	28	William Abraham, tailor.
Jan.	25	William Banester, tanner.
,,	25	Thomas Tomlinson, fletcher.
,,	25	Gruffin [Gruffith, M.B.] Dodd, sherman.

Jan. 20   Ellis Shawe, tanner.
Mar. 7   Christopher Morvill [Morveyll, M.B.], merchant.
[Nov. 28 ?] Robert Hope, tailor.
 „   28   Thomas Tetlowe [Tetlo, M.B.], merchant.
Mar. 4   Thomas Payne, saddler.
June 28   Richard Herbert [Herber, M.B.], coryer.
 „   28   John [Thomas erased, M.B.] Birkhened, embroiderer.
 „   28   William Thornton, merchant.
Oct. 9   William Fletcher, merchant.
 „   9   John [Thorneton, merchant, erased, M.B.] Jones, merchant.

1553-4 [1-2 M.] JOHN OFFLEY, MAYOR.

Ralph Bromley, coryer.
James Folloyn, merchant.
Roger Trowtbeck, merchant.
Richard Marshe, merchant.
David Richardson, tanner.
Thomas Hill, *alias* Fisher, butcher.
John Radley, butcher.
John White, baker.
Peter Litherland, tanner.
Justician Spark, merchant.
Richard Trevor, goldsmith.
Robert Dutton, ironmonger.
William Wilcock, tanner.
Robert Lawton, merchant.
Randle Bennet, sherman.
Robert Jenins [? Jevins], merchant.
Thomas Harwar, goldsmith.
John Hixon, weaver.

1554-5 [1-2 P. & M.] FULKE DUTTON, MAYOR.

Nov. 8   Richard Cooke, merchant.
 „   8   Christopher Smith, tailor.
 „   8   Richard Darwall, glover.
 „   8   John Done, pewterer.
 „   8   Thomas Leeche, barber.
Jan. 22   Richard Harpur, gentleman.
 „   22   William Gerrard, esquire.
Feb. 19   William Bastwell, bowyer.
 „   19   John Wright, butcher.
 „   19   William Brid [Brulle, M.B.], tanner.

Feb.	19	Robert Annion, butcher [tanner, M.B.].
Mar.	7	Edward Wright, skinner.
„	7	Robert Urmeston, founder.
„	7	Thomas Alcock, tailor.
Apr.	8	Thomas Mosse, merchant.
July	4	Richard Fisher, hooper.
„	4	Richard Heydocke, joiner.
„	4	William Mutton, goldsmith.
„	4	Richard Litherland, tanner.
„	18	Nicholas Rowson, merchant.
„	18	John Midleton, ironmonger.
„	18	Richard Leeche, ironmonger.
„	18	Richard Colly, ironmonger.
„	18	Thomas Bildon the younger, ironmonger.
„	18	Christopher Walker, sherman.
Aug.	1	Roger Davemport, gentleman.
„	1	William Dodd, merchant.
„	1	Thomas Horton the younger, skinner.
Sep.	18	William Golborne, gentleman.
„	18	William Radford, merchant.
„	18	William Grymsdich, merchant.
Oct.	8	Richard Granwall, weaver.
„	8	William Fletcher, weaver.

1555-6 [2-3 P. & M.] JOHN SMITH, Mayor.

Nov.	5	Roger Sonky, yeoman.
„	5	Thomas Gest, tallow-chandler.
„	5	John Eaton, beer-brewer.
„	5	Thomas Bennet, cordwainer.
„	5	John Johnson, milner.
„	7	Thomas Bruse, water-leader.
„	7	William Rogerson, draper.
„	7	John Milner, tailor.
„	7	Wilham Twisse, beer-brewer.
„	7	Robert Carrier, tailor.
„	7	Richard Radley, shoemaker.
„	7	William Hancock, currier.
„	12	Thomas Meykin, shoemaker.
„	12	Thomas Sandford, innkeeper.
„	12	Thomas Shotleworth, yoman, *alias* dytcher.
„	—	John Person [Pierson, M.B.], fishmonger.
M. after F. of S. Martin		John Andrewe, shoemaker.
„	„	Robert Stobbes [Stubbs, M.B.], shoemaker.

M. after F. of S. Martin		John Tilston, shoemaker.
„	„	Richard Perry, tailor.
F. before F. of S. Kath. the Virgin.		John Massy, miller.
„		William Halle, yeoman.
„	„	Thomas Malpas, innkeeper.
„	„	Edward Thatcher, labourer.
Jan.	20	Randle Anderton, cooper.
„	20	George Shalcrofte, merchant.
„	20	Oliver Vos [Vouse, M.B.], tailor.
„	20	Nicholas White, mariner.
„	20	John ap Ries, smith.
„	20	Nicholas Wright, baker.
Mar.	10	Richard Case, yeoman.
„	10	John Edwards, tailor.
„	10	Thomas Lynacre, cooper.
„	10	William Griffith [Gruffith, M.B.], butcher.
„	23	Clement Grey, ironmonger.
„	23	John Carter.
„	23	Robert Brerewod, glover.
May	20	Thomas Pole, barber.
„	20	Peter Wright, baker.
June	16	Richard Huet [Hughet, M.B.], cordwainer.
„	16	John Stevenson, bowyer.
„	16	Hugh Massy, smith.
Aug.	—	Peter Colman, *alias* Cotes, yeoman.
„	3	John Barnes, tanner.
„	3	Thomas Robinson, weaver.
„	31	John Yerworth [Yarworth, M.B.], gentleman.
„	31	John Thornton, merchant.
„	31	Ralph Trevor, goldsmith.
„	31	Hugh Thomas, butcher.
Oct.	9	John Eaton, haberdasher.
„	9	Roger Holve, beer-brewer.
„	15	Henry Raborne, glover.
„	15	Thomas ap Lle[wely]n, yeoman.
„	15	William Lle[welyn], shoemaker.
„	15	Ralph Madock, baker.
„	15	Thomas Lewes, mercer.

1556-7 [3-4 P. & M.] JOHN WEBSTER, Mayor.

John Lowe, glover.
Richard Pewe, ironmonger.
William Massy, merchant.

William Cradock, smith.
John Hooton, butcher.
John Floyd, mercer.
Hugh Williams, mercer.
Robert Powell, mercer.
James Battrich, ironmonger.
Ralph White, sherman.
Ralph Cowper, sherman.
William Stokes, joiner.
James Gitton, sherman.
John Tasker, joiner.
William Garfild, joiner.
David ap Bennet, joiner.
Robert Nicholas, fletcher.
Robert Savage, beer-brewer.
Thomas Langley, beer-brewer.
Richard Deane, tanner.

1557-8 [4-5 P. & M.] WILLIAM BIRD, Mayor.

John Meredeth, tailor.
Richard Cowper, ironmonger.
John Robinson, dyer.
Hugh Cally, sherman.
Randle Lloyde, gentleman.
Thomas Lynyall, mercer.
Robert Eaton, baker.
Edward Hancock, baker.
Richard Thornton, ironmonger.
John Asmor, tailor.
Richard Barker, smith.
John Dobbe, cordwainer.
John Pillen, merchant.
William Croughton, gentleman.
William Steale, grocer.
Randle Leche, merchant.
James Banester, embroiderer.
William Costerdyne, merchant.
Henry Maynwaringe, draper.
George Sedgewick, merchant.
David Madock, tanner.
William Johnson, smith.
William Walle, ironmonger.
Thomas Bavand, merchant.
Richard Bavant, merchant.

Griff Jenins [? Jevins], merchant.
Henry Moneley, tallow-chandler.
Randle Bostock, barber.
Thomas Newton, shoemaker.
Richard Wright, draper.
John Rathburne, baker.
Robert Crosse, tailor.
Richard Lingley, shoemaker.
John Whithed, glover.
William Pick, painter.
Richard Holbruck, baker.
Randle Eaton, draper.
Randle Ince, shoemaker.
Richard Smith, weaver.
John Dannold, baker.
Richard Bird, tanner.
Robert Chamblen, tanner.
Ralph Mayo, *alias* Baxter, webster.
Edward Brid, tanner.
Thomas Towers, smith.

1558-9 [6 P. & M.–1 Eliz.] SIR LAURENCE SMITH, KNIGHT, MAYOR.

Nov. 13		Hugh Aldersey, merchant.
—		John Ridley, draper.
—		Richard Davies, draper.
—		John Richards, draper.
—		Thomas Walle, haberdasher.
—		John Allen, draper.
—		David Phillips, mercer.
Nov. 14		John Allyngton, ironmonger.
Dec.	1	William Smith, glover.
,,	1	William Denson, baker.
Jan.	23	John Robinson, yeoman.
Feb.	9	Edmund Annyon, hoper.
,,	9	Richard Cowton, saddler.
——	23	Richard Newhall, pewterer.
—		Geoffrey Bickley, slater.
—		Thomas Finlowe, glover.
Apr.	18	Richard Pope, corviser.
,,	18	Richard Thornton, tanner.
,,	18	Ralph Jenson, tanner.
—		William Tayler, tanner.
—		Richard Brassey, smith.
—		John Jones, merchant.

—	William Grene, tallow-chandler.
—	Humphrey Weston, glover.
—	John Grice, glover.
—	Ralph Rogerson, bowyer.
—	Richard Bolland, butcher.
May 6	Ralph Radford, merchant.
June 12	Richard Radley, baker.
Aug. 28	Thomas Ellome, clerk and tayler.
,, 28	Nicholas Massy, draper.
,, 28	Richard Whitlegg, smith.
—— 12	Richard Massy, mercer.
12	George Buxy, corviser.
12	John Glegg, tanner.

1559–60 [1–2 Eliz.] HENRY HARDWARE, Mayor.

James Haughton, ironmonger.
John Fisher, gentleman.
Robert Femey, corviser.
William Christian, fishmonger.
Roger Lea, ironmonger.
Peter Hues, tailor.
John Fletcher, baker.
Bartholomew Tayler, fishmonger.
Thomas Walle, innkeeper.
Thomas Nicholson, merchant.
Robert Burstow, merchant.
James Parker, glover.
Thomas Radford, merchant.
Thomas Gruff, baker.
Thomas Hughson, glover.
William Kirkes, corviser.
William Cally, mercer.
Richard Gittens, salter.
Robert Brock.
John White, baker.
Hamon Johnson.
Laurence Browne.
John Bolland.
John Robinson.

1560–1 [2–3 Eliz.] WILLIAM ALDERSEY, Mayor.

James Cornell.
John Powell, ironmonger.
William Gruff, weaver.

Richard Tyerer, glover.
Richard Meales, yoman.
Thomas White, glover.
Thomas ap Lle[wely]n.
Thomas Heward, merchant.
William Goodman s. of Adam Goodman, alderman.
John Johnson, cowper.
George Whitoff.
Adam Bles, mercer.
Richard Duglas, barber.
Edward ap Robin.
William Richardson.
Hugh Spark, fletcher.
Edmund Smith s. of Thomas Smith, alderman.
Fulke Aldersey s. of William Aldersey, alderman.
Randle Bulkley, tailor.
Randle Williamson.
Robert Thornley.
Thomas Holme, smith.
John White, sherman.
Thomas ap Hue, sherman.
Thomas Bromley, butcher.
Ralph Tomlinson, cowper.
John Moore.
Roger Horton, sherman.
Robert Weston, sherman.
John Robinson, dyer.

1561-2 [3-4 Eliz.] JOHN COWPER, Mayor.

Robert Evans, tailor.
William Tayler.
John Tayler, *alias* Darbyshier.
John Powell.
Richard Raburne, corviser.
Robert Heath.
John Andrewe, smith.
John Symonds.
John Jenson, shoemaker.
Richard Robinson.
Richard Fisher.
Ralph Rosingreve.
Thomas Simcock, smith.
Thomas Leche, ironmonger.
Richard Catterall, weaver.

Richard Hoker, merchant.
Ralph Tonge, fishmonger.
Roger Bradshawe, plumber.
William Johnes s. of Robert Johns, alderman.
John Hall, baker.

1562-3 [4-5 Eliz.] RANDLE BAMVILE, Mayor.

William Shurlock.
Robert Monxfild, skinner.
Richard Woodcock, tanner.
Thomas ap David ap Kenrick.
Guy Curmyne, smith.
Thomas Lache, cowper.
Thomas Barker, embroiderer.
Humphrey Renolds, draper.
Ralph Snede, esquire.
George Snede, esquire.
Paul Chauntrell, mercer.
Robert Huntington, baker.
Thomas Wright, ironmonger.
John Lle[wely]n, glover.

1563-4 [5-6 Eliz.] Sir LAURENCE SMITH, Knight, Mayor.

Oct. 26	Robert Leche, barber, p. of Richard Leche, barber.
,, 26	Richard Cally [Kelly, M.B.], painter, p. of Thomas Poole, painter.
,, 27	Richard Welde, sherman, p. of Henry Fynchet, sherman.
Nov. 5	David Johns, saddler, p. of William Fletcher, saddler.
Jan. 13	John Glover, sherman, p. of William Dod, sherman.
June 13	William Shevington, painter, p. of Richard Hallwoode, painter.
July 13	George Phillips, shoemaker, p. of John Cocke of Chester, shoemaker.
,, 17	William Clough of Chester, cook.
Aug. 11	Henry Grimsdich, shoemaker, p. of Thomas Blith, shoemaker.
,, 11	Thomas Fletcher, glover, p. of Peter Fletcher, glover.
,, 13	John Thomas, mercer, p. of Robert Powell, mercer.
Sep. 22	Thomas Blanchard, baker, p. of John Blanchard, baker.
,, 22	Thomas Janson, butcher, p. of Richard Brine, butcher.

38 THE ROLLS OF THE FREEMEN OF [1564-6

Sep. 22 John Cotgreve, milner, servant of Ralph Goodman the elder, alderman.
Oct. 2 Richard Bridge, fishmonger, p. of William ———.
„   5 Richard ap Owen [Ries ap Howen, M.B.], mercer, p. of Richard Barton, mercer.

1564-5 [6-7 Eliz.] RICHARD POOLE, Mayor.

James Glaseor, gentleman.
Stephen Woods, fishmonger.
Ralph Tilston, shoemaker.
John Shurlock, shoemaker.
John Kempe, smith.
Thomas Edwards, shoemaker.
Richard Eaton, cowper.
Robert Woods, cowper.
Richard Hogge, merchant.
Roger Sydall, tailor.
Richard Smith, shoemaker.
Randle Whitby, sherman.
Thomas Barrowe, glover.
William Glasior, esquire.
Thomas Gremsdich.
John Grymsdiche.
Phillip Walker, sherman.
Sir Henry Sidney, knight.

1565-6 [7-8 Eliz.] THOMAS GREENE, Mayor.

Richard Johnson, *alias* Conley, shoemaker.
Thomas Lathom, weaver.
John Tayler, saddler.
Richard Doby, glazier.
Michael Smith, merchant.
Roger Calcot, smith.
John Lingley.
John Hatton, cardmaker.
David Momford, founder.
Robert Walle, ironmonger.
Henry Houghton, ironmonger.
Peter Newall, tanner.
Richard Harford, tanner.
Robert Wildinge, mercer.
Roger Lynyall, hatmaker.
William Huntington, tanner.

Robert Asmore, tailor.
Robert Wright, ironmonger.
Thomas Moston, ironmonger.
John Rosingreve, pewterer.
Richard Ledsham, pewterer.
John Williamson, skinner.
Robert Grymesdich, merchant.
Richard Wilson, shoemaker.
Robert David, glover.
William Crougton, sherman.
Peter Cowper, baker.
John Bacon, yeoman.

1566–7 [8–9 Eliz.] Sir WILLIAM SNEDE, Knight, Mayor.

Randle Johnes.
Richard Fletcher, glover.
William Harrison.
John Longton, hatmaker.
John Tilston, mercer.
John Moores, shoemaker.
John Fulin, merchant.
Robert Lea, tailor.
John Henshawe, yeoman.
Thomas Spencer.
Richard Spencer, gentleman.
Peter Maynwaringe, merchant.
William Browne, merchant.
Ralph Crane, stringer.
Thomas Warmincham, saddler.
John Skynner, hatmaker.
Thomas Tarleton, weaver.
Thomas Rogerson, glover.
Thomas Haselwall, hewster and smith.
William Crosse, glover.
Edward Gill, glover.
Hugh Bildon.
John Tarleton, tallow-chandler.
William Villam, tailor.
John Jeffrey, *alias* Hixon, yeoman.
William Kent, yeoman.
Francis Godlof, bookbinder.
Richard Yockinge, innkeeper.

1567-8 [9-10 Eliz.] RICHARD DUTTON, Mayor.

Dec. 5 Peter Wright, skinner, p. of Thomas Orton of Chester, skinner, and s. of Ralph Wright of Chester, mercer, defunct.
Jan. 13 Arthur Chauntrell, sherman, p. of Henry Annyon of Chester, sherman.
Jan. 22 Thomas Birchenshed [Birkenhead, M.B.], shoemaker, p. of Robert Askow of Chester, shoemaker.
Feb. 9 Valentine Broughton, mercer, p. of Alderman Thomas Bellin of Chester, mercer.
„ 9 William Pixley, mercer, p. of Alderman John Webster, mercer, defunct.
„ 10 Anthony Hanky, mercer, s. of Alderman John Hankie of Chester, and p. of Alderman John Webster of Chester, mercer.
„ 10 Edward ap Richard, cardmaker, p. of John Psyvall [? Percival] of Chester, cardmaker, defunct.
Mar. 15 Thomas Dob, sherman, p. of William Dodd of Chester, sherman.
Apr. 6 John Aldersey, merchant, s. of Alderman William Aldersey of Chester, merchant.
„ 6 William Aldersey s. of Ralph Aldersey of Chester, alderman, defunct.
„ 6 Robert Stevens, glover, p. of Gilbert Whithed of Chester, glover, defunct.
„ 6 William Aldersey s. of Alderman Thomas Aldersey of Chester, defunct.
„ 6 David Chalner s. of John Chalner of Chester, merchant.
„ 15 John Smith of Chester, barber, s. of Hamnet Smith, late of Chester.
June 15 Roger Radford s. of Ralph Radford of Chester, defunct.
„ 15 Adam Johnson s. of Hamnet Johnson of Chester.
„ 15 Robert Barrowe s. of Thomas Barrowe of Chester.
„ 16 Thomas Waite } ss. of George Weite of Chester,
„ 16 Robert Weite } defunct.
[Another s. of George, Raffe Weite, is referred to in this entry.]
„ 19 Alexander Wildinge, shoemaker, p. of George Buxy of Chester, shoemaker, on report of George Buxy and Thomas Pyllyn, alderman of the Shoemakers. [This report was afterwards found to be false, and Alexander Wildinge was disfranchised on 30th Aug., 1568, by Order of Assembly.]
Aug. 31 Richard Knee of Chester, merchant.

Sep. 9 Robert Pillin s. of Thomas Pillin of Chester, gentleman, defunct, upon report of Elizabeth Goodman, wife of John Pillin of Chester, merchant, deceased, to whom he had been p., and also upon report of Thomas Pillin, merchant, to whom he had also been p.
„ 10 Thomas Kempe, merchant, p. of Alderman Adam Goddman, merchant.
„ 16 William Pillin, merchant, p. of James Pillin of Chester, merchant.
„ 23 William Bulkeley, merchant, s. of William Bulkeley, late of Chester, tailor.
„ 23 Robert Barton, glover, s. of John Barton of Chester, glover.
„ 23 James Knowlesley, s. of William Knowlesley, late of Chester, painter and barber.
Oct. 4 Richard Glover of Chester, dyer, p. of Evan Denevet of Chester, dyer, defunct.
„ 4 Roland Williams, tailor, p. of Griff Tudder of Chester, tailor.
„ 7 Thomas Blethin [or Plethin, M.B.], baker, p. of William Whithed of Chester, baker.
„ 12 William Knight, "ut forensicus" [as a foreigner; "clerk" erased.]

1568-9 [10-11 Eliz.] WILLIAM BALLE, MAYOR.

John Platt, tailor.
William Balle.
Richard Richardson, *alias* Locker, furbur.
Richard Whithed, baker.
William Barton, mercer.
Ralph Warmingham, saddler.
Thomas Persivall, saddler.
Peter Newall, merchant and draper.
Ralph Jaman, draper.
Thomas Parry, ironmonger.
William Crosse, weaver.
Thomas Foxe, merchant.
Thomas Meoles, weaver.
Randle Ewlowe, shoemaker.
William Ramesden, clothworker.
Robert Snagg, gentleman.
William Bushell.
Roger Grice, glover.

David Dannold, baker.
Thomas Smith, sherman.
William Cotgreve, innkeeper.
Thomas Holbruck, butcher.
Thomas Brerewood, glover.

1569-70 [11-12 Eliz.] SIR JOHN SAVAGE, KNIGHT, MAYOR.

Dec. 20 John Dutton, gentleman, s. of Fulke Dutton, alderman.
„ 20 Edward Trevor s. of John Trevor, goldsmith.
„ 20 Ralph Coldok, shoemaker, s. of Richard Coldock, shoemaker.
Jan. 14 William Burgeny, p. of Roger Lingley of Chester, shoemaker, defunct.
Mar. 13 William Shepperd, innkeeper, s. of Richard Shepperd of Chester, innkeeper.
Apr. 6 John Fyton, ironmonger, p. of John Alington of Chester, ironmonger.
„ 6 Richard Newall, tanner, s. of Richard Newall of Chester, tanner, defunct.
„ 6 Richard Tilston, shoemaker, s. of John Tilston of Chester, shoemaker.
May 23 Robert Smith, goldsmith, s. of Laurence Smith of Chester, goldsmith.
„ 23 Geoffrey Granno [or Gromwall, M.B.], tailor, s. of —— Gromwall of Chester, weaver, defunct.
„ 23 Henry Annion, tanner, s. of Henry Annyon of Chester, tanner, defunct.
„ 23 John Pope, shoemaker, s. of Richard Pope of Chester, shoemaker.
„ 23 ‡Roger Basford s. of Roger Basford of Chester, tailor.
„ 23 Richard Sponne, tanner, p. of John Barnes, tanner.
„ 23 William Blanchard, baker, p. of Robert Whithed, baker.
„ 23 George Bircheley· of Chester, yeoman.
July 3 Hugh Kenrick, joiner, p. of William Stokes, joiner.
„ 3 John Allen, embroiderer, p. of James Banester, embroiderer.
„ 3 Thomas Aldersey s. of William Aldersey, alderman.
„ 3 Ralph Smith s. of Thomas Smith, alderman.
„ 3 Roger Smith, mercer, s. of Roger Smith, mercer.
„ 3 Ralph Balle, merchant, s. of Thomas Balle, merchant.
„ 3 Nicholas Ketle s. of Thomas Ketle, dyer.
„ 18 Ralph Dod, sherman, s. of William Dod of Chester, sherman.

July	15	William Marten, draper, } ss. of Edward Marten, draper.
,,	15	John Marten, draper,
,,	15	William Fletcher, tanner, s. of Thomas Fletcher, tanner, defunct.
Sep.	15	Richard Bebinton, butcher, s. of Thomas Bebinton, butcher.
,,	15	Thomas ap Ithell p. of Richard Brine.
,,	15	Henry Pemberton, glover, p. of John Barton, glover.
,,	27	Henry Harpur, gentleman, "because he wilbe of Counseil wth this Cyty."
Oct.	11	William Fletcher, shoemaker, p. of Randle Ince of Chester, shoemaker.
,,	11	Thomas Werden, beer-brewer, p. of Thomas Burges of Chester, beer-brewer.

1570–1 [12–13 Eliz.] SIR LAURENCE SMITH, KNIGHT, MAYOR.

Dec.	16	John Weston, butcher, s. of John Weston of Chester, butcher.
,,	16	Thomas Gill s. of John Gill, fletcher.
Jan.	4	Richard Pemberton p. of William Lynacar of Chester, shoemaker, defunct.
,,	8	Thomas Cowper, draper, p. of John Ridley of Chester, draper.
,,	8	Ralph Hulton [Hilton, M.B.] s. of Robert Hilton of Chester, shoemaker, defunct.
,,	9	Thomas Fletcher, shoemaker, s. of William Fletcher of Chester, shoemaker, and p. of Alderman Randle Bamville, draper.
,,	24	David Mered[ith], *alias* Lloyde, draper, p. of John Allen of Chester, draper.
,,	22	Richard Harrison, sherman, p. of Henry Annion of Chester, sherman.
,,	22	William Dymock s. of William Dymock the elder of Chester, merchant.
,,	22	Richard Grymsdich s. of Richard Grymsdich of Chester, alderman, defunct.
,,	22	John Richards, sherman, p. of Richard Gitten of Chester, sherman, defunct.
,,	22	Richard Goose, draper, p. of Humphrey Renolds of Chester, draper.
Apr.	10	Robert Caren, hoper, p. of Phillip C—— of Chester, hoper.
May	2	John Tayler, tanner, s. of Thomas Tailer, *alias* Lancasher of ———

May   9 Ralph Harrison s. of John Harrison of Chester, smith.
June 18 James Hatton, butcher, s. of Thomas Hatton of Chester, pinner, defunct, and p. of Robert Lewes of Chester, butcher, defunct.
„   27 John Wright s. of Ralph Wright of Chester, chapman, defunct.
„   27 Edmund Dawby, glazier, s. of Richard Dawby of Chester, glazier.
Aug. 20 Stephen Gruffi, alias William, glover, p. of Richard Caldey of Chester, glover.
Sep.   3 Richard Rathburne of Chester, merchant.
„   3 Roger Darwall, glover, ⎫ ss. of Richard Darwall of
„   3 Robert Darwall, glover, ⎭   Chester, glover.
Oct.   9 George Brid, tanner, p. of William Brid, defunct.
„   9 Thomas Bavand, tanner, p. of William Bri—— [? Baxter], alias Meo of Chester, tanner.
„   9 William Sandford of Chester, tailor.
Aug.   6 William Dannold, draper, p. of Nicholas Massy of Chester, draper.

1571-2 [13-14 Eliz.] JOHN HANKEY, Mayor.

Nov. 12 Robert Cowper, baker, p. of John Whithed of Chester, baker.
„   26 Nicholas Hallewell, baker, p. of Richard Modesley of Chester, baker.
Jan.   9 George Antrobus, cowper, p. of Robert Phillipps of Chester, cowper.
„   21 Richard Bromley, saddler, s. of Ralph Bromley of Chester, linen draper, and p. of William Fletcher of Chester, saddler.
„   21 Humphrey ap Robin, ironmonger, p. of Edward ap Robyn, ironmonger.
„   21 Henry Johnes, saddler, p. of Daniel Jones of Chester, saddler.
„   21 Robert Halle, founder, p. of Gilbert Knowles of Chester, founder.
„   21 Thomas Brabant, cowper, p. of Edmund Annyon of Chester, cowper.
Mar. 31 Thomas ap John, ioyner [? junior], ironmonger, p. of John Thornton of Chester, ironmonger.
Apr.   9 Robert Smith, plumber, p. of John Bradshaw of Chester, plumber.
May 21 William Irby, tanner, s. of John Irby, and p. of William Bridd of Chester, tanner.

June 25	William Wright, baker, p. of Thomas Goret of Chester, baker, defunct.
Aug. 10	William Fletcher of Churton, co. Ches., sherman, and p. of Robert Modesley of Chester, sherman.
June 30	Robert Amery, ironmonger, s. of Robert Amery of Chester, ironmonger, defunct.
" 2	Roger Gest, ropier, p. of Alderman Thomas Bavand of Chester, ropier.
" 2	William Clough, weaver, s. of William Clough, late of Chester, weaver.
Aug. 11	Randle Hanky, merchant, s. of Hugh Hankey of Chester, merchant, defunct.
Sep. 1	Richard Coddington of Chester, peddler.
" 22	William Rogerson, draper, s. of William Rogerson of Moston, co. Ches., gentleman, defunct, and p. of Alderman Hugh Rogerson, draper.
Oct. 2	Richard Leighe, potticarier, p. of William Kally of Chester, apothecary, defunct.
" 7	Thomas Button of Chester, yeoman.
" 7	Richard Cotton, mercer, p. of Adam Bles of Chester, mercer.
" 10	George Calcot, ironmonger, p. of Alderman William Aldersey of Chester, ironmonger.

1572-3 [14-15 Eliz.] ROGER LEY, MAYOR.

Richard Lea, stringer.
John Tilston, shoemaker.
Richard Newall, pewterer.
Randle Newas, pewterer.
William Hocknell, mercer.
Henry Longton, hatmaker.
Hugh Evans, ironmonger.
Henry Pimrose, tailor.
William Hurst, stringer.
Richard Helin.
Robert Ince, shoemaker.
Richard Bromfild, draper.
Ralph Rathburne, draper.
John Burton, draper.
Robert Hodgson, shoemaker.
Richard Annyon, draper.
John Browne, glover.
Owen ap Ellis, ironmonger.
Mathew Evans, plumber.

William Corkill, chandler.
William Eaton, yeoman.
Richard Byram, weaver.
William Tayler, weaver.
George Cowper, ironmonger.
Robert Hodson, yeoman.
William Coventry, merchant.
Thomas Cowley, tanner.
Ellis Johnes, ironmonger.

1573-4 [15-16 Eliz.] RICHARD DUTTON, Mayor.

Oct. 27 Thomas Norcot, skinner, p. of John Williamson of Chester, skinner.
,, 27 John Hallewell.
,, 27 Laurence Rawlinson.
,, 27 Griffin ap David ap Lloid.
Dec. 19 Peter Smith, weaver, p. of William Fletcher of Chester, weaver.
,, 20 Nicholas Bremes of Handbridge.
Jan. 13 William Kirks, shoemaker, p. of William Kirkes of Chester, shoemaker.
,, 20 Richard Marks of Chester, cowper.
,, 23 William Churton, draper, p. of John Allen of Chester, draper.
,, 29 John Rathburne, ironmonger, p. of Richard Bavand of Chester, ironmonger.
Feb. 1 William Wildinge, glover, p. of Robert Brerewood of Chester, glover.
,, 1 Thomas Dannold, glover, s. of Richard Dannold of Chester, baker, defunct, and p. of Peter Fletcher of Chester, glover.
,, 1 William Hodgson, smith, p. of Roger Calcot of Chester, smith.
,, 1 Richard Dawby, glazier, s. and p. of Richard Dawby, late of Chester, glazier.
,, 1 John Asbruck, glover, p. of Alderman John Harvy of Chester, glover.
,, 8 Robert Ollerhed, hatmaker, p. of John Lovet of Chester, hatmaker.
Apr. 30 Thomas Penteny, barber, p. of Richard Leche of Chester, barber.
,, 30 Godfrey Hough, tailor, p. of Robert Evans of Chester, tailor.
,, 30 John Thomas, butcher, p. of Roger Brine of Chester, butcher.

[1573-4]

Apr. 30		William Crosse, baker, p. of Thomas Fletcher of Chester, baker.
May	3	Robert Poole of Chester, gentleman.
,,	3	George Hulton of Chester, yeoman.
,,	5	Hugh David, *alias* Baugh, of Chester, mariner.
,,	7	William Giell of Chester, mariner, p. of John Warton of Chester, mariner.
,,	7	Richard Foxley of Handbridge, tailor.
,,	8	Richard Haselwall of Handbridge.
,,	10	William Fletcher, shoemaker, s. of William Fletcher of Chester, shoemaker, defunct.
,,	10	John Hale s. of Roger Hale of Chester, sergeant of the keys, defunct, and p. of Richard Coock of Chester, shoemaker.
July	3	Ralph Modesley, sherman, s. of Randle Modesley, and p. of Robert Modesley of Chester, sherman.
,,	5	Robert Wilson, smith, p. of Thomas Hulme of Chester, smith.
,,	14	Alex. Harison, chirurgeon, servant of the Queen.
,,	14	Richard Brookes, smith.
,,	27	John Williamson, *alias* Staples of Boughton, tailor.
Aug.	11	Richard Lightfoote, weaver, p. of William Fletcher of Chester, weaver.
,,	11	John Marten, weaver, p. of John Hixon of Chester, weaver.
,,	11	John Corne of Handbridge, glover.
,,	11	Thomas Vernon s. of Ralph Vernon of Chester, shoemaker.
,,	13	Hugh Grymesdich of Chester.
,,	13	William Robinson of Chester.
,,	13	William Duccar of Chester.
,,	28	Robert Molston, carrier.
,,	28	Ralph Molston s. of above Robert Molston.
,,	31	Thomas Damport, "extra le Barrs Ciℓ Cestr et infra libertaℓ ejusdem."
Sep.	11	Henry Glasior of Chester, osteler.
,,	13	Thomas Deane of Chester, weaver.
,,	13	Thomas Coventrey of Chester, mariner.
,,	13	John Deane, shoemaker, p. of Richard Huet of Chester, shoemaker.
,,	13	John Harrison, weaver.
,,	13	Brian Bland of Chester, mariner.
,,	13	William Wolfe, cowper, s. of Richard Wolfe, late of Chester, cowper.
,,	21	Thurstan Hollinshed, servant of William Gerrard, esquire, recorder of Chester.

Sep.	27	William Croxson [Crosson, M.B.] of Chester, weaver.
,,	27	Richard Carter of Chester, mariner.
Oct.	1	John Wildinge of Chester, innkeeper.
Sep.	4	John ap Lle[wely]n, joiner, s. of Lle[wely]n ap Griff, and p. of William Stokes of Chester, joiner.
,,	4	Edward Lle[wely]n, joiner, p. of Hugh Kenrick of Chester, joiner.
,,	4	David ap Thomas, glover, p. of John Horton of Chester, glover.
Oct.	6	John Assherwod [or Ashwodd], weaver [bowyer, M.B.], of Bridg North, co. Salop.
,,	9	William Radcliffe of Chester, merchant.
,,	9	John Walley of Chester, mariner.
,,	9	John Bennet of Chester, mariner.
,,	9	Nicholas Wright of Chester, weaver.
,,	9	Henry Turner of Chester, water-leader.
,,	11	Thomas Ellam of Chester, singer.
,,	11	John Foxall of Chester, weaver.
,,	11	John Ryder, glover, p. of Peter Fletcher of Chester, glover.
,,	11	Roland Barnes, mercer, p. of Paul Chantrell of Chester, mercer, and s. of Richard Barnes of Chester, tanner.
,,	11	William Trallock.
,,	11	Robert Trallock.
,,	11	John Geste.
,,	11	Robert Fazakerley.
,,	11	Francis Sefton.
,,	11	John Occle of Chester, yeoman, servant of Henry Harpur of Chester, esquire.
,,	12	James Banester of Chester, public notary.
,,	12	Walter Nowell of Chester, shoemaker.
,,	12	Robert Turner, tailor, p. of John Asmore of Chester, tailor.
,,	12	Thomas Dodd of Boughton, yeoman.
,,	12	Thomas Deane, *alias* Wright, of Chester, baker.
,,	12	John Sowthworth [Sothorne, M.B.], weaver, p. of John Meall of Chester, weaver.
,,	12	Thomas Sowthorthue [Sothorne, M.B.] of Chester, weaver.
,,	12	James Banian of Chester, yeoman.
,,	13	Roger Whatton of Spitle Boughton, wheelwright.
,,	13	Edward Thomas, ironmonger, p. of Alderman John Cowper, ironmonger.
,,	13	William Hulton, shoemaker, s. of [Robert?] Hulton, late of Chester, shoemaker.
,,	13	Roger Chauntrell of Chester, shoemaker.

1574–6]   THE CITY OF CHESTER   49

Oct. 15   John Houghton, innkeeper, s. of William Houghton of Chester, innkeeper, defunct.

1574–5 [16–17 Eliz.] SIR JOHN SAVAGE, KNIGHT, MAYOR.

John Twis, sherman.
Richard Boydell, joiner.
Richard Wright, sherman.
Robert Edwards, ironmonger.
Henry Thornton, merchant.
Thomas Fisher, shoemaker.
Thomas Morgan, cook.
Robert Hatton, butcher.
William Calkin, tailor.
Henry Scarsbridge, joiner.
Thomas Carden, tanner.

1575–6 [17–18 Eliz.] HENRY HARDWARE, MAYOR.

Oct. 24   Peter Bennet of Chester, shoemaker, p. of Thomas Byrchenshaw of Chester, shoemaker, defunct.
Nov. 22   Thomas Rixon, officer, s. of Randle Rixon of Chester, officer, defunct.
Dec. 5   Henry Hocknell, tailor, p. of John Milner of Chester, tailor.
„   5   Thomas Kempe, smith, p. of John Kempe of Chester, smith.
„   5   Edward Yonge, shoemaker, p. of John Coorke of Chester, shoemaker.
„   12   John Tayler, weaver, p. of Thomas Deane of Chester, weaver.
Jan. 10   John Harvy s. of John Harvy of Chester, alderman.
„   10   Richard Tilston p. of Alderman Roger Lea of Chester, ironmonger.
„   10   William Throp s. of Thomas Throp, sergeant of the keys, and p. of Edward Wright of Chester, skinner.
„   10   Thomas Richardson s. of William Richardson, *alias* Locker, of Chester, furbur.
„   13   Robert Ewley, skinner, s. of Hugh Ewley of Marston, co. Ches., and p. of Thomas Monxfild of Chester, skinner, defunct.
„   13   Richard Wells, late of Shrewsbury, weaver.
„   14   William Cally, sherman, p. of Roger Tailor of Chester, sherman, defunct.
Apr. 28   John Pulford, joiner, } pp. of William Sto¹
„   28   Henry Scarsbrig

50 THE ROLLS OF THE FREEMEN OF [1576–7

May 4 William Stevenson, joiner, p. of Richard Boydell of Chester, joiner.
„ 4 John Pulford, joiner, p. of Richard Boidell, joiner.
„ 16 Richard Marten, draper, s. of Edward Marten of Chester, draper, and servant of William Pixley, mercer, and afterwards of Alderman John Cowper, ironmonger.
July 5 William ap Richard, clothier.
„ 11 John Watkinson, beer-brewer, p. of Thomas Burges of Chester, beer-brewer.
„ 11 Robert Glover, beer-brewer, p. of Thomas Burges of Chester, beer-brewer.
„ 19 Roland Marshe p. of John Marshe of Chester, glover.
Aug. 15 Thomas Wykes, weaver.
„ 27 Robert Phillips, hatmaker, p. of Thomas Lyniall of Chester, hatmaker.
Sep. 17 Anthony Gremsdich, merchant, s. of Richard Grymesdich of Chester, merchant.
„ 17 John Ley, tailor, p. of Robert Gill of Chester, tailor.
„ 17 Richard Sefton, tanner, p. of William Meo of Chester, tanner.
„ 24 Robert Evans, glover, p. of Alderman John Harvy of Chester, glover.
Oct. 2 John Nicoll, baker, p. of Richard Modesley of Chester, baker.
„ 8 Ralph Golburne, founder, p. of Gilbert Knowles of Chester, founder.
„ 9 Richard Broster, tanner, s. of Richard Broster of Chester, tanner, and p. of William Croston of Chester, gentleman.
„ 10 Griffin Sownds, butcher, p. of Thomas Jenson of Chester, butcher.

1576–7 [18–19 Eliz.] JOHN HARVY, Mayor.

Edward Lloid, mercer.
Robert Shurlock, shoemaker.
William Prichard, butcher.
Henry Yonge, shoemaker.
Robert Ratcliffe, merchant.
John Warton, merchant.
John Hulton, shoemaker.
Thomas Gardner, cowper.
Thomas Wilson, sherman.
John Bostock, capper.

John Churton, sherman.
Richard Sawnders, bowyer.
William Harvy.
Hamon Sothorne, draper.
Fulke Smith, merchant.
Henry Marten, fishmonger.
Ralph Barlow, linen-draper.
Edward ap David, glover.
John Birth, butcher.
Thomas Fisher, *alias* Hill, butcher.
John Milner, pursuivant.

1577–8 [19–20 Eliz.] THOMAS BELLIN, Mayor.

John Bellin, tailor.
Solomon Smith, merchant.
Richard Warmingham.
Jesper Gillam, yeoman.
Ralph Radford, tanner.
Richard Aldersey.
Edmund Jenson, butcher.
John Bebinton, butcher.
Ralph Edge, shoemaker.
Edward Poole, merchant.
John Ratcliffe.
Arthur Cuxton.
Hamon Bennet, tanner.
Richard Bryne, butcher.
Edward Marten, draper.
John Wade, butcher.
John Wright, tanner.
Richard Shevington, joiner.
Ralph Finchet, sherman.
Ralph Mort, saddler.
John Davy, butcher.
John ap Rees, cowper.
David Bennet, joiner.
John Woodes, baker.
Thomas Balle.
Robert Woodcock, tanner.
Thomas Carter, tailor.
Henry Pigot, ironmonger.
Ralph Williamson, skinner.
Richard Clough, weaver.
Paul Chauntrell, mercer.

Richard Rathburne.
Ralph Johnson, glover.
Robert Cooke, glover.
Thomas Bowier, yeoman.
John Brid.
Thomas Pate, sherman.
—— Powell, tailor.
Thomas Richardson, shoemaker.
Barnabas Poole, gentleman.
Peter Buxy, shoemaker.
Nicholas Buxy, shoemaker.
William Penny, fletcher.
Richard Tilston, shoemaker.

1578-9 [20-21 Eliz.] WILLIAM JEWET, Mayor.

Simon Smith, furbur.
William Dowby, shoemaker.
Richard Meycock, pewterer.
David Evans, pewterer.
Arthur Marten, glover.
Evan ap Hoell, glover.
Thomas Newport, shoemaker.
Robert Fisher, smith.
Henry Hamnet, draper.
William Tilston, mercer.
James Grymsdich, draper.
William Holland, mercer.
Ralph Bithell, tanner.
John Throp, tailor.
William Congley, stringer.
Ralph Horton, sherman.
William Kinge, baker.
John ap Shone, baker.
Thomas Vernam, weaver.
Thomas Heath, cowper.
Henry Coz, glover.
John Probin, ironmonger.
John Dewsbery, embroiderer.
John Tayler, cowper.
Humphrey Phillips, tailor.
George Woodward, yeoman.
John Hyne, chandler.
Geoffrey Cooke, fishmonger.
Evan ap David, glover.

Hugh Cromp, baker.
Francis Higinson, yeoman.
Robert Jonson, glover.
Edward Huet, beer-brewer.

1579–80 [21–22 Eliz.] WILLIAM GOODMAN, DIED, AND HUGH ROGERSON, SUCC., MAYORS.

Nov. 3 Edward Bennet, shoemaker, p. of William Lea of Chester, shoemaker.
„ 3 Laurence Brid, tanner, p. of Richard Brid of Chester, tanner.
„ 10 William ap Richard, baker, p. of William Denson, late of Chester, baker.
Jan. 11 Henry Shaw, tanner, s. of Ellis Shaw of Chester, tanner.
„ 11 Henry Annyon, tanner, s. of John Annion, late of Chester, tanner.
„ 11 Robert Persivall, cardmaker, s. of Randle Persivall, late of Chester, cardmaker.
Mar. 3 Richard Looker, chandler, p. of Alderman Thomas Grene of Chester, tallow-chandler.
„ 8 William Sale, tailor, p. of Christopher Smith of Chester, tailor.
Apr. 7 John Lenard, tailor, p. of John Milner of Chester, tailor.
„ 11 John Richardson, *alias* Richards, *alias* Barker, tanner, p. of Richard Woodcok of Chester, tanner, and s. of David Richards, *alias* Barker, of Chester, fishmonger.
„ 11 John Williams, mercer, p. of John Tilston of Chester, mercer.
May 14 Robert Church, tailor, p. of William Sandford of Chester, tailor.
„ 20 Ralph Hyne, tanner, p. of Alderman William Brid of Chester, tanner.
July 16 John Bastwell, bowyer, s. of John Bastwell, late of Chester, bowyer.
Aug. 30 Laurence Warmingham, saddler, s. of Laurence Warmingham, late of Chester, saddler.
„ 30 William Dodd, draper, p. of Alderman William Hamnet of Chester, draper.
„ 30 Gilbert Hancock, saddler, s. of William Hancock of Chester, currier, and p. of Thomas Warmingham, saddler.

Aug. 30 Robert Foxall, hatter, p. of Thomas Lynyall of Chester, hatter.
Oct. 3 William Hixon, weaver, s. of John Hixon of Chester, weaver.
,, 3 Thomas Meoles, weaver, s. of Thomas Meoles of Chester, weaver, defunct.
,, 3 Henry Trafford, late of Chester, baker.
,, 10 Richard Dod, draper, p. of Richard Wright of Chester, draper.
,, 10 John White, glover, p. of Humphrey Weston of Chester, glover.
,, 10 Richard Vaws, tailor, s. of Oliver Vaws of Chester, tailor, defunct.
,, 11 William Cawdie, glover, s. of Richard Cawdie of Chester, glover.
,, 12 William Hine, shoemaker, p. of Thomas Richardson of Chester, shoemaker, defunct.
,, 3 Ralph Dicus, weaver, p. of Thomas Deane of Chester, weaver.
,, 13 Arthur Bennet, yeoman, servant of William Glaseor of Chester, esquire.

1580-1 [22-23 Eliz.] WILLIAM BIRD, Mayor.

Thomas Hulme, gentleman.
William Lecester, mercer.
Fulke Ries, mercer.
Richard Arrowsmith, shoemaker.
Thomas Rivington, yeoman.
Richard Evanson, weaver.
Hugh Gruffi', tailor.
James Balle, smith.
George Browne, founder.
Thomas Bryne, butcher.
Richard James, butcher.
William Liverpoole, pinner.
Edmund Gamull, gentleman.
Peter Williams, sherman.
William Witten, sherman.
Richard Rogerson.
Thomas Jones, sherman.
Edward Gruff', tailor.
John Wildon, innkeeper.
William Modesley, baker.
Edward Brid, ironmonger.

Richard Hanmer, ironmonger.
Christopher Goodman, gentleman and preacher, &c.
Richard Offley, merchant.
William Offley, merchant.
Hugh Offley, merchant.
John Rogers, grocer.
Alex. Cotes, gentleman.
Roger Bell, yeoman.
Thomas Rogers, *alias* Rogerson, draper.
Henry ap Richard, chandler.
John Fromwey, barber.
Richard Tayler, mercer.
Thomas Alcock, tailor.
Thurstan Held, baker.
Richard Howell, yeoman.
John Johnson, silk weaver.
John Lightfot, glover.

1581-2 [23-24 Eliz.] RICHARD * BAVAND, Mayor.

James Kempe, joiner.
John Nutter, draper.
Robert Dodd.
Ralph Birkhened, gentleman.
Richard Banester, haberdasher.
Thomas Robinson, weaver.
Fulke Ledsham, draper.
Thomas Dawson, ironmonger.
Thomas Allerton, ironmonger.
Ralph Key, draper.
John Wright, draper.
John Smith, draper.
John Litherland, tanner.
William Nilley, weaver.
Richard Richardson, *alias* Wever.
Griffin Richard, weaver.
John Bryne, butcher.
Edward Burges, cowper.
James Eccles, slater.
Hugh Skinner, slater.
Richard Geste, slater.
Thomas Booth, slater.

* Canon Morris gives this Mayor's name as Robert. On the other hand, Ormerod, Hemingway, and the Roll of Freemen give it as Richard.

Richard Scons, slater.
Thomas Goose, slater.
Laurence Meirick, slater.
Thomas Morris, slater.
Hugh Brickhill, slater.
John Kynsley, slater.
William Kneckell, slater.
John Gardner, slater.
Thomas Cadell, slater.
William Garnet, slater.
William Warton, slater.
Robert Catterall, slater.
Nicholas Banester, slater.
Launcellot Llen, slater.
Richard Jaman [? Janian], slater.
William Walshe, slater.
Hugh Ussherwood, slater.
John Cowper, weaver.
Peter Street, yeoman.
John Taylor, *alias* Sars, yeoman.
Edward Kilso, saddler.
Ralph Cowper, sherman.
William Congley, cowper.
Thomas Bebinton, butcher.
William Ollerhed, wright.
Anthony Enowe, yeoman.
Peter Price, plumber.
Ralph Rathburne, tanner.
William King, tanner.
John Bettrich, tanner.
Richard Williamson, skinner.
Henry Trafford, smith.
Robert Williamson, smith.
John Thornton, merchant.
Thomas Smith, gentleman.
Edward Smith, gentleman.
Randle Throp, cowper.
Robert Grice, hatmaker.
John Hancock, tailor.
William Thickins, merchant.
Richard Battrich, tailor.
Thomas Ticer, clothworker.
Richard Bavand, ironmonger.
Edward ap Thomas ap dd [David], glover.

1582-3 [24-25 Eliz.] WILLIAM STILES, Mayor.

Nov. 21 William Linton, servant of the Reverend Father in God, William, Bishop of Chester.
Dec. 17 William Coldock, shoemaker, s. of Richard Coldock of Chester, shoemaker, defunct.
„ 17 George Heath, shoemaker, s. of Robert Heath of Chester, shoemaker.
Jan. 10 ‡Thomas Yonge s. of Ralph Yonge.
„ 10 Thomas Egerton, shoemaker, s. of Ralph Egerton, and p. of Edward Yonge of Chester, shoemaker.
„ 19 Henry Hardware, merchant, s. of Alderman Henry Hardware of Chester, merchant.
„ 19 George Ithell, baker, p. of Thomas Plethin of Chester, baker.
Feb. 6 John Farror, linen-draper, late of Bridge Trafford, co. Ches.
„ 22 Henry Tetlowe, merchant, s. of Thomas Tetlowe of Chester, merchant.
„ 28 William Richardson, *alias* Locker, cutler, s. of William Richardson, *alias* Locker, cutler.
„ 28 Peter Richardson, *alias* Locker, cutler, s. of Richard Richardson, *alias* Cutler [*sic*].
Apr. 11 Ralph Allen, shoemaker, p. of John Andrew of Chester, shoemaker.
„ 11 William Allen, pewterer and founder, p. of Gilbert Knowles of Chester, founder.
May 11 Richard Gitton, merchant, s. of Richard Gitton of Chester, merchant, defunct.
„ 23 Hugh Williams, glover, s. of Hugh Williams of Chester, mercer, and p. of Richard ——, glover.
June 10 Simon Richardson, fishmonger, s. of David Richardson of Chester, fishmonger, and p. of Robert David of Chester, glover, defunct.
„ 11 John Gest, ironmonger, p. of Richard Marshe of Chester, ironmonger and ropier.
„ 11 Peter Wright, tailor, p. of Ralph Calveley of Chester, tailor, and s. of Robert Wright of Chester, butcher, defunct.
„ 28 Phillip Phillips, hatter, p. of Robert Phillips of Chester, hatmaker.
July 9 John Seale of Chester, tailor.
„ 10 Nicholas Sands of Chester, milner.
„ 10 John Fraunces of Chester, tanner, p. of William Meo, *alias* Baxter, of Chester, tanner.

Aug. 13		Godfrey Wynne, butcher, p. of Thomas Fisher, *alias* Hill, of Chester, butcher.
,,	16	William Foster, mercer, p. of Paul Chauntrell, mercer, and s. of Ralph Forster, merchant, defunct.
,,	21	Edward Sefton, tailor, p. of Robert Hill of Chester, tailor.
,,	22	George Walmesley, tailor, at the request of Thomas Egerton, esquire, "solicitor" to the Queen, and Thomas Walmesley, esquire, sergeant-at-law to the Queen.
Sep.	3	Robert Malpas, shoemaker, p. of Randle Ince of Chester, shoemaker.
,,	11	John Kinge, ironmonger, s. of William Kinge of Chester, baker.
,,	11	Thomas Tilston, hatmaker, s. of John Tilston of Handbridge, yeoman, defunct, and p. of John Tilston of Chester, hatmaker.
,,	11	William Hand, tailor, p. of William [Sanford?] of Chester, tailor.
Oct.	1	John Litler, draper, p. of John Allen of Chester, draper.
,,	2	Griffin Evans, silk weaver.
,,	5	Thomas Radford, yeoman, s. of Roger Radford of Chester, tanner, defunct.
,,	5	John Molson, tanner, p. of Henry Annion of Chester, tanner.

1583-4 [25-26 Eliz.] ROBERT BREREWOOD, Mayor.

Oct. 21 Richard Stockton, smith, s. of Hugh Stockton of Chester, smith.
Nov. 6 Edward Powell, smith, p. of John Kempe of Chester, smith.
Dec. 18 John Annion, cowper, s. of Edmund Annion of Chester, cowper, defunct.
Jan. 3. James Sale, shoemaker, s. of William Sale of Hargreve Stubbs, co. Ches., and p. of William Kirkes of Chester, shoemaker.
,, 4 Thomas Bastwell, haberdasher, s. of John Bastwell the younger of Chester, currier, defunct.
,, 16 Edward Howell, ironmonger, s. of Howell Mathew [*sic*], and p. of Humphrey Probin of Chester, ironmonger.
,, 28 William Lea, shoemaker, s. of William Lea of Chester, shoemaker.

[1583-4] THE CITY OF CHESTER 59

Jan. 29 John Leeche, mercer, p. of William Pixley of Chester, mercer.
Feb. 4 Randle Bingley, sherman, s. of John Bingley of Chester, sherman.
„ 10 William Wright, baker, s. of Peter Wright of Chester, baker.
„ 10 William Adams, baker, p. of William Kinge, the elder, of Chester, baker.
„ 12 John Brerewood, glover, s. of Robert Brerewood of Chester, mayor and glover.
„ 14 John Annion, shoemaker, p. of John Shurlocke of Chester, shoemaker, defunct.
„ 27 Thomas Bird, tanner, s. of William Bird of Chester, alderman and tanner.
„ 28 Edward Dutton, gentleman, s. of Richard Dutton, late of Chester, alderman.
Mar. 2 Christopher Conway, goldsmith, s. of Peter Conwaie of Chester, goldsmith, and p. of William Mutton of Chester, goldsmith, defunct.
„ 11 Robert Ridley, brickman, p. of William Gest of Chester, brickman, defunct.
„ 31 Ralph Halwood, barber, } ss. of Richard Halwood of
„ 31 Nicholas Halwood, barber, } Chester, barber, defunct.
Apr. 1 Hugh Fletcher, butcher, p. of Roger Brine of Chester, butcher.
„ 23 Peter Warburton of Northwiche, co. Ches., esquire.
June 20 John Peerson, weaver, p. of Thomas Deane of Chester, weaver.
July 11 Thomas Carter, tailor, p. of John Loy of Chester, tailor.
„ 28 John Wright, draper, s. of Nicholas Wright of Chester, baker, and p. of Ralph Rathburne of Chester, draper.
„ 28 ‡Thomas Cowmishe s. of Phillip Cowmishe of Chester cowper, defunct.
July 28 ‡Edward Tailer s. of Roger Tailor of Chester, sherman, defunct.
Sep. 19 Randle Foxall, weaver, p. of John Foxall of Flowkersbrooke, co. Ches., weaver.
Oct. 6 Thomas Chalner s. of Robert Chaln' of Chester, merchant, defunct.
„ 6 John Eaton, yeoman, keeper of the Northgate Gaol.
„ 12 William Granwall, weaver, s. of Richard Granwall of Chester, weaver.
„ 12 John Lloyd, weaver, s. of Thomas Lloid of Chester, weaver, defunct.

Oct. 12 Lewis Roberts, ironmonger, p. of Richard Marshe of Chester, ironmonger, defunct.
„ 12 Fulke Carter, baker.
„ 12 Richard Twis, sherman.
„ 14 Richard Deane, weaver, s. of Thomas Deane of Chester, weaver, defunct.

1584-5 [26-27 Eliz.] VALENTINE BROUGHTON, MAYOR.

Mar. 27 William Dod, sherman, s. of Griffin Dod of Chester, sherman.
Nov. 9 Cuthbert Gerrard, gentleman, s. of Sir William Gerrard of Chester, knight, defunct.
„ 10 Gilbert Gerrard, esquire, s. and h. of Sir William Gerrard of Chester, knight, defunct.
„ 16 Richard [Rice also, M.B.] Bennet, dyer, s. of Bennedict ap Shone, and p. of Laurence Sherington of Chester, dyer.
„ 16 Thomas Harbotle, mercer, p. of Paul Chantrell of Chester, mercer.
Jan. 5 Thomas Christian, cowper, s. of William Christian of Chester, cowper, defunct.
„ 5 William Leene [Lyne, M.B.], cowper, p. of Thomas Lynacre of Chester, cowper.
„ 5 John Scons [Sconce, M.B.], cowper, p. of William Christian, defunct.
„ 8 Ralph Done, esquire.
„ 8 Thomas Balle, shoemaker, p. of Richard Wilson of Chester, shoemaker.
„ 12 John Ketle, dyer, s. of William Ketle of Chester, dyer.
Feb. 1 Thomas Lenard, shoemaker, p. of Robert Marten of Chester, shoemaker, defunct.
„ 8 Thomas Whitby, wright.
„ 8 Richard Shurlock, shoemaker, p. of William Shurlock of Chester, shoemaker.
„ 12 Jesse Smith, draper, s. of Oliver Smith of Chester, draper and merchant.
„ 24 William Arrowsmith of Caernavon, mercer, s. of Gilbert Arrowsmith of Chester, sergeant of the keys, defunct.
„ 25 John Lucas, glover, s. of George Lucas of Chester, glover, defunct.
Mar. 1 John Andrewe, smith, s. of John Andrewe of Chester, smith, defunct.

[1584-5] THE CITY OF CHESTER 61

Mar. 12 John Rathburne, joiner, p. of Richard Boydell of Chester, joiner.
„ 20 Randle Bellin, mercer, s. of Thomas Bellin of Chester, alderman and mercer.
„ 20 Robert Hancock, smith, s. of Robert Hancock of Chester, smith, defunct.
„ 24 William Plomb, tailor, p. of Ralph Calveley of Chester, tailor.
Apr. 29 John [Rogers *alias*, M.B.] Rogerson, hosier [draper, M.B.], s. of William Rogerson, *alias* Rogerson [*sic*] of Chester, hosier.
May 7 Roger Lunt, tailor, p. of John Asmore of Chester, tailor, defunct.
„ 10 Thomas ap John, glover, p. of John Annion of Chester, glover, defunct.
„ 11 Robert Davison, butcher, p. of Thomas Holbruck of Chester, butcher.
June 8 Robert Farrington, currier, p. of John Lingley of Chester, currier.
„ 8 Henry Wilson, tanner, p. of William Huntington of Chester, tanner, defunct.
„ 9 John Eaton } ss. of John Eaton of Chester, beer-
„ 9 Thomas Eaton } brewer, defunct.
„ 9 Thomas Lynaker, cowper, s. of Thomas Linacre of Chester, cowper.
„ 22 John White, joiner, s. of John White, mariner, and p. of Richard Boydell of Chester, joiner, defunct.
„ 25 Henry Harries, weaver.
„ 25 William Bostock, innkeeper, s. of Ralph Bostock of Chester, innkeeper.
July 14 William Lowe, shoemaker, p. of William Kirks of Chester, shoemaker.
„ 14 Hugh Wilkinson, sherman, p. of William Fletcher of Chester, sherman.
„ 14 Thomas Bennet s. of Thomas Bennet of Chester, innkeeper and shoemaker.
„ 20 William Jackson, sawyer.
Aug. 2 Laurence Gremesdich of London, merchant, s. of Richard Gremesdich the younger of Chester, merchant, defunct.
„ 2 Robert Walle, ironmonger, s. of William Walle of Chester, alderman and ironmonger.
„ 2 Thomas Halwood of London, ironmonger, s. of Robert Halwood of Chester, barber, defunct.
„ 6 Patrick Thomason, butcher, p. of Richard Bryne of Chester, butcher, defunct.

Aug. 30   John Poole, hatter, p. of John Allen of Chester, hatmaker.
„ 31   William Ince, shoemaker, ⎱ ss. of Randle Ince of
        Richard Ince, saddler,   ⎰ Chester, shoemaker.
„ 31   Richard Annyon, butcher, s. of John Annyon of Chester, tanner, defunct.
Sep. 6   George Bellen s. of George Bellen of Chester, shoemaker, defunct.
„ 13   Thomas Jackson s. of Thomas Jackson of Chester, tailor, defunct.
„ 20   William Edwards, baker, p. of John Blanchard of Chester, baker.
„ 29   Richard Frawnces, shoemaker, p. of Alexander Wildinge of Chester, shoemaker.
Oct. 11   Thomas Birth of Chester, butcher, s. of John Birth of Chester, butcher.
„ 11   Robert Leene [Leyne, M.B.], tailor, p. of Robert Evans of Chester, tailor.
„ 13   Humphrey Hurste p. of Thomas Werden of Chester, beer-brewer.

1585-6 [27-28 Eliz.] EDMUND GAMULL, Mayor.

Richard Balle, tailor.
John Ridley.
John Jonson.
Robert Warton, weaver.
Randle Dodd, yeoman.
Robert Cally, sherman.
George Ravenscrofte, ironmonger.
Richard Browne, tailor.
William Barnes, tanner.
Richard Carington, beer-brewer.
John Rawlin, tanner.
Richard Bird, tanner.
John Drinkwater, ironmonger.
William Banester, tanner.
Hugh Banester, tanner.
Thomas Burges, dyer.
Robert Bassenet, yeoman.
Richard Peycock, merchant.
Robert Jones, draper.
Edward Blacon, tailor.
Ralph Fletcher, butcher.
John Lightfoote, wright.

Richard Garfild, joiner.
Robert Ashton, tanner.
Thomas Tomlinson, cowper.
Robert Johnson, tanner.
Richard Bennet, shoemaker.
Robert Golburne, ironmonger.
Robert Radford, merchant.
William Ridley, draper.
Griffin ap Thomas, butcher.
Ralph Crosse, glover.
William Payne, tailor.
Thomas Tetlowe, merchant.

1586-7 [28-29 Eliz.] WILLIAM WALLE, Mayor.

Thomas Betson, milner.
Richard Blagg, smith.
William Styles, mercer.
Lord Fardinando Strange.
John Leeche.
Thomas Allen, embroiderer.
John Stretch, innkeeper.
Richard Braband, cowper.
John Prenton, dyer.
John Looker, tallow-chandler.
Thomas Andrewe, shoemaker.
Richard Button, butcher.
John Madocke, butcher.
John Eaton, tailor.
John Moyle, draper.
Roger Bryne, butcher.
John Boydell, draper.
John ap David, baker.
John Stiles, draper.
Robert Offley, gentleman.
Thomas Offley, gentleman.
Richard Bennet, tanner.
John Sprowson, hatmaker.
Edward Hedock, clerk.
Hugh Hyne, chandler.
Thomas Harvy, glover.
Thomas Bruce, glover.
Thomas Cooke, glover.
John Smarley, yeoman.
Humphrey Yonge, yeoman.

Owen Williams, linen-draper.
Robert Mosse, tailor.
Richard Hallwall, smith.
John Lache.

1587-8 [29-30 Eliz.] ROBERT BREREWOOD, Mayor.

Oct. 16 John Walker, glazier, s. of Christopher Walker of Chester, sherman.
„ 16 James Massy s. of Thomas Massy, late of Chester, glazier.
„ 19 William ap Thomas, glover, p. of Richard Darwall of Chester, glover.
„ 24 William Johnson, smith, s. of William Johnson of Chester, smith.
„ 31 William Madock, glover, s. of William Madock of Chester, glover.
Nov. 15 John Stiles, mercer, s. of William Stiles, late of Chester, alderman and mercer.
Dec. 19 Thomas Stapleton, gentleman, servant of the most noble Lord Strange.
„ 19 George Flowers, pewterer.
Jan. 10 William Christian of the Isle of Man, beer-brewer, and p. of John Watkins of Chester, beer-brewer.
„ 12 Henry Newbot, sherman, p. of Ralph Modesley of Chester, sherman.
„ 12 Ralph Sekerson, fishmonger, p. of William Cotgreave of Chester, innkeeper and fishmonger.
„ 12 William Sawnders, bowyer, p. of Richard Saunders of Chester, bowyer.
„ 23 Thomas Moldinge, tanner, p. of David Dymock of Chester, tanner.
Feb. 7 Thomas Case, yeoman, s. of Richard Case, sergeant of the keys.
„ 9 Otes Conilow.
„ 12 Thomas Wright, draper, p. of Nicholas Massey of Chester, draper, and s. of Nicholas Wright, baker.
„ 12 Richard Wright, baker, s. and p. of Nicholas Wright of Chester, baker, defunct.
Mar. 5 Robert ap Edward, glover, p. of Thomas Finlow of Chester, glover.
„ 21 James Radford, butcher, p. of John Thomas of Chester, butcher.
Apr. 11 John Walshman, baker, p. of Robert Whithed, late of Chester, baker.

Apr.	30	*John Glynne.
May	17	Dudley Yerworth s. of John Yerworth of Chester, esquire, defunct.
„	17	Roger Kinge, shoemaker, p. of Nicholas Buxy, shoemaker, and s. of William Kinge, the elder, of Chester, baker.
„	17	John Hinton, baker, p. of John Danald, baker, and s. of Thomas Hinton of Chester, capper, defunct.
June	13	Randle Ince, draper, p. of Nicholas Massy, draper, and s. of Randle Ince of Chester, shoemaker.
July	2	Thomas Pricket, embroiderer, p. of John Dewsbury of Chester, haberdasher.
„	2	Thomas Smith, hatter, p. of John Tilston of Chester, hatmaker.
„	10	*Richard Powell, fletcher.
„	23	John Cowper, hatter, s. of Ralph Cowper of Chester, sherman, and p. of John Tilston of Chester, hatmaker.
Sep.	17	Richard Barnes, tanner, s. of John Barnes of Chester, tanner.
„	17	Thomas Annyon, butcher, s. of Robert Annion of Chester, butcher, defunct.
„	17	George Cotton, shoemaker, p. of Robert Heath of Chester, shoemaker.
„	24	Thomas Thornton, merchant, s. of Ralph Thornton of Chester, merchant and ironmonger, defunct.
„	27	*Edward Johnson, *alias* Currier, wheelwright.
„	28	John Stonier, wright.
Oct.	3	Edward Button, butcher, s. of Thomas Button of Chester, water-leader, defunct.
„	3	Randle Bromley, butcher, s. of Thomas Bromley of Chester, butcher, defunct.
„	4	Robert Gruffeth, butcher, s. of Hugh Griff of Chester, butcher, defunct, and p. of Richard Bebinton of Chester, butcher.

1588-9 [30-31 Eliz.] ROBERT BROCK DIED, AND WILLIAM HAMNET, SUCC., MAYORS.

Nov.	4	Ralph Oty, baker, s. and p. of Henry Ottie of Chester, baker.
Dec.	17	William Helly, yeoman, servant of the Mayor.
Jan.	18	Thomas Wright, hatmaker, s. of Peter Wright of Chester, baker, defunct, and p. of Robert Foxall of Chester, hatmaker.

Jan.	18	John Rigmayden, baker, p. of William Wright of Chester, baker.
Feb.	5	William Denwall, draper, p. of James Gremesditch of Chester, draper and hosier.
„	19	William Glover, tailor, p. of Roger Sidall of Chester, tailor.
„	22	John Fletcher, tanner, p. of Ralph Hine of Chester, tanner.
Mar.	19	John Hitchenson, hatmaker and haberdasher, p. of John Allen of Chester, hatmaker and haberdasher.
„	26	Thomas Annyon, butcher, s. of Edmund Annion of Chester, cowper, defunct, and p. of Thomas Brine of Chester, butcher.
„	26	William Andrew, tanner, p. of Ralph Rathburne of Chester, tanner, defunct.
Apr.	11	Robert Pemberton, tanner, p. of Henry Annion, the elder, of Chester, tanner.
„	20	Richard Sale, tailor, p. of Christopher Smith of Chester, tailor, defunct.
„	17	Thomas Ireland, dyer, p. of John Robinson of Chester, dyer.
„	21	Thomas Ketle, dyer, s. of William Ketle of Chester, dyer.
May	6	William Garrat, mariner.
„	26	Anthony Warmingham, saddler, p. of Ralph Warmingham of Chester, saddler, defunct.
July	10	John Morres, beer-brewer, p. of John Ratcliffe of Chester, beer-brewer.
„	12	*John Burton, wright.
„	22	Richard Anglizer, cowper, p. of Thomas Heathe of Chester, cowper.
„	29	William Pemberton, sherman, p. of William Witten of Chester, sherman.
„	31	George Harpur, ironmonger, p. of Robert Walle of Chester, ironmonger.
Aug.	6	John Shurlock, tailor, s. of Robert Shurlock, and p. of Ralph Calveley of Chester, tailor, defunct.
„	11	Ralph Bird, brickman, s. of William Bird, the younger, of Chester, tanner, defunct, and p. of William Geste of Chester, brickman, defunct.
„	18	Thomas Prenton, baker, s. of Urian Prenton of Chester, baker.
„	20	Richard Cally, saddler, p. of David Johns, late of Chester, saddler, defunct.
Sep.	1	John Laton, cardmaker, ⎫
„	1	William Laton, cardmaker, ⎬ ss. of Randle Laton of Chester, cardmaker.
„	1	Randle Laton, cardmaker, ⎭

1589–90] THE CITY OF CHESTER 67

Sep. 1 John Lingley, shoemaker, s. of Richard Lingley of Chester, shoemaker.
„ 15 Robert Edmond, glazier, p. of Edmund Dawby of Chester, glazier.
„ 19 Phillip Peereson, ironmonger, p. of William Forster of Chester, ironmonger.
Oct. 9 William Dodd, mercer, p. of Valentine Broughton of Chester, alderman and mercer.

1589–90 [31–32 Eliz.] WILLIAM COTGREVE, Mayor.

Oct. 13 Thomas Tilston, shoemaker, s. of Ralph Tilston of Chester, shoemaker, defunct.
„ 14 William Meisam, sherman, p. of Randle Whitbye of Chester, sherman.
Nov. 26 William Butler, slater, p. of Robert Trollock of Chester, slater.
Dec. 22 John Halwood, tailor, servant of Sir Gilbert Gerrard, knight, Master of the Rolls to the Queen at Westminster.
Jan. 2 John Owen, mercer, s. of Owen ap John Owen of Llangullan, co. Anglesey, clerk, and p. of John Tilston of Chester, mercer and alderman.
„ 10 Thomas Walshe, cowper, p. of Thomas Carden of Chester, cowper.
„ 12 Thomas Ince, shoemaker, s. of Randle Ince of Chester, shoemaker.
Feb. 10 John Hughes, ironmonger, p. of Humphrey Probin of Chester, ironmonger.
„ 12 Richard Radley s. of Richard Radley of Chester, shoemaker, defunct.
„ 13 *Thomas Watson, merchant.
„ 14 *Randle Stockton of London, dyer.
Mar. 11 *Richard Greves, tailor.
„ 19 William Harvy, butcher, p. of Edward Wright, *alias* Janson, of Chester, butcher.
Apr. 13 William Bird of Chester, butcher, p. of Richard James of Chester, butcher, and s. of John Bird of Chester, tanner.
„ 30 Randle Phillips s. of George Phillips of Chester, shoemaker, defunct, and p. of Richard [Vause ?], tailor.
May 5 Ralph Johnson, smith, s. and p. of William Johnson of Chester, smith, defunct.
June 11 Richard Ireland, plasterer, servant of Gilbert Gerrard, esquire, s. and h. of Sir William Gerrard, knight, defunct.

July   6   William Richardson, hatter, p. of John Allen of
            Chester, hatmaker.
 „   10   Thomas Johnes, baker, p. of John Blanchard of Chester,
            baker, defunct.
 „   10   Edward Griffeth, baker, p. of John Johns of Chester,
            baker, defunct.
 „   13   *George Woodes of Chester, yeoman.
 „   24   John Holker, glover, s. of Richard Holker of Chester,
            merchant, defunct.
Aug.   11   John Smith, barber-surgeon, p. of Thomas Mercer of
            Chester, barber-surgeon.
 „   18   William Whitle, tanner, p. of John Barnes of Chester,
            tanner.
Sep.   2   Phillip Harrison, weaver, p. of John Harrison of
            Chester, weaver.
Oct.   1   *Robert Lloyd, yeoman, servant of David Yale, doctor
            of laws and Chancellor to the Diocese of Chester.
 „   14   John Gest, ropier, s. of Roger Gest of Chester, ropier.

1590-1 [32-33 Eliz.] WILLIAM MASSY, Mayor.

Oct.   23   *Thomas Orton of Chester, yeoman.
Nov.   13   William Glynne, ironmonger, p. of Ellis Johnes of
            Chester, ironmonger.
 „   23   Robert Blease, apothecary, p. of Adam Blis of Chester,
            mercer and apothecary.
 „   3   John Williams, p. of John Hanky, alderman and tanner,
            defunct.
Dec.   29   Rice Coytmore, mercer, p. of John Williams of
            Chester, mercer.
Jan.   7   Thomas Lea, shoemaker, ⎫ ss. of William Lea of Ches-
 „   7   John Lea, shoemaker,   ⎭   ter, shoemaker.
 „   20   John Corne, tailor, p. of Thomas Carter of Chester,
            tailor.
 „   22   *James Broster, yeoman.
 „   26   John Greene, tallow-chandler, s. of William Greene of
            Chester, tallow-chandler.
 „   26   Thomas Looker, tallow-chandler, p. of Richard Looker
            of Chester, tallow-chandler, defunct.
Feb.   3   Owen Johnes, mercer, p. of Valentine Broughton of
            Chester, mercer.
 „   3   Robert Johnes, merchant, p. of Richard Rathburne the
            elder, of Chester, merchant.
 „   3   Owen ap Harry, ironmonger, p. of John Fyton of
            Chester, ironmonger.

Feb.	9	Simon Newas, pewterer, s. of Richard Newas, late of Chester, pewterer.
,,	22	John Molson, draper, p. of Ralph Jenins of Chester, draper, and Elene, his wife.
,,	26	Henry Clough, tailor, s. of William Clough of Chester, coock.
July	13	Richard Drihurst, ironmonger, p. of Richard Bavand of Chester, alderman and ironmonger.
Aug.	4	Thomas Weston, glover, s. of Humphrey Weston of Chester, glover, defunct.
,,	9	Robert Sym, mercer, p. of Roland Barnes of Chester, mercer.
,,	9	Robert Heward, merchant, p. of Thomas Heward of Chester, merchant.
,,	9	Hugh ap Griffeth, glover, p. of John Orton of Chester, glover, defunct.
,,	27	John Norman, baker, p. of Peter Wright, late of Chester, baker.
,,	30	Lawrence Leicester, gentleman.
Sep.	6	Edward Yonge, ironmonger, p. of Robert Amery of Chester, ironmonger.
,,	28	William Massy s. of William Massy of Chester, alderman and merchant.
,,	28	John Bavand s. of Richard Bavand of Chester, alderman and ironmonger.
Oct.	5	Robert Fletcher, hatmaker, s. of John Fletcher of Chester, merchant.

1591-2 [33-34 Eliz.] THOMAS LYNYALL, Mayor.

Oct.	18	William Alcock, yeoman, s. of Thomas Alcok, late of Chester, tailor.
Nov.	11	Thomas Chalner, baker, p. of John Woodes of Chester, baker, defunct.
,,	10	Richard Newton, brickman, s. of Thomas Newton of Chester, shoemaker, defunct.
,,	25	Robert Cowper, baker, p. of William Kinge of Chester, baker.
,,	26	John Walsh, slater, p. of William Walshe of Chester, slater.
Jan.	12	George Okes, merchant, p. of William Aldersey of Chester, merchant and alderman.
,,	19	William Ashton, mercer, p. of Paul Chauntrell of Chester, mercer.
,,	28	Rowland Davies, yeoman.

Feb.	3	Richard Dannold, baker, s. of John Dannold, baker, defunct.
,,	3	John Gregory, glover, p. of Richard Fletcher of Chester, glover.
,,	24	Randle Walker, sherman, s. of Christopher Walker of Chester, sherman.
,,	24	Thomas Edmonds, joiner, p. of Hugh Kenrick of Chester, joiner.
Mar.	13	John Lea, merchant, p. of Thomas Lynyall of Chester, alderman and merchant.
,,	13	John Wright, cowper, p. of Thomas Garden of Chester, cowper.
,,	13	Henry Totty, cowper, p. of John Prees of Chester, cowper.
,,	23	William Hulme, stationer.
Apr.	14	Edward Clappam, merchant.
,,	21	Edward Bathowe, clothier.
May	29	Richard Booth, wright.
July	3	John Bithell, smith, p. of Ralph Bithell, late of Chester, smith.
,,	10	John Wilcok, shoemaker, p. of Ralph Hulton of Chester, shoemaker.
,,	10	Edward Hall, shoemaker, s. of William Hall, late of Chester, yeoman.
,,	10	Ralph Saunders, shoemaker, s. of Thomas Saunders, *alias* Steward, late of Chester, merchant.
,,	11	Henry Bedford, merchant, p. of Richard Knee of Chester, merchant.
July	21	Paul Langton, butcher, s. of John Langton of Chester, haberdasher, defunct.
,,	24	Peter Lawton of Chester, yeoman.
Aug.	2	Henry Bennet, innkeeper.
,,	3	Lawrence Hey, tanner, s. of Robert Hay, and p. of Thomas Bird of Chester, tanner.
,,	15	Hugh Dod, yeoman, s. of Griffin Dod of Chester, sherman.
,,	30	John Allen, servant of Sir Henry Harrington, knight.
Sep.	11	John Smith, cutler, s. of Richard Richardson [*sic*], late of Chester, cutler.
,,	22	John Lay, chandler, p. of Henry Prichard of Chester, chandler, defunct.
Oct.	9	Hugh Richardson, shoemaker, s. of William Richardson of Chester, shoemaker, defunct.
,,	9	John Birchened, shoemaker, s. of Thomas Birchened of Chester, shoemaker, defunct.
,,	9	William Urmeston, shoemaker, s. of Robert Urmeston of Chester, pewterer, defunct.

[1592-3]   THE CITY OF CHESTER   71

Oct. 9 Nicholas Ince of Chester, s. of Randle Ince of Chester, shoemaker.
„ 10 Lewis Jones, silk-weaver.
„ 12 William Grafton of Chester, gentleman.
„ 12 Dannold Callister, p. of Hugh Cally of Chester, sherman, defunct.
„ 12 Richard Partington, tailor, p. of Robert Hill of Chester, tailor.
„ 12 John Asbruck, tailor, p. of Humphrey Phillips of Chester, tailor.
„ 12 John Lingley, goldsmith, s. of John Lingley of Chester, goldsmith.
„ 12 Thomas Pooley, servant of Edward Halsall, esquire, sheriff of Chester.

1592-3 [34-35 Eliz.] JOHN FYTON, Mayor.

Oct. 23 John Johnes, gentleman.
„ 28 William Tayler, glover, p. of William Balle, alderman and glover.
Nov. 8 Roger Lea s. of Robert Lea, tailor and "officiar," defunct.
„ 14 Edward Throp, hatmaker, s. of Thomas Throp, sergeant of the keys.
„ 28 William Halliwell, weaver, p. of John Hixon, weaver.
Dec. 1 George [Bowes?] merchant, p. of William Massy, alderman and merchant.
Jan. 3 Richard Buxy, shoemaker, } ss. of George Buxy of
„ 3 John Buxy, shoemaker, } Chester, shoemaker, defunct.
Feb. 14 Edward Smith of Chester, smith, p. of Robert Williams of Chester, smith.
„ 19 Robert Bennet, draper, s. of David Bennet of Chester, joiner, defunct, and p. of Thomas Fletcher of Chester, alderman and draper.
„ 19 Randle Fernough, ironmonger, p. of John Kinge of Chester, ironmonger.
„ 26 Thomas Browne, slater, p. of Robert Fazakerley of Chester, slater.
Mar. 5 Evan ap Thomas, sherman, p. of Ralph Modesley of Chester, sherman.
„ 7 George Bunbury, shoemaker, s. of Richard Bunbury, merchant, defunct.
Apr. 3 James Annyon, tailor, p. of George Walmesley of Chester, tailor.

Apr. 21 Lewis Williams, tailor, p. of John Throp of Chester, tailor.
„ 23 William Salusbury, joiner, s. of Thomas Salusbury, esquire, defunct.
May 29 William Seale of Chester, mariner, s. of John Seale of Chester, mariner, defunct.
„ 29 Grifin Johnes, sherman, p. of Thomas Jones of Chester, sherman.
June 13 John Griffeth, beer-brewer, s. of Richard Griff of Chester, glover, and p. of Thomas Werden of Chester, beer-brewer.
„ 15 Edward Brock, tanner, s. of Robert Brock of Chester, alderman, and p. of Richard Spon of Chester, tanner.
„ 25 John Bingley s. of John Bingley of Chester, sherman.
„ 25 Christopher Chalner of Chester, s. of John Chalner of Chester, merchant.
„ 25 William Bird s. of Edward Bird of Chester, tanner.
July 18 George Bird, draper, p. of Richard Dodd of Chester, draper.
Aug. 25 Richard Catherall, weaver, s. of Richard Catherall of Chester, weaver, and p. of John Harrison of Chester, weaver.
Sep. 3 William Tarleton, weaver, s. of Thomas Tarleton of Chester, weaver.
„ 23 Richard Rogerson s. of Hugh Rogerson of Chester, alderman.
Oct. 1 John Englefeld, shoemaker, p. of Henry Yonge of Chester, defunct.
„ 1 William Clough, shoemaker, s. of William Clough of Chester, cook.
„ 3 William Bird s. of William Birde of Chester, tanner, defunct.
„ 3 John Deane, tanner, p. of William Bird of Chester, tanner.
„ 3 Henry Fells, merchant, "ut forensecus per congreg."
„ 3 Edward ap Prichard, merchant, p. of William Massy of Chester, alderman and merchant.

1593-4 [35-36 Eliz.] DAVID LLOYD, MAYOR.

Thomas Throp.
Thomas Johnson, shoemaker.
William Brock, gentleman, s. of Robert Brock, alderman.
Richard Bunbury.

Ralph Ellam.
William Annyon, tanner.
Peter Fletcher, tailor.
Richard Modesley, sherman.
John Tayler, tanner.
Ralph Dod, draper.
Thomas Johnson, boatman.
Thomas Asmore.
Humphrey Ellice.
Peter Blake.
Peter Selvy, *alias* Blakey, yeoman.
William Lynyall, tanner.
Laurence Jenson, tanner.
Thomas Bird, tanner.
John Burnet, butcher.
William Gremesdich, shoemaker.
John Powell, wright.
William Gitton, sherman.
Richard Bridges, dyer.
John Halle, baker.
James Downham, yeoman.
John Granwall, sherman.
David Midleton, hatmaker.
David Allen, shoemaker.
John Harrison, sherman.

1594-5 [36–37 Eliz.] FOULK ALDERSAY, Mayor.

Thomas Dalbie.
Robert Rogerson.
Thomas Williams.
William Hinckes, butcher.
William Geste, ropier.
William Colly.
John Ashton, baker.
William Bennet, baker.
Thomas Lynyall, tanner.
William Prenton, hatmaker.
David ap Edward, cowper.
Thomas Markes, cowper.
Peter Tilston, draper.
Richard Gregorie, goldsmith.
Henry Maynwaringe, clerk.

Apr. 2 Richard Barrowe, butcher, p. of Richard Roberts of Chester, butcher.

Apr.	9	John Doole, butcher, p. of Roger Bryne of Chester, butcher.
May	22	Thomas Ledsham, tailor.
,,	22	John Hutchens, tailor.
,,	23	Thomas Calcott, s. of George Calcott, merchant.
,,	23	Laurence Waynwright.
June	11	John Cooke, glover, s. of Richard Coocke of Chester, defunct.
,,	11	Richard Weston of Chester, glover, s. of Humphrey Weston of Chester, glover, defunct.
,,	31	Richard Snede, draper, p. of Henry Hamnet of Chester, draper.
Aug.	5	William Johnes, smith, p. of James Balle of Chester, smith.
,,	8	Peter Goose, draper, s. of Richard Goose of Chester, draper, defunct.
,,	21	William Hewys s. of Peter Hewys of Chester, tailor.
,,	27	William Newhouse s. of Richard Newhouse of Chester, ironmonger, defunct.
Sep.	6	William Bostock, draper, p. of Ralph Rathburne of Chester, draper.
,,	24	Thomas Woodes, beer-brewer, p. of Thomas Werdes of Chester, beer-brewer.
,,	26	John Barlowe, mercer, p. of John Williams of Chester, mercer.

1595–6 [37–38 Eliz.] WILLIAM ALDERSEY, Mayor.

Oct.	27	Henry Gest, ropier, s. ⎫ of Roger Gest of Chester,
,,	27	Roger Gest, ropier, p. ⎭ ropier, defunct.
,,	27	John [Roger, M.B.] Fazakerley, shoemaker, p. of Richard Huet of Chester, shoemaker, defunct.
,,	27	Richard Wildinge, shoemaker, p. of Alex. Wilding, shoemaker, and s. of Robert Wildinge of Chester, mercer, defunct.
,,	27	Ralph Penny, hatmaker, p. of John Tilston of Chester, hatmaker.
Nov.	4	Richard Finchet, sherman, s. of Henry Finchet, sherman, defunct.
,,	4	Thomas Cowper, sherman, s. of Ralph Cowper the elder, of Chester, sherman.
,,	4	Henry Pye, joiner, p. of Henry Scarsbrick of Chester, joiner.
,,	10	Bradford Throp, shoemaker, s. of Thomas Throp, sergeant of the keys, and p. of Peter Buxy, shoemaker.

Nov. 10		Randle Adshed, turner.
Dec. 5		Thomas Wilcock, saddler, s. of Thomas Wilcock of Chester, tanner, defunct.
,,	5	‡Simon Stockton, cutler, s. of Hugh Stockton of Chester, smith.
,,	6	James Fletcher, glover, s. of Richard Fletcher of Chester, glover.
,,	12	John Tony, glover, p. of Robert Brerewood of Chester, alderman and glover.
—		Valentine Barker s. of Thomas Barker.
Jan.	9	Thomas Colton s. of Richard Colton of Chester, saddler.
,,	13	Thomas Woodes s. of Robert Woodes of Chester, cowper, defunct.
,,	13	Robert Smith, weaver, s. of Richard Smith of Chester, weaver, defunct.
,,	15	William Richardson, dyer, p. of John Prenton of Chester, dyer.
,,	16	Edward Bennet, tanner, p. of John Frances of Chester, tanner.
,,	16	William Hunt, ironmonger, p. of Richard Bavand of Chester, alderman and ironmonger.
—		Robert Walker, tailor.
—		John Higgen, joiner, p. of John Taylor of Chester, joiner.
Mar.	8	Robert Mawburne, p. of William —— of Chester, alderman.
,,	8	John Madock s. of Ralph Madock of Chester.
,,	8	John Lenard, shoemaker, p. of William —— of Chester, shoemaker.
,,	22	Ralph Wright s. of John Wright.
,,	22	John Blanchard s. of Thomas Blanchard.
Apr. 14		Griffin ap Harry, ironmonger, p. of Richard Bavand of Chester, alderman, and Jane, his wife.
,,	19	William Hancock, barber, s. of William Hancock of Chester, turner, and p. of Ralph Hedwod.
,,	22	Randle Bavand, ironmonger, s. of Richard Bavand of Chester, alderman.
,,	22	Richard Rathburne, innholder, s. of Richard Rathburne of Chester, alderman.
,,	22	Richard Massy s. of William Massy, late of Chester, alderman and merchant.
May 10		Edward Blinston, baker, p. of Robert Cowper of Chester, baker.
—		John Fletcher s. of William Fletcher of Chester, tanner.

May 25 William Spenne, ironmonger, p. of Robert Amery of Chester, ironmonger.
June 4 George Kenyough, weaver, p. of Robert Wareton of Chester, weaver.
„ 14 Thomas Bostock, beer-brewer, p. of John Watkins of Chester, beer-brewer.
July 9 John Ratcliff s. of John Ratcliff, beer-brewer.
„ 9 Geoffrey Wareton.
„ 9 George Comes.
„ 9 William Grenefield.
„ 9 Robert Ince, draper.
„ 10 Edward Newby, weaver.
„ 10 Phillip Cottingham, house-wright.
„ 12 Richard Cowley of Handbridge, yeoman.
„ 15 William Christian, glover, p. of Robert Brerewood of Chester, alderman and glover.
Sep. 1 Edward David, saddler, p. of Gilbert Hancok of Chester, saddler.
„ 3 Edward Orton, merchant, s. of John Orton of Chester, glover, defunct.
„ 3 ‡Robert Cawdey, glover, s. of Richard Cawdey of Chester, glover, defunct.
„ 10 Thomas Ryder, shoemaker, p. of Edward Bennet of Chester, shoemaker.
„ 28 John ap Shone, tanner, p. of John Richardson, *alias* Barker of Handbridge, tanner.
Oct. 7 William Coytmore, merchant, p. of Foulk Aldersey of Chester, alderman and merchant.
„ 11 Edward Meredith, ironmonger, p. of John Fyton of Chester, alderman and ironmonger.
„ 14 Robert Bassinet, embroiderer, p. of John Dewsbury of Chester, embroiderer.
„ 15 Foulk Gillam s. of Thomas Gillam of Chester, embroiderer.

1596-7 [38-39 Eliz.] THOMAS SMITH, Esquire, Mayor.

Nov. — William Manninge, gentleman.
— ‡Kenrick ap Evan, gentleman.
Dec. 10 Hugh Glaseour of Chester, esquire.
„ 10 George Robins of Chester, gentleman.
„ 15 Thomas Nicoll, tanner, p. of William Bird of Chester, alderman and tanner.
Jan. 8 William Harvey, glover, s. of Robert Harvey of Chester, glover, defunct.

Jan.	11	Hector Modesley of Chester, shoemaker.
„	11	Henry Leene, shoemaker, p. of Peter Bennet of Chester, shoemaker.
„	13	Richard Barnes, farrier.
„	18	Randle Halle, shoemaker, p. of Robert Heath of Chester, shoemaker, defunct.
„	31	Thomas Eaton, smith, p. of G—— Curmyn of Chester, smith.
Feb.	2	William Jenson, smith, p. of William Johnson of Chester, smith.
„	17	Thomas Jenson, smith, p. of Simon [Cronry?] of Chester, smith, defunct.
„	26	John Smith s. of Michael Smith of Chester, merchant.
Apr.	1	Hugh Jenkin, tanner, p. of Richard Bennet of Chester, tanner.
„	5	William Halle, hatter, p. of Robert Phillipps of Chester, hatter.
„	5	‡Hugh Harvy s. of John Harvy, alderman and glover, defunct.
„	6	Peter Drinkwater of Chester, ironmonger.
May	10	John Monxfield, skinner, p. of William Throp of Chester, skinner.
„	13	John Gruffeth, ironmonger, p. of Thomas Eaton of Chester, ironmonger, defunct.
„	18	Humphrey Dale, yeoman, servant of Thomas Smith, mayor of the city.
June	3	William Betson of Chester, mariner.
„	21	Richard Birchleye, girdler, s. of George Birchleye of Chester, yeoman, defunct.
„	21	Richard Goose, draper, s. of Richard Goose of Chester, draper, defunct.
July	29	Thomas Taylor, baker, p. of Henry Trafford of Chester, baker, defunct.
„	29	John Rogers s. of Robert Rogers, professor of theology, defunct.
„	29	Henry Taylor.
Aug.	3	Hugh Harvy, glover, s. of John Harvy, defunct.
„	3	John Hoo, mariner, p. of Robert Ratcliff of Chester, mariner.
„	3	Edmund Taylor, draper, p. of Randle Ince of Chester, draper.
„	4	William Ratcliffe s. of William Ratcliffe of Chester, merchant, defunct.
„	9	Mark Styles s. of William Styles of Chester, alderman, defunct.
„	11	John Robinson s. of John Robinson of Chester, dyer.

Aug. 11 John Fernaugh, baker, p. of William King the younger, baker.
„ 17 James Smith of Chester, yeoman, s. "naturalis" of John Smith of Chester, alderman, defunct.
„ 23 Christopher Hoole, mariner.
„ 25 Thomas Sutton, servant of Peter Warburton, sergeant-at-law.
Oct. 4 Richard Smith, smith, p. of Urian Ryder of Chester, smith, defunct.
„ 10 Ralph Pricket, embroiderer, p. of Thomas Prycket of Chester, embroiderer.

1597-8 [39-40 Eliz.] [Sir JOHN SAVAGE, Kt., died, and] THOMAS FLETCHER, succ., Mayors.

Jan. 16 Robert Amery, ironmonger, s. of Robert Amery of Chester, ironmonger.
„ 19 Theodore Tomlinson ⎫ ss. of Thomas Tomlinson of
„ 19 Joseph Tomlinson ⎭ Chester, fletcher.
„ 19 Lawrence Ditchfielde, ironmonger, p. of Robert Walle the younger, of Chester, ironmonger, defunct.
„ 23 Robert Basforde s. of John Basforde of Chester, merchant, defunct.
Feb. 10 Richard Shone, tallow-chandler, p. of Thomas Case of Chester, tallow-chandler.
„ 13 David Denevet of Chester, yeoman.
„ 17 Edward Kitchen, gentleman.
Apr. 17 Thomas Milner, hatmaker, s. of John Milner of Chester, tailor.
May 6 Arrat Watt, wright.
„ 9 Joseph Fazakerley, slater, s. of Robert Fazakerley of Chester, slater.
„ 10 Henry Crosby, yeoman.
„ 22 Thomas Stanier, wright, p. of John Stanney of Chester, wright.
„ 22 Ralph Richardson, butcher, p. of Robert Hatton of Chester, butcher.
„ 22 Abraham Scons, fishmonger and cowper.
June 3 Randle Hulme, paynter, p. of Thomas Chalner of Chester, painter, defunct.
„ 3 Ralph Hulme, smith, s. of Thomas Hulme of Chester, smith.
„ 7 Thomas Wattkynes of Chester, beer-brewer.
„ 9 Randle Janyon, slater, p. of Robert Fazakerley of Chester, slater.

Aug.	19	Randle Bies, mercer, s. of Adam Bies of Chester.
„	19	Thomas Bies, mercer, mercer.
„	27	John Lunne, tailor, p. of John Throp of Chester, tailor.
„	27	William Moscroft, beer-brewer.
„	30	William Mountford, founder, s. of David Mountford of Chester, founder, defunct.
July	4	Antony Symcocke, smith, s. of Thomas Symcocke of Chester, smith, defunct.
„	17	Thomas Harrison, sherman, s. of Richard Harrison of Chester, sherman, defunct.
„	20	John Richardson, dyer, s. of William Richardson of Chester, dyer, defunct.
„	26	Robert Cowper, baker, s. of Peter Cowper of Chester, baker.
„	31	Edward Wade, shoemaker, p. of Richard Bennet of Chester, shoemaker.
Aug.	1	Roger Kinge, baker, p. of William Kinge, the elder, of Chester, baker.
„	3	Thomas Frauncis, cook, at the request of William Booth and Thomas Venables, esquire.
„	7	William Ryder of Newton, co. Ches., yeoman.
„	9	Cuthbert Amont, saddler, p. of Edward Kilshe, alias Gilson of Chester, saddler.
„	10	John Harpur, ironmonger, p. of George Harpur of Chester, ironmonger.
„	14	Stephen Albrighte, loriner.
„	17	Richard Ampson, cook.
„	21	Richard Barlowe, shoemaker, p. of Thomas Tilston of Chester, shoemaker.
„	30	Robert Boydell s. of Richard Boydell of Chester, joiner, defunct.
Aug.	30	John Tylston, hatmaker, s. of John Tylston of Chester, hatmaker, defunct.
Sep.	7	Thomas Fletcher s. of William Fletcher of Chester, tanner.
„	11	William Newboulte, tailor, p. of Robert Hill of Chester, tailor.
„	22	William Allen, draper, s. of John Allen of Chester, defunct, and p. of John Litler of Chester, draper.
Oct.	2	William Gamulle, merchant, s. and p. of Edmund Gamuell of Chester, alderman and merchant.
„	2	Edward Allen, merchant, s. of John Allen, draper, defunct, and p. of David Lloyd of Chester, alderman and draper.

1598-9 [40-41 Eliz.] RICHARD RATHBURNE, Mayor.

Oct. 17 Thomas Whitle, shoemaker, p. of William Lea of Chester, shoemaker, defunct.
„ 30 Ralph Tonge, shoemaker, s. of Ralph Tonge of Chester, fishmonger, defunct.
Nov. 13 William Jones, shoemaker, s. of Henry Jones of Chester, saddler, defunct.
„ 16 Foulk Shevington s. of William Shevington of Chester.
„ 20 William Huntington, tailor, s. of Robert Huntington of Chester, baker, and p. of John Halwood of Chester, tailor.
Dec. 1 Robert Grice, glover, s. of Roger Grice of Chester, glover.
„ 11 Henry Phillippes, tailor.
„ 14 John Pickes, hatmaker, s. of —— Picke of Chester, merchant, defunct.
„ 14 Edward Williamson, hatmaker, s. of John Williamson of Chester, skinner.
Jan. 16 Thomas Mory, shoemaker, p. of John Andrewe of Chester, shoemaker.
„ 25 Robert Buxy, shoemaker, s. of George Buxy of Chester, shoemaker.
Feb. 1 Peter Wignall, innholder.
„ 9 Richard Dicus, weaver, p. of George Dicus of Chester, weaver.
„ 20 William Basford s. of John Basford of Chester, tailor, defunct.
„ 20 Robert Sevell, joiner, p. of William Garfeild of Chester, joiner, defunct.
„ 20 Edward Lea, glover, p. of —— —— of Chester, glover.
Mar. 18 John Pymrose, tailor, s. of William Pymrose of Chester, tailor.
May 18 Hugh Byrchley, scrivener, s. of George Byrchley of Chester, defunct.
„ 22 Hugh Williamson, mercer, p. of John Owen of Chester, mercer.
„ 22 Humphrey Jackson, draper, p. of John Moyle of Chester, draper.
June 1 Nicholas Garsey, glazier, p. of Edward Dalby of Chester, glasier.
„ 7 William Johnson.
„ 25 John Barnes s. of John Barnes of Chester, tanner, defunct.

June	26	Richard Sponne, tanner, s. of Richard Sponne of Chester, tanner.
,,	27	John Maddock, barber, p. of Robert Leeche of Chester, barber.
July	2	Richard Case s. of Richard Case of Chester, sergeant of the keys, defunct.
		†Sir John Savage, knight.
,,	7	William Crancke.
,,	20	William Hunte, ironmonger, p. of Richard Bavand of Chester, alderman.
,,	23	John Robinson, dyer, s. of John Robinson of Chester, dyer, defunct.
Aug.	13	Foulk Radford s. of —— Radford of Chester, defunct.
,,	13	William Leeche, draper, p. of Henry Hamnett of Chester, draper.
,,	20	Thomas Bunbury s. of —— Bunbury of Chester, defunct.
,,	20	Richard Coldocke s. of Richard Coldocke of Chester, —— defunct.
,,	26	David Thomas, tailor, p. of Humphrey Phillipps of Chester, tailor.
,,	26	George Blinston, baker, p. of John Crompe of Chester, baker, defunct.
Sep.	24	Robert Kelly s. of —— Kelly of Chester, defunct.
Oct.	1	William Humfrey, tallow-chandler, p. of Thomas Looker of Chester, tallow-chandler.
,,	8	Thomas Flemynge, shoemaker, p. of Thomas Newport of Chester, shoemaker.
,,	8	John Edwardes s. of John Edwardes of Chester, tailor.
,,	9	John Moulsdale, yeoman, p. of William "Do." of Chester, mercer, defunct.

1599–1600 [41–42 Eliz.] HENRY HARDWARE, Esquire, Mayor.

†Richard, bishop of Chester.

Mar.	26	Robert Dannold, hatmaker, s. of John Dannold of Chester, baker, defunct, and p. of Phillip Phillipps of Chester, hatmaker.
Apr.	23	William Weston, glover, s. of William Weston of Chester, defunct, and p. of William Weston of Chester.
,,	23	Edward Dod, butcher, s. of John Dod of Chester, pewterer, defunct, and p. of Robert Termond of Chester, butcher, defunct.

Apr.	22	William Dawson, hatmaker, s. of —— —— of Chester, defunct, and p. of John Tilston of Chester, hatmaker, defunct.
May	10	Peter Taylor, dyer, s. of Andrew Taylor of Chester, defunct.
„	14	Thomas Warton s. of William Warton of Chester, wright, defunct, and p. of John Sproson, hatmaker.
Dec.	14	Ellis Williams, gentleman, clerk of the Pentice.
Jan.	17	John Wyldinge, tailor, p. of William Hand of Chester, tailor.
Feb.	5	Robert Lytherland, merchant, s. of Peter Lytherland of Chester, merchant [tanner written above], defunct.
„	5	William Poole, barber, s. of Thomas Poole of Chester, painter.
„	5	John Locker, cutler, s. of Richard Locker of Chester, cutler, defunct.
„	5	Robert Marckes, cowper, s. of Thomas Marckes of Chester, cowper.
„	7	Arthur Thomas, glover, p. of Robert Berewood of Chester, alderman.
„	7	Paul Johnson, glover, p. of William Ball of Chester, alderman, defunct.
„	10	Griffith Jones, sherman, p. of Thomas Johnes of Chester, sherman.
„	14	William Griffith, servant of David Trevor, gentleman.
Mar.	12	Foulk Williams, mercer, p. of Richard Coitmore of Chester, mercer.
„	28	Robert Culleigne, gentleman.
May	27	Richard Deane, shoemaker, s. of Richard Deane of Chester, tanner, defunct.
June	17	John Tasker, joiner, s. of John Tasker of Wisewall, co. Lanc., yeoman.
„	21	William Saunders, plumber.
„	23	John Allington s. of John Allington of Chester, ironmonger, defunct.
„	27	Randle Borowes, ironmonger, s. of Randle Borowes of Alperom, co. Ches., yeoman, and p. of William Glynne of Chester, ironmonger.
„	27	William ap Hugh, joiner, s. of Hugh ap David of Whitford, co. Flint, yeoman, defunct, and p. of Robert ap Hugh of Chester, joiner.
July	1	Robert Smith s. of Robert Smith of Chester, goldsmith.
„	3	Robert Coldocke, clerk, s. of Richard Coldocke of Chester, shoemaker, defunct.
Oct.	9	Adam Cayne [Cane, M.B.], p. of Richard Gosse of Chester, hosier.

1600-1] THE CITY OF CHESTER 83

July 8 William Pemberton p. of Peter Litherland of Chester, tanner, defunct.
„ 21 Richard Shurlocke s. of John Shurlocke of Chester, shoemaker, defunct.
Aug. 22 John Askew, shoemaker, s. of Robert Askewe of Chester, defunct.
„ 27 Robert Seale [*alias* Smith, M.B.], yeoman, s. of John Seale of Chester, mariner, defunct.
Sep. 9 Gilbert Eaton, beer-brewer, s. of Thomas Eaton of Chester, beer-brewer.
„ 15 William Fisher, innholder, s. of Thomas Fisher of Chester, innholder.
„ 18 Richard Bannester, carpenter, s. of Nicholas Bannester of Chester, wright.
„ 23 John Walker, beer-brewer, p. of Thomas Revington of Chester, beer-brewer.
„ 27 Edward Stonnley, shoemaker, p. of Ralph Allen of Chester, shoemaker.
Oct. 7 John Annion, draper, p. of William Denwall of Chester, draper.
„ 9 Peter Pennant, mercer, p. of Valentine Broughton of Chester, alderman.

1600-1 [42-43 Eliz.] ROBERT BREREWOOD, Mayor.

George Salte, plumber.
Humphrey Lyniall, shoemaker.
Peter Bennet, maltster.
Hugh Johnes, yeoman.
William Litherland, yeoman.
John Lewes, pewterer.
Randle Kelsall, innholder.
Robert Goodicar, shoemaker.
William Bavand, tanner.
John Edwards, draper.
John Whitby, innholder.
Richard Bennet, cowper.
Thomas Harrison, cowper.
John Berscowe.
William Richardson, cowper.
Edmund Bromley, chandler.
Peter Dawson, hatmaker.
William Lea, yeoman.
John Lyniall, merchant.
Thomas Hatton.

1601 [43- —Eliz.] RICHARD BAVAND, Mayor.

> Robert Trollocke, slater.
> Edward Coventry, sherman.
> Henry Dutton, sherman.
> Richard Barrowe, glover.
> Ralph Davies, joiner.
> George Howell, hatmaker.
> John Younge, tailor.
> Robert Massy, beer-brewer.
> Arthur Urmeston, shoemaker.
> John Amote, shoemaker.
> John Harrison, shoemaker.
> William Whitehead, shoemaker.
> Edward Lyniall, shoemaker.
> Robert Berry, merchant.
> Richard Stannley, glover.
> John Coddington.
> William Birtles, cowper.
> Thomas Lawton, esquire, *in lege erudit.*
> Thomas Gamull, gentleman.
> Robert Brocke, gentleman.
> Charles Fitton, merchant.
> Michael Bavand, merchant.
> Richard Edmondes, yeoman.
> Randle Smith.
> Samuel Bastwell.
> John Twis, tailor.

1601-2 [— -44 Eliz.] JOHN RATCLIFFE the Elder, Mayor.

> Henry Ball, hatmaker.
> Robert Hilton, hatmaker.
> William Radford, tanner.
> John Smith, yeoman.
> William Ince, hatmaker.
> John Taylor, ironmonger.
> Richard Baily, beer-brewer.
> John Ryder.
> William Johnson, pewterer.
> William Frauncis, tanner.
> William Higgenson.
> John Leonard, smith.
> Robert Whitehead, gentleman.
> John Ashton, innholder.

Erasmus Preece, beer-brewer.
William Jennion, clocksmith.
John Garner, smith.
John Andrewe, beer-brewer.
Ralph Mosse, baker.
Thomas Kinge, baker.
Arthur Figes, ironmonger.
Roger Llen, dyer.
Nicholas Modsley.
David ap Hugh, tailor.
Thomas Orton, yeoman.
William Orton, apothecary.
Hugh Wynne, ironmonger.
Robert Holywell, smith.
Richard Wade, butcher.
Edmund Challenor, tanner.
Thomas Wyate, glazier.
Robert Barton.
Robert Whitbie, gentleman.
William Bucke, chirurgeon.
John Leene, tanner.
William Skellington, slater.
Thomas Harvy, millener.
Richard Carigge, mercer.
Thomas Denson, baker.
Richard Chauntrell, hatmaker.
Robert Gwynne, gentleman.
Richard Prymatte, yeoman.
Thomas Lowe, hatmaker.
William Throppe, skinner.
Roger Hancocke, tailor.
William Wildinge, hatmaker.
Randle Glover.
Richard Gawlther, yeoman.
Robert Fletcher, hatmaker.
Robert Ollerhead, hatmaker.
Joseph Tegin, yeoman.
Thomas Coventry, tailor.
Richard Lewis, beer-brewer.
Randle Brine, mercer.
Robert ap Jevan.
Robert Glover.
Roger Taylor, *alias* Darbyshier, yeoman.
John Garnett, yeoman.
Henry Pemberton, shoemaker.
Robert Guyle, mariner.

George Jewett, yeoman.
Robert Branie, butcher.
John Whytoffe, weaver.
John Bostocke.
Francis Hogeskine, hatmaker.
Robert Halle, shoemaker.
Thomas Sponne, ironmonger.
Arthur Harrison, hatmaker.
William Scons, slater.
William Hand, weaver.
Thomas Steevenson, tailor.
Thomas Dewesbury, embroiderer.
Edward Owen, ironmonger.

1602-3 [44 Eliz.-1 Jas. i.] HUGH GLASEOUR, Esquire, Mayor.

Nathaniel Woodward, chirurgeon.
Thomas Boyer, shoemaker.
Thomas Sayer, millner.
John Maddocke, yeoman.
Lawrence Massy, ironmonger.
Robert Fletcher, shoemaker.
John Aldersey, ironmonger.
Thomas Amerie, ironmonger.
John Anthrobus, cowper.
William Newton, mercer.
Richard Newall, yeoman.
William Younge, shoemaker.
Peter Taylor, butcher.
John Kennion, cowper.
William Aldersey, merchant.
Roger Davies, butcher.
Thomas Marshe, yeoman.
Richard Walker, turner.
Richard Owen, mercer.
Hugh Motterom, yeoman.
Richard Bythell, yeoman.
Richard Breides, yeoman.
Richard Barker, embroiderer.
Thomas Fletcher, cowper.
William Ellis, } brothers.
John Ellis,
Richard Mullineux, weaver.
William Sparke, ironmonger.

Roger Lea, cowper.
William Taylor, weaver.
Phillip Moyle, yeoman.

1603-4 [1-2 Jas. i.] JOHN ALDERSAIE, Mayor.

William Byrome, weaver.
Thomas Goose, hosier.
Samuel Bennet, shoemaker.
William Kinge, baker.
Richard Hall, baker.
Valentine Fletcher, tanner.
John Cowper, baker.
William Dodd, hatmaker.
William Fletcher, glover.
Robert Furbarr, beer-brewer.
William Knee, merchant.
William Fletcher, draper.
William Mullinex, draper.
James Hamlyn, yeoman.
William Johnes, threadmaker.
Thomas Glegge, tailor.
Robert Greene, yeoman.
Thomas Johnes, smith.
William Fleete, tailor.
Henry Radford, yeoman.
William Cooke, fishmonger.

1604-5 [2-3 Jas. i.] EDWARD DUTTON, Esquire, Mayor.

Oct. 16 William Wall p. of William Wall, alderman, defunct, and afterwards p. of Robert Wall, alderman and ironmonger.
„ 23 David Tonnay p. of David Edwards of Chester, glover.
„ 23 John Grice, glover, s. of Roger [or Robert] Grice of Chester, glover, defunct.
„ 23 Richard Hall p. of William Denwall of Chester, draper.
—— 16 William Croughton p. of Thomas Johnson of Chester, shoemaker.
„ 16 Richard Calcott, joiner, s. of George Calcott of Chester, merchant.
—— 23 John Finley, glover, s. of Thomas Finley of Chester, glover, defunct.

Jan.	7	John Sale, shoemaker, s. of James Sale of Chester, shoemaker.
,,	7	Richard Newporte, shoemaker, s. of Thomas Newporte, shoemaker.
,,	10	Thomas Massy, draper, s. of Nicholas Massy of Chester, draper.
,,	10	William Phillipps, hatmaker, s. of Robert Phillipps of Chester, hatmaker, lately defunct.
,,	10	William Orton, glover, s. of John Orton of Chester, glover, defunct.
,,	10	William Malpasse, shoemaker, s. of Robert Malpasse of Chester, shoemaker.
,,	10	Richard Jennion p. of William Butler, slater.
,,	10	Robert Rutter, draper, p. of John Litler of Chester, alderman and draper.
,,	16	George Hilton, shoemaker, s. of George Hilton of Chester, yeoman, defunct.
Mar.	7	Richard Scons p. of John Scons of Chester, cowper.
,,	7	Thomas Williams p. of John Maddocke of Chester, butcher.
,,	7	Richard James, butcher, s. of Richard James of Chester, butcher, defunct.
,,	11	Thomas Wrighte, ironmonger, s. of Thomas Wrighte of Chester, ironmonger, defunct.
,,	11	Roger Wilkinson p. of Lewis Roberts of Chester, ironmonger.
,,	18	Henry Tilston, hatmaker, s. of Richard Tilston of Chester, shoemaker, defunct.
,,	18	Robert Chauntrell, sherman, s. of Arthur Chauntrell of Chester, sherman.
,,	18	Ralph Graunge, carrier.
,,	19	Ralph Warminsham p. of Anthony Warminsham of Chester, saddler.
,,	21	Edward Gueste, pewterer, s. of Roger Gueste of Chester, ropier.
Apr.	3	George, lord bishop of Chester.
,,	16	William Lowe p. of William Whittle of Chester, tanner.
,,	16	Richard Litherland, tanner, s. of Peter Litherland of Chester, tanner.
,,	20	John Lloyd p. of John Moyle of Chester, draper:
,,	17	William Parsonage p. of Thomas Williams of Chester, hatmaker.
,,	24	John Willson, smith, s. of Robert Willson of Chester, smith.
,,	24	Thomas Knowles the fletcher s. of James Knowles of Chester, joiner, defunct.

[1605–6] THE CITY OF CHESTER

Mar.	29	William Broomfield, hatmaker, s. of Richard Broomfield of Chester, hatmaker, defunct.
May	27	Nicholas Johnes, saddler.
June	6	George s. of John Wrighte of Chester, draper, defunct.
,,	19	Robert Wrighte, fustian weaver, s. of Richard Wrighte of Chester, draper, defunct.
,,	19	Ralph Willson p. of William Lyniall of Chester, tanner.
,,	19	Thomas Parker, merchant, p. of John Aldersey of Chester, alderman.
,,	17	Randle Midleton, vintner, s. of John Midleton of Chester, merchant, defunct.
Sep.	18	Hugh Wicksteed, glover, p. of Robert Brerewood of Chester, alderman and glover, defunct.
Oct.	1	John Tyrer, yeoman, s. of Richard Tyrer of Chester, glover, defunct.
,,	1	Lawrence Rathbone, ironmonger, s. of John Rathbone of Chester, ironmonger, defunct.
,,	7	Randle Dodd, sherman, s. of Griffin Dodd of Chester, sherman, defunct.
		†Thomas Beedle, booer.
,,	7	William Hewitt, yeoman, s. of Richard Hewitt of Chester, shoemaker, defunct.
,,	9	John Dodd p. of Thomas Revington of Chester, beer-brewer.
,,	9	Robert Hall p. of Randle Fernall of Chester, ironmonger.
,,	10	Edward Parker, gentleman.
,,	8	Thomas Aldersaie, merchant, p. of William Aldersaie of Chester, alderman and merchant.
,,	9	John Moran of Chester, yeoman.
May	14	Richard Taylor, clothworker [shoemaker, M.B.], s. of John Taylor of Chester, shoemaker, defunct.

1605–6 [3–4 Jas. i.] JOHN LITLOR, Mayor.

Oct.	31	William Moores p. of William Aston of Chester, mercer.
,,	31	Thomas Llen, alias Baghe, joiner, s. of Edward Llen, alias Baghe of Chester, joiner.
Nov.	14	Roger Burrs p. of Thomas Wrighe of Chester, hatmaker.
,,	21	William s. of Ralph Rathbone of Chester, tanner, defunct.

Dec. 14		William Holiewell p. of Thomas Ledshame of Chester, tailor.
,,	19	Robert Lowe p. of William Bennet, Chester, baker.
,,	28	William Younge, saddler, s. of Henry Younge of Chester, shoemaker, defunct.
Jan.	8	Daniel Throppe, shoemaker, s. of William Throppe of Chester, skinner.
,,	8	Hugh Taylor, shoemaker, s. of John Taylor of Chester, cowper.
,,	15	William Catterowe, joiner, s. of Robert Catterowe of Chester, defunct.
,,	15	Richard Grymbsditch, shoemaker, s. of Hugh Grymbsditch of Chester, defunct.
,,	20	John Hinde, hatmaker, s. of Ralph Hinde of Chester, tanner, defunct.
Feb.	4	Robert Roberts p. of Thomas Case of Chester, tallowchandler, defunct.
,,	19	Isaac Thomas p. of Ralph Modesley of Chester, sherman, defunct.
,,	25	Edward Broster, shoemaker, s. of Richard Broster of Chester, tanner, defunct.
Mar.	4	Robert Thorneley p. of Robert Leeche of Chester, barber, defunct.
,,	10	Thomas Hutchins p. of James Annion of Chester, tailor, defunct.
,,	17	Robert Thomason p. of Henry Scarsebricke of Chester, joiner.
,,	17	Robert Scarsebricke, joiner, s. of Henry Scarsebricke of Chester, joiner.
Apr.	8	William Deane, yeoman, s. of Thomas Deane of Chester, weaver, defunct.
,,	28	Robert Millner p. of Thomas Barrowe of Chester, glover, defunct.
,,	28	Roger Whitehead p. of John Hinton, baker.
May	5	James Whittacres p. of John Moyle of Chester, draper.
,,	5	Phillipp Done p. of John Greene of Chester, tallowchandler.
,,	6	Thomas Johnes, sherman, s. of Thomas Johnes of Chester, sherman.
,,	14	John Bennett p. of Arthur Chantrell of Chester, sherman.
Apr.	19	John Golborne, yeoman, s. of Ralph Golborne of Christleton and late of Chester, pewterer.
,,	19	David Evans, pewterer, s. of David Evans of Chester, pewterer.
,,	19	Thomas Locker, cutler, s. of Thomas Locker of Chester, cutler.

Apr. 19		Richard Locker, cutler, s. of Peter Locker of Chester, cutler, defunct.
May 19		Christopher Gardner p. of David Evans of Chester, pewterer.
June 6		Thomas Holmes, smith, s. of Thomas Smith [*sic*] of Chester, smith.
,,	6	John Griffith p. of William Jeinson of Chester, smith, defunct.
July	1	Robert Coddington, tanner, s. of Richard Coddington of Chester, capper, defunct.
,,	9	Edward Fitton, gentleman, s. of John Fitton of Chester, alderman, defunct.
,,	9	Edward Eaton, ironmonger, p. of John Fitton of Chester, alderman, defunct.
,,	9	Edward Phasackerley p. of William Leicester of Chester, alderman and mercer.
,,	9	John Phillipps, merchant, p. of John Aldersey of Chester, alderman, defunct.
,,	9	Thomas Jones, cooke, servant of the Bishop of Chester.
,,	9	George Brooke, esquire.
,,	9	John Greene, pursuivant.
,,	9	Thomas Mersland, yeoman.
,,	9	Robert Thornton, weaver.
,,	14	Isaac Warminsham, sherman, s. of Thomas Warminsham of Chester, saddler, defunct.
,,	17	Hugh Hanky p. of William Fletcher, sherman, defunct.
,,	19	Thomas s. of Robert Whitbie, gentleman, and clerk of the Pentice.
,,	24	William Ball, glover, s. of John Ball of Chester, defunct.
,,	24	William Coldocke, shoemaker, s. of William Coldocke of Chester, shoemaker, defunct.
,,	24	John Massie, draper, s. of Nicholas Massie of Chester, draper.
Aug. 19		John Byrom, weaver, s. of Richard Byrom of Handbridge, weaver.
,,	19	Mathew s. of William Richardson, dyer, defunct.
,,	19	John Challenor s. of Christopher Challenor of Chester, milner.
Sep. 15		William Catterowe, cooper, s. of Robert Catterowe of Chester, carpenter, defunct.
,,	15	William Plethin, hatmaker, s. of Thomas Plethyn of Chester, baker, defunct.
,,	15	Henry Darwall, glover, s. of Roger Darwall of Chester, glover.
,,	15	John Tilston, glover, s. of Richard Tilston of Chester, ironmonger, defunct.

Sep. 22 Randle Morgan p. of William Thomas of Chester, glover.
„ 22 Arthur Bolland p. of Paul Chauntrell, mercer, defunct.
„ 22 Christopher Bleas p. of Roland Barnes, mercer, defunct.
„ 22 Ralph Bleas p. of Robert Bleas of Chester, mercer.
„ 24 Richard Johnson, yeoman.
„ 24 John Leivesley, yeoman.
Oct. 2 Henry Kewquicke p. of Robert Wareton, weaver.
„ 2 William Willson p. of Ralph Finchett, sherman.
„ 9 John Lorawnce p. of Richard Roberts, butcher.

1606–7 [4–5 Jas. i.] PHILLIP PHILLIPPS, MAYOR.

Oct. 21 Richard Bird, tanner, s. of George Bird of Chester, tanner, defunct.
Feb. 23 ‡John Smith, shoemaker, s. of Robert Smith of Chester, goldsmith.
Oct. 24 James Dawson, *in artibus magister*.
„ 20 ‡Edward Pemberton, shoemaker, s. of Richard Pemberton of Chester, shoemaker.
Nov. 22 Miles Somner p. of Thomas Revington, beer-brewer.
„ 26 Roland Johnson p. of George Harpur, ironmonger.
Jan. 26 Richard Pemberton p. of Richard Lingley of Chester, shoemaker, defunct.
„ 26 Thomas Tomlynson, cowper, s. of Thomas Tomlynson of Chester, cowper.
„ 30 John Edwards p. of John Barnes, tanner.
Feb. 3 Anthony Reive, tailor.
„ 9 John Ryder, tallow-chandler, s. of John Ryder of Chester, glover, defunct.
Mar. 10 Richard Robinson, shoemaker, s. of Richard Robinson of Chester, shoemaker, defunct.
„ 24 Laurence Fletcher, glover [gentleman, M.B.], s. of John Fletcher of Chester, merchant, defunct.
Apr. 16 Edward Savage, esquire, s. of Sir John Savage, knight, citizen and alderman of Chester, defunct.
„ 16 Sir Thomas Savage, knight, s. of Sir John Savage of Rock Savage, knight, sheriff of the county of Cheshire, and alderman of the city of Chester.
May 5 William Gregorie p. of William Lea, shoemaker, defunct.
„ 24 John Frammall, barber, s. of John Frammall of Chester, barber, defunct.
June 9 Griffin Edwards p. of Christopher Conway of Chester, goldsmith, defunct.

June	12	Thomas Kinge, ironmonger, s. of John Kinge of Chester, ironmonger, defunct.
,,	12	John Croughton p. of Thomas Wright of Chester, hatmaker.
,,	26	Richard Hinde p. of Hugh Hinde, tallow-chandler, defunct.
July	11	Thomas Corbin, yeoman, s. of William Corbin of Broadlane, co. Flint, yeoman, and p. of Ellis Williams of Chester, gentleman, and late clerk of the Pentice, defunct, and afterwards p. of Robert Whitbie, gent., clerk of the Pentice.
,,	17	Thomas Taylor, yeoman, s. of Richard Taylor of Chester, apothecary.
,,	14	James Byrom, clerk, s. of Richard Byrom, weaver, defunct.
,,	14	Richard s. of Henry Cooe, glover, defunct.
,,	18	Thomas Massie p. of William Whittle, tanner.
,,	24	William Harrison p. of Lewis Williams of Chester, tailor.
,,	27	Roger Barrowe, glover, s. of Thomas Barrowe, glover, defunct.
,,	29	David Roberts p. of Robert Aṁ [Amery], ironmonger.
Aug.	17	Thomas Orton, glover, s. of John Orton, glover, defunct.
,,	18	Egidius Crosse, hatmaker, s. of William Crosse of Chester, glover.
Sep.	17	John Parkensonn, gentleman.
Oct.	5	William Smallshaw p. of William Butler, slater.
,,	7	Ralph Radford, merchant, s. of Ralph Radford of Chester, tanner, defunct.
,,	8	Edward Griffith, clothier, p. of Edward Bathoe, cloothier.
Nov.	8	Anthony Lunt, gentleman.
,,	8	Robert Potter, cook.
Oct.	10	Thomas Hawkeshawe [Hakeshawe, M.B.] p. of Thomas Wright of Chester, hatmaker.
,,	10	Thomas Robinson, weaver.
,,	12	James Apleton, yeoman.

1607-8 [5-6 Jas. i.] SIR JOHN SAVAGE, KNIGHT, MAYOR.

—		Richard Smith, cutler, s. of ——
Dec.	21	Peter Cotterell, pewterer, p. of William Allen.
Oct.	29	Hugh Johnes p. of Hugh Lloyd, tailor.
,,	29	John Higgnett p. of Richard Partington, tailor.
Jan.	16	John Maddocke p. of John Barnes of Chester, tanner.

Mar.	11	Paul Cotton [Colton, M.B.], butcher, s. of Richard Cotton, defunct, and p. of William Bird, defunct.
,,	11	William Higginson p. of Thomas Fisher, butcher.
,,	11	John Finchett, sherman, s. of Ralph Finchett, sherman.
,,	11	Thomas Walshe p. of Robert Hatton, butcher.
,,	11	Robert Brocke, beer-brewer,⎫ pp. of John Ratcliffe
,,	11	Robert Parker, beer-brewer,⎭ the elder, alderman.
,,	23	George Revington, beer-brewer,⎫ ss. of Thomas Revington of Chester,
,,	23	John Revington, beer-brewer,⎭ beer-brewer.
Apr.	18	Thomas Crosse, shoemaker, s. of William Crosse, baker, defunct.
——	—	John Holywell, p. of —— —— of Chester, tailor.
May	9	John Williams, glover, s. of Hugh Williams of Chester, glover.
,,	25	*Edmund Haywood, linen-draper.
June	6	Richard Robinson, glover, s. of John Robinson, dyer, defunct.
,,	10	William Conwaie, merchant, p. of Foulk Aldersey, alderman and merchant.
,,	28	John Lloyd, mercer, p. of John Mowsdale.
Aug.	8	Lawrence Crooke p. of Thomas Tomlynson, cooper.
,,	9	John Bingley, sherman, s. of Randle Bingley, sherman.
,,	9	John Johnes, baker, s. of John Johnes, baker, defunct.
,,	9	Richard Annyon p. of John Rigmarden, baker.
,,	27	Thomas Whitehead p. of John Francis, tanner.
,,	27	Henry Ramsden, tailor, p. of John Throppe, and s. of William Ramsden, clothworker, defunct.
,,	3	Richard Tottie p. of Richard Francis, shoemaker.
Sep.	20	George Cally, musician.
,,	20	Thomas Farrington, currier, s. of Robert Farrington, currier, defunct. [This entry is cancelled in rough note-book.]
,,	20	Ewan Tellet p. of William ap Hugh, joiner.
,,	24	Hugh Johnson, merchant, s. of Adam Johnson, draper, defunct.
Oct.	12	John Kente, tailor, s. of Thomas Kente of Chester.
Sep.	24	John s. of Thomas Dodd, saddler, defunct.
,,	24	Thomas Parsonage p. of Thomas Williams, hatmaker.
,,	24	Foulk Salisburie, ironmonger, p. of Richard Bavand of Chester, ironmonger, defunct, and afterwards of Lewis Roberts of Chester, alderman and ropier.
July	26	John Welshman p. of John Welshman, baker.

1608-9 [6-7 Jas. i.] WILLIAM GAMULL, Mayor.

    Randle Higginson, beer-brewer.
    Thomas Price, goldsmith.
Dec. 14 William Fletcher p. of James Downeham of Chester, weaver.
Jan. 17 Edward Massy, merchant, s. of William Massy of Chester, alderman and merchant, defunct.
,, 25 John s. and p. of Rice Booth of Chester, carpenter.
Feb. 3 William Hield, baker, s.   ⎫ of Thurstan Hield of
,, 8 Richard Rathbone, baker, p. ⎬ Chester, baker.
,, 8 Thomas Homfreyes, yeoman.
Mar. 14 John Chantrel, joiner, s. of Roger Chantrel of Chester, shoemaker, defunct.
,, 23 Thomas Johnes p. of John Owen of Chester, mercer.
,, 23 William Taylor, yeoman, s. of Richard Taylor of Chester, apothecary.
May 10 John Burton, candlemaker, s. of John Burton of Chester, draper, defunct.
,, 15 William Booth p. of Lewis Johnes of Chester, silk-weaver.
,, 15 Thomas Davies p. of Phillip Cottingham of Chester, carpenter.
,, 25 William Bagh, *alias* Llen, s. of John Bagh, *alias* Llen, of Chester, joiner, defunct.
June 8 John Ball p. of Robert Cowper of Chester, baker.
,, 13 Thomas s. of James Bannester of Chester, embroiderer, defunct.
,, 23 Thomas Vawes.
,, 5 John Whitbie p. of Ralph Mosley of Chester, cloth-worker, defunct.
July 6 David s. of Owen Ellis of Chester, ironmonger, defunct.
    Richard James, butcher.
    Thomas Wright.
    Thomas Knowles, ironmonger.
    William Bell.
    William Dannold, sherman.
    Randle Dannold, glover.
    Thomas Dannold, glover.
    Christopher Dannold, glover.
    John Harrison.
    Thomas Grosvenor.

96 THE ROLLS OF THE FREEMEN OF [1609-11

1609-10 [7-8 Jas. i.] WILLIAM LEICESTER, Mayor.

John Garrard, carpenter.
Edward Farrar, weaver.
William Bannester.
Robert Millington, baker.
Randle Whitbie, candlemaker.
Thomas Taylor, smith.
Thomas Williamson, tanner.
Richard Weeram, blacksmith.
Robert Woodcocke, shoemaker.
Thomas Ince, glover.
Edward Towers, beer-brewer.
Richard Ouldham, smith.
Richard Bromley, butcher.
Richard Younge, beer-brewer.
Robert Phillipps, hatmaker.
Lawrence Fletcher, glover.
Robert Sprowston, hatmaker.
Hugh Taylor, innholder.
Hamnett Bennett, saddler.
Ralph Wall, ironmonger.
Ralph Mynshall, shoemaker.
Robert Huggenson, glover.
Edward Wall, ironmonger.
John Ketley [? Tetley], butcher.
Thomas Johnes, beer-brewer.
Richard Cally.
Robert Kirkman.
John Christian, slater.
Edward Calcott, turner.
William Lurtinge, hatmaker.
William Hand the younger, tailor.
William Plombe the younger, tailor.
Phillip Moores, tailor.
Edward Reignaldes, draper.
William Kinge, tailor.
Edward Williams, innholder.
Thomas ap Robert, hatmaker.
Ralph Plethyn, hatmaker.

1610-1 [8-9 Jas. i.] THOMAS HARVEY, Mayor.

Moises Dalbie, glazier.
Peter Crosse, glover.
Thomas Booer, shoemaker.

		William Ball.
		William Huntington, shoemaker.
		John Stockton, glover.
		Thomas Fromall.
		Thomas Baghe, hatmaker.
		Thomas Williamson, tailor.
Dec.	7	Ralph Hinde, shoemaker, s. of Ralph Hinde, tanner, defunct.
,,	11	John Ormeston p. of William Modesley, baker.
,,	14	Thomas Grimsdich p. of Peter Case of Chester, draper.
,,	14	Thomas Griffith p. of John Coke of Chester, glover.
,,	28	Thomas Shevington p. of Ralph Prickett, embroiderer.
Jan.	23	Thomas Robinson p. of William Poole, barber.
,,	28	Francis Trevis, draper, ——— ——— Litlor, ald.
—		Robert Jeinson, shoemaker.
—		Richard Laurenson, hatmaker.
Apr.	7	John Tellett p. of William Ince, saddler.
,,	12	Richard Wall, silkeman, s. of Robert Wall, alderman, defunct.
,,	16	Robert Hoose, baker, s. of William Hoose, baker, defunct.
July	4	Thomas Holland, mercer, s. of William ———, of Chester, mercer.

Daniel Wright, shoemaker.
John Pikyvanne, cardmaker.
Henry Trafford, hatmaker.
Roger Lea, draper.
Daniel Lea, hatmaker.
Thomas Heyward, sherman.
Richard Carington.
Adam Kempe, baker.
Richard Aldersey, gentleman.
Richard Leicester, mercer.
Thomas Gillam the younger.
William Manley, mercer.
Richard Darwall, glover.
Michael Shepheard, glover.
John Allen, gentleman.

1611-2 [9–10 Jas. i.] JOHN RATCLIFFE, Mayor.

David Rogers, draper.
Tobias Smith, draper.
Humphrey Lloyd, merchant.
John Leech, mercer.

William Case, gentleman.
John Brereton, gentleman.
Ralph [Thorneley or Thornton?], bricklayer.
Edward Smith, cutler.
George Fernihaugh, mercer.
Peter Ince, draper.
Randle Ince, shoemaker.
Henry Hockenhull, baker.
Thomas Fisher, draper.
John [Bargeley?], dyer.
William Smith.
Henry [Tytlen?], beer-brewer.
John Roberts, butcher.
Roger Tayler, milner.
Thomas Pemberton, merchant.
Edward [Fichecale -hill?].
John Brerewood, grocer.
John Mountford, pewterer.
James Wild[igge?], preacher.
John Blanchard, yeoman.
Thomas ———— ————
John Woodes, maltster.
Thomas Deane, shoemaker.
William Done, ironmonger.
Edward Bostock, ironmonger.
Peter Smith, beer-brewer.
John Harvie, glover.
John Brooke, ironmonger.
John Dobbe, glover.
Thomas Croftes, hatmaker.
Christopher Tilston.
Henry ————, mercer.
Thomas ————rchley, mercer.

1612-3 [10-11 Jas. i.] ROBERT WHITBIE, Gentleman, Mayor.

Dec. 29 John Johnson p. of Richard Brydge of Chester, dyer.
Jan. 4 Henry s. of George Monxfield of Chester.
 „   22 Ralph Lightfoote p. of William Bennet of Chester, baker.
 „   26 James Battrich p. of Lewis Roberts, alderman.
Feb. 18 Hugh Leighe p. of Edward Bathoe of Chester, clothier.
Apr. 7 Edward Croftes p. of Thomas Wareton of Chester, hatmaker.

[1613-4] THE CITY OF CHESTER

Apr. 13 Thomas Caldwell p. of Thomas Weston of Chester, glover.
„ 13 George Caldwell p. of John Madock, butcher.
„ 21 Robert Fletcher p. of John Blanchard of Chester, baker.
„ 22 Thomas s. of Richard Fletcher of Chester, glover.
„ 22 John s. of Thomas Dannold of Chester, glover, defunct.
„ 22 Edward s. of Edward Davies of Chester, glover.
„ 27 William Whytle p. of William Whyttle of Chester, tanner.
June 30 William s. of Thomas Eaton of Chester, beer-brewer, defunct.
July 9 John s. of John Francis, tanner.
„ 9 Thomas s. of Ralph Johnson of Chester, smith.
„ 10 Richard Richardson p. of Richard Chauntrell of Chester, feltmaker.
„ 21 William s. of Ralph Golborne of Chester, pewterer.
„ 31 Thomas Wright, clockmaker, s. of Richard Wright of Chester, draper.
Aug. 3 John Eccleston, yeoman, servant of Robert Whitbie, mayor.
„ 3 William s. of Henry Hamnett of Chester, draper.
„ 18 Robert s. of John Francis the elder, tanner.
„ 18 Thomas Inglefield p. of Robert Roberts, tallow-chandler.
Sep. 6 Edward Whitby, esquire, s. of Robert Whitby, mayor of the city.
„ 27 Henry Edwardes p. of William Fletcher, glover.
Oct. 6 Thomas Gilbert p. of John Locker, cutler.
„ 6 Robert s. of Ralph Radford, tanner.
„ 6 Thomas Deane p. of Richard Taylor, clothworker.
„ 8 Thomas s. of Richard Kney, merchant.
„ 9 William Richardson p. of John Ratcliffe, alderman.
„ 12 Robert Harvie, ironmonger, s. of Thomas Harvie of Chester, alderman.

1613-4 [11-12 Jas. i.] WILLIAM ALDERSEY THE YOUNGER, MAYOR.

Oct. 19 Thomas Croughton p. of William Denwall of Chester, draper.
Nov. 10 John s. of John Looker of Chester, tallow-chandler.
Dec. 3 James s. of William Walsh, slater, defunct.
„ 10 Thomas Beedle p. of Thomas Beedle of Chester, bowyer, defunct.

Dec.	10	William Bennet p. of Richard Sponne the elder, tanner.
Jan.	3	John Prenton, dyer, s. of John Prenton, dyer, defunct.
,,	7	George Halliwell p. of William Hallwod, tailor, defunct.
,,	7	Robert Wildinge, tailor, s. of Alexander Wildinge, shoemaker.
,,	7	John Nicholl, tailor, s. of John Nicholl, baker, defunct.
Feb.	4	Robert Crosse, glover, s. of William Crosse, glover.
,,	10	Joseph Leighe, chirurgeon, s. of Richard Leighe, chirurgeon.
,,	21	Joseph ap Jevan, hatmaker, s. of Robert ap Jevan, glover.
,,	26	Richard s. of Roger Basford of Chester, tailor.
Mar.	21	Daniel Bavand, esquire, s. of Richard Bavand, alderman, defunct.
,,	17	William s. of Ralph Tomlinson, butcher.
,,	17	Robert Tassie p. of James Fletcher of Chester, glover.
,,	29	Richard Corbin p. of William Denwall, draper.
Apr.	4	John s. of Thomas Johnes, clothworker.
,,	4	Jevan Johnes, p. of Thomas Johnes, clothworker.
,,	21	William Parrie, glover, s. of Edward Parrie of Chester, glover.
,,	21	Richard s. of Richard Meycocke, pewterer.
,,	21	Peter Hatton p. of John Burton of Chester, wright.
,,	29	John Knowles p. of John Madock of Chester, baker.
May	9	John Smith, feltmaker, s. of Ralph Smith, merchant.
,,	16	Richard Bridges, dyer, s. of Richard Brydges, dyer.
,,	16	Christopher Barnand p. of Richard Brydges, dyer.
June	11	John Leonard p. of Thomas Bird, tanner.
,,	20	William Baylie p. of Hugh Crumpe, baker.
,,	27	Robert s. of Robert Nicholas, fletcher.
Aug.	5	Christopher s. of Nicholas Hallwood of Chester, barber.
,,	5	John Taylor p. of William Hancocke of Chester, barber.
,,	20	William Bennet, tailor.
,,	30	Edward Parry p. of Owen Harries, ironmonger, defunct, and afterwards of Arthur Figes, ironmonger.
Sep.	9	Thomas s. of James Massie.
,,	23	William Gleg p. of William Aldersey the younger, lately mayor.
Oct.	3	William Curbisley p. of Thomas Ince, shoemaker, for 5 years and afterwards for rest of 7 years p. of Thomas Ryder, shoemaker.
,,	7	Humphrey Johnes, tailor, p. of Hugh Johnes.

Oct. 10 John Banckes.
„ 13 John s. of Roger Siddall, tailor.
„ 13 Randle Olton p. of Thomas Linall, tanner, and afterwards of John Fraunces the younger.

1614–5 [12–13 Jas. i.] WILLIAM ALDERSEY THE ELDER, MAYOR.

Nov. 5 William Phillippes, tailor, s. of Humphrey Phillippes, tailor, defunct.
„ 14 John Johnson, shoemaker, s. of Ralph Johnson, smith, defunct.
„ 25 John Seale, tailor, s. of John Seale, tailor, defunct.
„ 28 John Bathoe, clothworker, p. of Randle Finchet.
„ 28 Thomas s. of John Williams, mercer, defunct.
„ 29 William Dutton, gentleman, s. of Edward Dutton, alderman.
„ 29 Randle Dimmocke, gentleman, s. of William Dimmocke of Hawarden, co. Flint, gentleman.
Dec. 15 William Ball, yeoman, s. of William Ball, alderman, defunct.
„ 15 Alexander Hinde, tallow-chandler, s. of Hugh Hinde, tallow-chandler, defunct.
Jan. 9 Lawrence Miller p. of John Poole, hatmaker.
„ 9 Ralph Morgan p. of Richard Rider, shoemaker.
„ 16 William Edwards p. of William Sparke, ironmonger.
„ 16 Ralph Hilton p. of John Annion, draper.
„ 16 Michael Burges p. of William Whittle, tanner.
„ 16 Andrew Gamull p. of William Gamull, alderman.
„ 30 William s. of William Lea, ironmonger, defunct.
„ 30 Richard Robinson p. of Thomas Robinson the younger, weaver.
„ 30 Stephen Stiles, tailor, s. of John Stiles, mercer, defunct.
„ 30 Gabriel s. of Richard Weaver, draper.
—— 23 John Marshe p. of John Robinson, weaver.
„ 23 Thomas Moris, clothworker, p. of Randle Walker.
„ 23 John Davies p. of John Ratcliffe, alderman.
—— 23 John Hatton, ironmonger, p. of Lawrence Rathburne.
„ 23 Richard Tailor p. of Ralphe Mosse, baker.
May 26 Richard Kney, mariner, s. of Richard Kney, merchant.
„ 26 Thomas Warmingham p. of Anthony Warmingham, saddler.
„ 26 Roger Linall, hatmaker, s. of Roger Linall, hatmaker, defunct.
„ 26 David Plumbe p. of John Locker, cutler.

June	26	William Lache p. of William Messam, clothworker.
,,	26	George Dewesbury, embroiderer, s. of John Dewesburie, embroiderer, defunct.
,,	26	William Minor, vintner, p. of Robert Hall, ironmonger.
,,	26	William Fazakerley p. of John Fazakerley, defunct.
July	19	John Powell, smith, s. of Edward Powell, smith.
,,	19	John Tottie p. of William Skellington, slater.
,,	19	Thomas ap Jevan s. [*sic*] of Evan Powell, glover.
Aug.	14	John Crookes p. of Thomas Parcivall, saddler.
,,	14	Hugh Crumpe, baker, s. of Hugh Crumpe, baker.
,,	15	Sir Thomas Smith, knight.
,,	15	Robert Brerewood, esquire, *in legibus erud*, s. of John Brerewood, gentleman, defunct.
,,	15	William Saunders, gentleman, s. of —— Saunders, at the instance and request of Sir Thomas Savage, knight.
,,	15	William s. of Richard Robertes, butcher.
,,	15	William Hale, clothworker, p. of Robert Chauntrell.
,,	15	William Allen, shoemaker, s. of William Allen, pewterer.
,,	15	Thomas Gawne p. of Thomas Dannold, glover, defunct.
,,	15	John Garfield, joiner, s. of Richard Garfield, defunct.
Sep.	18	James Mutchell, tailor, p. of William Hande.
,,	18	John Crier p. of Nicholas Ince, maltster.
,,	18	William Drinckwater, ironmonger, s. of John Drinckwater, ironmonger, defunct.
,,	18	Henry Leonard, weaver, s. of Thomas Leonard, shoemaker, defunct.
,,	18	Edward Wright, barber-surgeon, s. of John Wright, skinner.
,,	18	Henry Brotherton p. of Randle Smith, clothworker.

1615-6 [13-14 Jas. i.] THOMAS THROPPE, Esquire, Mayor.

Oct.	30	Daniel Chaloner, sculptor, s. of Thomas Chaloner, painter.
,,	30	Thomas Williams, glover, s. of Hugh Williams, glover.
,,	30	Edward Harrie p. of Gilbert Eaton, beer-brewer.
,,	30	Joseph Lingley, goldsmith, s. of John Lingley, defunct.
Dec.	19	Kadwallader Edwardes p. of Ralph Holme, smith.
,,	19	Richard s. of Richard Hassellwall, mason.
,,	19	Richard Lloyd p. of Edward Fitton, ironmonger.
,,	19	Richard Critchley p. of Thomas Revington, beer-brewer.

Jan.	11	Miles Cooke p. of Thomas Massie, draper.
,,	11	Ralph Edge, chandler, s. of Ralph Edge, shoemaker, defunct.
,,	11	Robert Whitle p. of Thomas Weston, glover.
Feb.	5	Edward Tompson p. of Edward Blacon, tailor.
,,	5	Edward Bannester p. of Ralph Holme, smith.
,,	5	Robert Selbie, butcher, p. of Richard Wade.
,,	5	David Griffith p. of John Willson, smith.
Apr.	8	Richard Nicholl, tailor, s. of John Niccoll, tailor, defunct.
,,	8	James Ball, smith, s. of James Ball, smith.
,,	8	Peter Price, plumber, s. of Peter Piers [sic].
,,	8	Thomas Walshe, cooper, s. of Thomas Walshe, cooper.
,,	8	William Dawson, millioner, s. of Thomas Dawson, merchant.
,,	8	Edward Ball, millioner, s. of John Ball, glover, defunct.
,,	8	Paul Lloide, tailor, s. of Hugh Lloyd, tailor, defunct.
June	11	Richard Chetwood p. of John Tailor, ironmonger.
,,	11	John Carter, spurrier, p. of Stephen Albright.
,,	11	Richard Hickcocke p. of William Kinge, baker.
,,	11	David Bathoe p. of John Bristowe, tanner.
,,	18	Richard Lea, tanner,⎫ ss. of William Lea, ironmonger,
,,	18	Simon Lea, tanner, ⎭ defunct.
,,	18	John Deane, shoemaker, s. of John Deane, tanner.
,,	18	Phillip s. of William Plumbe.
,,	18	Richard Goughe, labourer, s. of Thomas Goughe, butcher.
Aug.	26	John Sier, barber, p. of Robert Thornley.
,,	26	John Poole, hatmaker, ⎫ ss. of John Poole, hat-
,,	26	Richard Poole, hatmaker,⎭ maker.
,,	26	George s. of Randle Vause, tailor.
,,	29	John Cowley p. of William Throppe the elder, skinner.
,,	29	John Tottie, cooper, s. of Henry Tottie, cooper.
,,	29	Robert Linaker, fishmonger, s. of Thomas Linaker, fishmonger.
,,	29	Henry Litherland, weaver, s. of Henry Litherland, tanner.
,,	29	Richard Bamber, beer-brewer, p. of John Ratcliffe, alderman.
Oct.	9	William Guile, mariner, s. of William Guile, sailor, defunct.
,,	9	William Andrew, feltmaker, s. of Thomas Andrew, shoemaker, defunct.

104 THE ROLLS OF THE FREEMEN OF [1619-20

Oct. 9 Robert Smith, feltmaker, s. of Robert Smith, defunct.
„ 9 Edward Tonna, glover, s. of John Tonna, glover, defunct.
„ 9 William Sprowston p. of Thomas Wright, feltmaker.

1619-20 [17-18 Jas. i.] HUGH WILLIAMSON, MAYOR.

Feb. 21 William s. of Thomas Rumer, and p. of William Wilson, sherman.
Jan. 31 Thomas s. of Thomas Lynaker, fishmonger and cooper.
Feb. 3 John s. of Robert Malbone of Chester, glover, and p. of John Gardner of Chester, smith and girdler.
„ 7 Jacob s. of Thomas Carter of Chester, tailor, and p. of Randle Ince, shoemaker.
„ 7 Coldson s. of Mr. Alderman Radcliff.
„ 22 Thomas s. of William Nicholls of Saughton on the Hill, and p. of Ralph Finchet of Chester, clothworker.
„ 24 Thomas } ss. of Randle Walker of Chester, cloth-
„ 24 Christopher } worker.
„ 24 Edward s. of Thomas Johnes of Chester, clothworker.
„ 24 Robert [s.] of Robert Adamson of Hellesby, co. Ches., yeoman.
„ 25 John s. of Richard Ampson of Chester, beer-brewer, and p. of William Edwards.
„ 28 Ralph s. of Raphe Fletcher, and p. of James Battriche.
„ 30 Richard s. of Richard Cowdocke, and p. of John
[sic] Hutchins, tailor.
Mar. 3 John Litler s. of George Litlor of Mouldsworth, co. Ches., and p. of Mr. Alderman John Litler, defunct.
Apr. 2 John s. of Thomas Powell of Ashton, co. Ches., and and p. of Robert Chauntrell, clothier.
— John s. of William Crewe of Elton, co. Ches., yeoman, and p. of Thomas Mersland, beer-brewer.
„ 6 Robert s. of Foulke Martin, and p. of Lawrence Crookes.
„ 7 Thomas s. of Randle Ince of Chester, draper.
„ 7 Griffith Williams s. of William ap Jevann Griffith of Llandesillo in Yale, co. Denbigh, and p. of William Whittle, tanner.
„ 25 Calvin s. of John Bruen, esquire, and p. of Robert Blease of Chester, mercer.
May 26 Thomas s. of Hugh Lloyd of Chester, tailor, " because he was a freeman's son."

June	9	Henry s. of Henry Wareton of Gresebie, co. Ches., yeoman, and p. of William Modesley, baker.
,,	19	Morris s. of Edward Robinson of Chester, brazier, and p. of Daniel Thropp, shoemaker.
,,	19	Robert s. of Robert Ridley of Chester, bricklayer.
,,	28	William s. of William Walshe of Chester, slater, and p. of William Hancocke.
July	4	Thomas s. of William Holford of Iscoyd, co. Ches., husbandman, and p. of Phillip Moore.
Aug.	4	Thomas s. of Edmund Rose of Liverpool, gentleman, and p. of David Roberts of Chester, ironmonger.
Oct.	12	Henry s. of John Hancock of Oxen, co. Ches., yeoman, and p. of Richard Sponne, tanner.
,,	12	Henry s. of —— Tottie of —— in Werrall, and p. of Ralph Wilson, tanner.
,,	12	Edward Barnes, servant of Hugh Jones, tailor.

1620–1 [18–19 Jas. i.] WILLIAM GAMULL, Mayor.

Nov.	21	Richard s. of Morgan Williams of Broughton, and p. of Richard Taylor, clothier.
,,	21	Jacob s. of John Lyngley of Chester, goldsmith, and p. of William Lurtinge, feltmaker.
Dec.	5	Thomas s. of Randle Walker of Buddworth, co. Ches., yeoman, and p. of Mr. Gilbert Eaton.
,,	13	Randle s. of Robert Farrington of Chester, currier, defunct, and p. of Raphe Moris.
	—	William s. of Richard Warmisham, goldsmith.
Jan.	5	Thomas s. of Richard Weaver, draper.
,,	30	Robert Waynewright, servant of Mr. Foulke Salisbury.
May	23	Nicholas Ratcliffe of Chester, gentleman.
July	26	Ellis Lewis s. of Lewis ap John Lewis of Carnarvon, and p. of Lewis Jones of Chester, silkweaver.
,,	30	William s. of Thomas Harryson of Saughall Massie, co. Ches., husbandman, and p. of Gilbert Eaton, beer-brewer.
Aug.	17	Robert s. of Robert Shurlocke of Sea——n [? Seacombe], co. Ches., defunct, and p. of Edward Bathoe, clothier.
,,	29	Richard s. of Richard Snead, draper, and p. of Thomas Fletcher, glover.
Sep.	28	Thomas s. of William Hand of Chester, tailor, and p. of Mr. William Gamull, mayor of the city.
,,	28	Christopher s. of Henrie Pye of Chester, joiner, defunct.
Oct.	3	Randle s. of John Annyon of Chester.

106 THE ROLLS OF THE FREEMEN OF [1621-2

Oct. 5 Robert s. of David Evans, pewterer, freeman of the city.
„ 5 Edward Johnes p. of Mr. Christopher Blease.
„ 5 Richard Bridge p. of Mr. Thomas Weston, glover.
„ 8 William Hilton p. of Mr. Thomas Bird, tanner.
„ 10 John Moreton p. of Richard Fletcher, glover.
„ 9 Ferdinand s. of John Taylor, *alias* Darbishire, late of Burton, co. Ches., butcher, and p. of Mr. John Ratcliffe, alderman.
„ 9 William s. of Edward Bradshawe of Chester, carpenter, deceased, and p. of William Smallshawe, slater.

1621-2 [19-20 Jas. i.] ROBERT WHITEHEAD, MAYOR.

Oct. 15 James Johnson p. of Lewis Johnes, silkweaver.
„ 19 John Jeffryes p. of Henry Totty, cooper.
Nov. 14 John s. of Erasmus Price of Chester, beer-brewer.
„ 23 Nicholas s. of Anthony Welshe.
Dec. 19 Thomas s. of Richard Fletcher of Chester, tailor, and p. of Peter Jenkin, clothworker.
Feb. 12 Richard s. of Raphe Richardson, butcher.
„ 12 Owen Morrice p. of William Catherall, fishmonger.
„ 18 Thomas Bradshaw p. of John Rigmarden, baker.
„ 18 Thomas Williamson p. of William Catherall, joiner.
Mar. 1 Henry Baxter p. of Thomas Deane, clothier.
„ 4 Richard s. of Thomas Bird, alderman.
„ 4 Richard Painter p. of Thomas Hitchens, tailor.
Apr. 2 Richard Rabon p. of William Crosse, glover.
„ 2 David Griffin p. of Godfrey Win, alderman.
„ 2 Thomas ap Robertes p. of John Wade, butcher, defunct.
„ 2 Richard Trafford p. of Thomas [Mercer ?], tallow-chandler.
„ 26 John s. of Thomas Sherott, late of Marston, co. Staff., and p. of John [Laughton ?], cardmaker.
June 12 Henrie s. of Lewis Jones, freeman of the city.
„ 12 John s. of John Ashton, baker.
July 1 Daniel s. of Symon Goyton of —— in Ireland, and p. of Thomas Gough of Chester, draper.
„ 1 Peter s. of Thomas Bennett of Frankby, co. Ches., yeoman, and p. of John Anyon and Raph Hulton, draper.
„ 1 John s. of John Bennett of Saughall Massie, and p. of Hugh Williamson, alderman.
„ 8 Edward s. of Edward Curlell of Chester.

July	15	Henrie s. of Richard Robinson of Chester, shoemaker.
,,	22	Mathew s. of Mathew Smith of Burton, yeoman.
Aug.	2	William s. of George Cowes of the [Holt ?], and p. of Thomas Hulmes, smith.
,,	14	Daniel s. of Rowland Gratbach of Whitechurch, and p. of Thomas Aldersey, merchant.
,,	28	John s. of John Mathew of Hargreve, co. Ches., and p. of Robert Lowe, baker.
Sep.	5	William s. of James Bromfild [or Bromefild] of ——, and p. of Moses Dalby, glazier.
,,	25	Philip s. of James Roland of Peckforton, and p. of John Aldersey of Chester, ironmonger.
,,	24	Robert s. of John Whitehead of Greate Sutton.
Oct.	2	James s. of Robert Wilson of Wallasey, and p. of James Fletcher, yeoman.
,,	3	William s. of John Downes of Burton, yeoman, and p. of William Whitby, tanner.
Feb.	17	John s. of Thomas Taylor of Pickton, yeoman, and p. of Mr. Robert Blease, alderman and apothecary.

1622–3 [20–21 Jas. i.] SIR THOMAS SMITH, KNIGHT, MAYOR.

Oct.	14	William } ss. of Mr. Randle Hulme of this cittie,
,,	14	Randle } painter.
,,	14	Christopher } ss. of John Walker of Chester, glasier.
,,	14	William }
,,	14	Christopher s. of William Hilton, shoemaker, and p. of Thomas Johnes, clothworker.
,,	17	Richard s. of Bradford Throppe of Chester, shoemaker, and p. of Rafe Morgan, shoemaker.
Nov.	7	Thomas s. of John Hinton of Chester, baker.
,,	11	Charles s. of Mr. Richard Fletcher, glover and sheriff's peer of the city.
,,	16	William s. of William Whittle of this city, tanner.
,,	19	Rowland s. of Edward Greene of Pulton, gentleman, and p. of Mr. [Robert ?] Berry of Chester, alderman and merchant.
Dec.	17	Thomas s. of Randle Suker of Hanmer, husbandman, and p. of William Helds of Chester, baker.
,,	17	Richard s. of William Dod of Malpasse, yeoman, and p. of Michel Jones of Chester, saddler.
Jan.	16	John s. of John Wright of Huxley, husbandman, and p. of John Ratcliffe of Chester, alderman.

Jan. 16		Henry s. of John Powell of Chester, carpenter, defunct, and p. of Thomas Welsh, cowper.
Feb.	19	William s. of William Aldersey of O——, co. Salop, gentleman, and p. of Thomas Weston of Chester, glover.
„	20	Richard s. of John Walton of Gilden Sutton, co. Ches., yeoman, and p. of John Maddocks of Chester, baker.
Mar. 26		John s. of Raph Axon of Lancan, co. Ches., and p. of Peter Goose of Chester, draper.
Apr. 17		William s. of William Poynton of Kinsley, co. Ches., husbandman, and p. of William Modesley of Chester, baker.
May 13		George s. and p. of Richard Meacock of Chester, pewterer.
„	14	William s. of Robert Twisse of Handbridge, smith, and p. of Kadwallader Edwards, smith.
„	19	Thomas s. and p. of Richard Stockton of Chester, blacksmith.
„	24	Thomas s. of Robert Thomason of Wallasey, and p. of Edward Griffeth, clothworker.
„	26	John s. of Thomas Lowe of Chester, feltmaker, deceased.
June 10		Richard s. of Roger Kinge of Chester, "made free of the Companie of bakers."
„	13	Thomas s. of Henry Watt of Wallasey, co. Ches., tailor, and p. of Richard Taylor of Chester, clothworker.
„	30	John s. and p. of Thomas Jeynson of Chester, smith.
July 29		Luke s. and p. of Oats Conniley of Chester, beerbrewer.
„	30	Edward s. of Hugh Roberts of Hugmoore, co. Denbigh, yeoman, and p. of John Garnett of Chester, beerbrewer.
„	31	Thomas s. of William Bolton of Abra [? Abram] co. Lanc., and p. of Richard Lecester, mercer.
Aug. 25		Robert s. of William Johnson of Chester, smith and freeman of the city, and p. of Thomas Johnson, smith.
Sep. 26		Laurence s. of John Robinson, tailor.
Oct.	4	William s. of Thomas Burges of Chester, dyer.
„	4	William s. of John Hasselhurst of Namptwich, and p. of John Wildinge, tailor.
„	7	John s. of John Robinson of Chester, tailor.
„	8	Thomas s. of Peter Wirrall of Dunham on the Hill, co. Ches., gentleman.

1623–4] THE CITY OF CHESTER 109

Oct. 8 John s. of John Stubbes of the Witten, and p. of Thomas Ince of Chester, glover.
„ 8 John s. of Richard Hill of Wallasey, and p. of William Wildinge of Chester, feltmaker.
„ 9 Alexander s. of Roger Johnes of Wrexham, co. Denbigh, fletcher, and p. of Richard Powell of Chester, fletcher.
„ 9 George s. of Edward Crookes of Garstonne, co. Lanc., husbandman, and p. of Thomas Percivall of Chester, saddler. "The aforesaid George deposed before Mr. Maior that he hath served seaven yeares as an apprentice."
„ 9 William s. of Robert Fletcher of Hatherton, co. Ches., yeoman.

1623–4 [21–22 Jas. i.] JOSEPH BRERETON, Mayor.

Oct. 14 Richard s. of Edward Dutton of Chester, alderman, deceased.
„ 16 William s. and p. of Lewis Johnes of Chester, silkweaver.
„ 17 John s. of Henry Bassett of ——, co. Kent, and p. of John Harrison of Chester, tailor.
Nov. 7 Richard s. of Richard Radley of Chester, shoemaker, and p. of William Halliwell of Chester, weaver.
„ 20 John s. of Richard Radley, late of Chester, shoemaker, and p. of George Hilton of Chester, shoemaker.
„ 22 Thomas s. of Richard Herall of Frodsham, and p. of John Whitbie of Chester, clothworker.
„ 22 William s. of John Mory [or Morrey] of Morton, co. Ches., husbandman, defunct, and p. of Randle Bingley of Chester, clothworker.
Jan. 7 George Warrington p. of Thomas Marten [or Maslen], beer-brewer.
„ 28 Andrew Minshall p. of Robert Fletcher the younger, hatmaker.
„ 28 Thomas s. of Jo. Lester, and p. of William Phillips.
Mar. 8 William Watmoughe p. of William Salisbury, joiner.
„ 16 Thomas Throp, merchant, s. of Thomas Throppe, alderman, defunct.
Apr. 20 Robert Williams p. of Edward Harrys, beer-brewer.
May 5 Thomas s. of Edward Throppe of Chester, feltmaker, and p. of Hugh Halliwell, baker.
Apr. 9 James Wildinge p. of Robert Wildinge, tailor.
„ 12 Thomas s. of Edward Throppe [? duplicate entry. See May 5 above].

May 28 Symon s. of David Momford of Chester.
June 16 Richard Ashton s. of John Aston, and p. of Thomas Massy, draper.
„ 16 Ralph s. and p. of John Ashton, baker.
„ 16 William s. and p. of Ralph Mosse, baker.
„ 20 —— Martin p. of Charles Fytton, alderman.
July 8 Jo. s. of Hugh Lloyd, and p. of Edward Harryes. brewer, 109
Aug. 6 Robert Greage s. of Henry Greag, and p. of Hugh Leigh, clothier.
„ 12 John Edwards p. of John Andrew, beer-brewer.
„ 17 John s. of James Robinson of Chester, water-leader, and p. of Robert ap Hugh, joyner.
Sep. 7 Jo. s. of Richard Hall, and p. of Thomas Griffith.
„ 7 "Jo Owen s. of Owen dd. Lloyd," and p. of Jo Hallwood, tailor.
„ 8 Thomas s. of Jo. Ashbrook, tailor.

1624-5 [22 J. i.–1 C. i.] PETER DRINKWATER, MAYOR.

Thomas Drinkwater } ss. of the mayor.
Robert Drinkwater }
Fr. s. of J. Taylor.
Richard Annion, yeoman, s. of Thomas Annion, ——.
Laurence [Barrow ?] p. of William [Eddes ?], iron-monger.
Thomas Crosse p. of Thomas Tu——.
Thomas Woodfin p. of John Totty, slater.

Nov. 6 Jo. Edwards, brewer, p. of Jo. Andrewe, beer-brewer.
Dec. 2 Henry Barton, carpenter, p. of James Hamlin.
„ 9 William Fletcher, clothworker, p. of William Ince.
„ 12 Richard s. of John Lacy of Pickton, and p. of Richard Newport, shoemaker.
Jan. 13 Randle Bennett, shoemaker, s. of Robert Bennett, draper.
„ 13 Peter Marten, shoemaker, p. of Daniel Wright.
Mar. 17 Thomas Cook, carpenter, p. of Jo. Welshe [or Webster].
„ 17 Jo. Penny, butcher, s. of Ralph Penny.
Feb. 1 Richard s. of William Mercer, and p. of Alice Mercer, widow of the said William, chandler.
„ 4 William Morris p. of William Wilson, clothworker.
„ 15 William s. and p. of John Welsheman, baker.
„ 18 John s. of John Edwards of Cheweley, gentleman.

[1625-6]   THE CITY OF CHESTER   111

Feb. 22 Thomas s. of Richard Roberts, and p. of Thomas Fisher, butcher.
Apr. 25 George Fletcher p. of Jo. Dannold, glover.
May 5   Ralph Richardson p. of William Higginson.
„   18   John Gryce p. of John Roberts, butcher.
„   19   Phillip Sproston, feltmaker, s. of John Sproston, defunct.
June 13 Thomas s. of Hugh Whickstead.
„   13   Richard Urmeston p. of William Kinge, baker.
„   22   Roger Rogers p. of Ralph Wilson, tanner.
„   23   John Jones p. of William Bennett, tanner.
„   23   Henry Tyrer p. of William Catterall, joiner.
„   27   Thomas Bradley p. of Thomas Crofts, feltmaker.
„   27   Richard s. of John Dewsbury.
„   29   Robert Greene, feltmaker, s. of Robert Greene.
„   29   John Williamson, feltmaker, s. of John Williamson.
„   29   Edward Wildinge, feltmaker, s. of William Wildinge, feltmaker.
„   29   William Wildinge, tailor, s. of John Wildinge, tailor.
„   11   Edward s. of Edward Parrie.
Aug. 8 William s. of Edward Button, alderman.
July 13 William s. of John Sproston, feltmaker.
„   13   Jo. s. of Thomas Fletcher, shoemaker.
„   14   Thomas s. of James Downam, weaver.
Aug. 2 Thomas Dyas p. of John Ashbrooke, tailor.
„   2   Thomas Lloyd p. of John Stringer, slater.
Sep. 6 Sir John Savage, knight.
„   6   Francis Gamull.
„   6   Thomas Bavand.
July 8 John Quaile p. of John Maddocke.
„   9   Daniel Bore p. of William Richardson, innholder.
„   13   Richard Owen, *alias* Carden, p. of Thomas Jackson, smith.
„   14   Thomas Ryder, shoemaker, s. of Thomas Ryder, shoemaker.
Oct. 10 Jeffray s. of William Granwall.
„   10   Edward Moyle   } pp. of Thomas Williams, saddler.
„   10   William Williams }
Sep. 27 Richard Fletcher, glover, s. of James Fletcher.

1625-6 [1-2 C. i.] RANDLE MAINWARING, Mayor.

Sep. 24 John Fletcher, glover, s. of James Fletcher.
Oct. 6 William s. of Randle Lawton.
Nov. 3 Randle s. of Randle Higginson.
„   14   William Ashton, baker, p. of John Ashton.

Oct.	17	Richard Wall p. of Henry Kenkeat, weaver.
,,	17	Jo. Gatliffe p. of Thomas Syer, linen-draper.
,,	17	Brian Croston p. of John Poole, feltmaker.
Nov.	3	Thomas Millington p. of Thomas Bird, alderman.
,,	3	Richard s. of Richard Pemberton, shoemaker.
Oct.	14	Thomas s. of Thomas Masland, beer-brewer.
July	25	Hugh Win, glover, s. of Hugh Win, glover.
Jan.	3	Robert Blanchard, glover, s. of John Blanchard, baker.
Nov.	11	Robert s. of John Bavand.
Oct.	14	William Crofte p. of John Whitbie, sherman.
Jan.	9	Thomas Ley p. of Samuel Bennet, shoemaker.
,,	18	Hugh Allen p. of George Halliwell, tailor.
Feb.	3	Richard Heighfield p. of John Ratcliffe, alderman and beer-brewer.
,,	7	Thomas Whittle, tanner, s. of William Whittle, tanner.
,,	7	Thomas s. of Hugh Williams, glover.
,,	10	John Barton p. of Edward Thompson, tailor.
,,	10	Thomas Pilkington.
,,	13	John Watt p. of Thomas Farington, currier.
,,	15	Richard Blagge p. of Robert Ollerhead, feltmaker.
Mar.	6	Thomas Liniall p. of Hugh Whickstead, glover.
,,	27	Thomas Reece p. of Thomas Williams, linen-draper.
Apr.	4	John Bennett p. of Thomas Goose, draper.
—		John Simson.
,,	6	Thomas Madocke p. of Ralph Wilson, tanner.
,,	24	Thomas Eaton, beer-brewer, s.⎫ of Gilbert Eaton,
,,	24	George Hinckley p. ⎭ beer-brewer.
,,	27	William Edge p. of George [this is crossed out in M.B. and Ralph is inserted] Hilton, shoemaker.
May	12	Richard Johnson p. of Rowland Johnson, ironmonger.
,,	12	Edward Lightfoote p. of Ralph Lightfoote, baker.
June	19	Jo. Wright p. of Robert Thornley, barber chirurgeon.
—		Henry Bennett, draper, p. of William Allen, alderman.
,,	19	William Bavand, gentleman, s. of Randle Bavand, merchant.
,,	21	William s. of Nicholas Ince, alderman, and p. of William Gamull, alderman.
,,	21	Robert Ince, shoemaker, s. of Randle Ince, draper, defunct.
,,	21	Thomas Hinde, feltmaker,⎫ ss. of Randle Hinde, tanner,
,,	21	James Hinde, feltmaker, ⎭ defunct.
,,	21	William Bradshawe p. of William Locker, cutler.
,,	21	William Locker, cutler, s. of Thomas Locker.
July	3	Thomas Jones, smith, s. of Thomas Jones, smith.
,,	3	John Fleete p. of William Fleete, tailor.
,,	1	Edward Robinson, weaver, s. of Thomas Robinson.

[1627-8] THE CITY OF CHESTER 113

July 1 Robert s. of Richard Johnson, innholder, defunct.
,, 8 Thomas Thropp, shoemaker, s. of Randle Throp.
,, 28 William Appleton p. of Ralph Wall, ironmonger.
,, 31 John Marten p. of William Allen, shoemaker.
Aug. 3 Alexander Wildinge, feltmaker, s. of Alexander Wildinge, shoemaker.
,, 3 John s. of Richard Danold, baker.
,, 19 William Jones p. of Edward Bromley, tallow-chandler.
,, 22 Thomas Gaskin p. of Richard Gaskin, slater.
— — John Fleete, tailor. [? Dup. entry. See July 3 above.]
Aug. 22 Joseph Pricket, embroiderer.
,, 29 John s. of Peter Tilston, draper.
Sep. 5 Rowland Eakin [or Ykin] p. of William Danold, clothworker.
Oct. 2 James Badger p. of Thomas Maxland.
,, 9 Robert Woodcocke p. of John Danold, glover.
,, 10 John Cotton p. of John Knowles, baker.
— Henry Baylie.

1627-8 [3-4 C. i.] RICHARD DUTTON, Mayor.

Oct. 16 David s. of George Flowers.
,, 22 William Lewis p. of John Maddocke.
Dec. 18 Richard David p. of John Crew, beer-brewer.
,, 20 John Cheswis p. of William Sparke, alderman.
Jan. 10 Robert Deane p. of William Wildinge, feltmaker.
,, 11 Richard Litlor, gentleman, s. of Richard Litlor, gentleman.
,, 11 Hugh Anderton of Chester.
,, 12 Isaac s. of John Wright of Chester, draper and hosier, defunct.
,, 18 Randle s. of Thomas Ledsham.
Feb. 1 John Aldersey, gentleman, s. of William Aldersey, alderman, defunct.
,, 5 John s. of William Sparke of Chester, treasurer.
,, 5 George s. of William Dimmocke of Hawarden, and p. of Christopher Blease.
,, 5 Owen Hughes p. of William Aldersey, alderman, defunct.
,, 12 Hugh s. of Simon Stockton, cutler, defunct.
Mar. 7 Thomas s. of Richard Bennet, cooper, defunct.
,, 22 John Nicholl p. of John Roberts of Chester, butcher.
Apr. 2 Thomas Prenton p. of Richard Taylor of Chester, clothier.
,, 29 Samuel Bucke p. of Thomas Aldersey of Chester, merchant.

H

Apr. 29 John Ilyffe p. of Thomas Deane of Chester, weaver.
May 9 Marmaduke s. of Thomas Asmore, innholder, defunct.
„ 14 Thomas Cooke p. of Thomas Weston, glover, defunct.
„ 16 William s. of William Pue of Chester, joiner.
„ 24 John Davies p. of Thomas Lowe, feltmaker, defunct.
„ 24 John s. of David Proderough, glover, defunct.
„ 26 William Seale, butcher, s. of Robert Seale, yeoman.
June 6 John s. of John Blanchard, baker, defunct.
„ 10 Hugh Higinet s. of Hamnet Hygynet, defunct, and p. of William Meason, clothworker.
„ 10 Edward s. of Henry Phillips, tailor, and p. of Richard Hyne, tallow-chandler.
„ 25 William Rathbone p. of William Glegge, merchant, defunct.
„ 25 Robert Jones p. of Gilbert Eaton, beer-brewer, defunct.
„ 30 William Ryder s. of Thomas Rider the elder, shoemaker.
„ 30 Richard Tylston p. of William Poole, barber.
July 1 Peter s. of Samuel Bennet, shoemaker.
„ 10 John Heighfield p. of John Ratcliffe, alderman.
„ 22 Richard s. of Peter Goose, draper.
„ 22 Thomas s. of John Andrewe, beer-brewer.
„ 22 Lancelott Cowes p. of Gabriel Weaver, draper and hosier.
„ 29 Robert s. of John Mowson, tanner.
Aug. 19 John Dutton, gentleman, s. of Edward Dutton, alderman, defunct.
„ 19 Thomas Sparke p. of Thomas Bird, alderman.
Sep. 24 Evan Lewis s. of William ap John Lewis of Llanvaior, co. Denbigh, gentleman, defunct, and p. of Michael Jones, saddler.
Oct. 2 John ap Edward p. of Randle Walker, clothworker.
„ 3 Owen Ellice of Chester, vintner.
„ 6 John s. of William Kinge, baker, defunct.

1628-9 [4-5 C. i.] JOHN RATCLIFFE, Mayor.

Edward Leene s. of William Leenes.
Richard s. of John Sproston, feltmaker, defunct.
Randle Walker, shoemaker, s. of Randle Walker, clothworker.
Edward s. of Robert Coddington, tanner.
William Seale, slater, s. of John Seale, tailor.
Thomas s. of Thomas Harrison, cooper.
John Davies p. of Roger Kinge, baker.

John Joynson s. of Robert Jeinson, shoemaker.
Richard Totty p. of John Grice.
Thomas Mottershead p. of Humphrey Lloyd, alderman, defunct.
John Hine p. of Alexander Hine, tallow-chandler.
George Santhey p. of William Jones, linen-draper.
Richard Dickenson p. of Gilbert Eaton, beer-brewer, defunct.
Humphrey Denwall p. of David Hatton, butcher.
John Leivesley s. of John Leavesley, innholder, defunct.
Randle Brureton p. of John Blanchard, baker.
Thomas Birchenhead p. of William Parsonage, feltmaker.
Miles Pemberton p. of Thomas Fletcher, glover.
Hugh Hughes p. of Edward Reignolds, draper.
Ralph Leigh p. of Adam Kempe, baker, defunct.
George s. of Hugh Jones, innholder.
John Rowland p. of William Throppe, skinner.
Edward Broughton p. of Samuel Robinson, merchant.
Thomas s. of Richard Warmingham, goldsmith.
John Whitbie p. of Robert Adamson, clothworker.
Humphrey Streete p. of Cadwallider Edwards, smith.
Nicholas s. of Nicholas Ince, alderman.
Silvan Glegg p. of Joseph Lingley, goldsmith.
Ralph Sharples p. of Thomas Welsh, hooper.
John s. of William Smith, and p. of John Hatton, ironmonger.
Robert Caddocke p. of Anthony Reive, tailor.
William Williamson p. of Thomas Williamson, joiner.
Randle Modesley p. of Robert Warton, weaver.
Richard Baylye, tailor, s. of Richard Baylye, beer-brewer.
Raph Lloyd p. of Thomas Crosse, feltmaker.
Ralph Pike p. of William Bennet, baker.
John s. of John Ratclyffe, mayor of the city.
John s. of William Fletcher, glover.
Thomas Eaton the younger, p. of Thomas Eaton the elder, smith.
Evan Jones p. of Robert Sproston, feltmaker.
Thomas s. of James Annion, tailor, defunct.
Hugh Humpston p. of Thomas Hatton, shoemaker.
Edward s. of Thomas Mercer, tallow-chandler.
Richard Lewis p. of Edward Yonge, shoemaker.
Randle Turner p. of William Hand, tailor.
William Catterall s. of William Catterall, joiner.

1634-5 [10-11 C. i.] FRANCIS GAMULL, Esquire, Mayor.

Nov.	9	Francis Jones p. of William Hand of Chester, tailor.
,,	26	Arthur Pricket p. of Roger Burrowes, feltmaker. [This freeman has been originally shown as s. of Robert Pricket, carpenter, but this has been erased.]
,,	27	John Fletcher, skinner, s. of Robert Fletcher, feltmaker, defunct.
,,	23	Richard s. of Richard Kally.
,,	27	Stephen Nichollson p. of Thomas Welshman, glover.
Mar.	4	Edward Kinsey p. of John Wildinge, tailor.
Dec.	9	John Johnson p. of Thomas Crosse, ironmonger.
Jan.	7	William s. of William Allen, shoemaker.
,,	7	William Coldocke, maltster, s. of Richard Coldocke, shoemaker.
Feb.	3	William Bennet [s. crossed out] p. of John Bennet, mercer, defunct.
,,	17	Robert Davies p. of Ralph Hulton, draper.
,,	17	Thomas Moreton p. of Calvin Bruen, ironmonger.
Mar.	10	Thomas s. and p. of Edward Fisher, butcher.
,,	23	Robert Palin p. of John Maddocke, tanner.
,,	24	Daniel Woods p. of William Catherall, hooper and fishmonger, defunct.
,,	31	Anthony Nicholl, smith, s. of Thomas Nicholl, tanner, defunct.
,,	31	Robert s. of Edward Guest, ropier.
,,	31	Samuel s. of Robert Ince, draper, and p. of Daniel Gaiton, draper and hosier.
,,	10	Ralph s. of Ralph Mosse, baker.
Apr.	14	George Rowlin p. of Randle Smith, clothworker.
May	27	John Hind p. of Edward Fisher, butcher.
June	5	James Bamber p. of William Watmough, joiner.
,,	8	George Pulford p. of William Horton, glover.
,,	8	William Ball the younger, glover, s. of Thomas Ball, glover.
,,	10	Thomas Lloyd p. of Christopher Tilston, feltmaker.
,,	10	William Yonge, baker, } ss. of William Yonge, shoe-
,,	10	John Yonge, shoemaker, } maker, defunct.
,,	10	Thomas s. of Isaac Warmincham, tailor, defunct, and p. of John Barton, tailor.
July	8	Richard Markes, cooper, s. of Thomas Markes, cooper.
,,	9	William s. of William Jones, linen-draper.
,,	20	Richard Woodcock } pp. of Edward Roberts, beer-
,,	20	John Hayes } brewer.

July	22	Thomas Darwall p. of James Battriche, ironmonger, defunct.
„	22	John Bastwell, glover, s. of Samuel Bastwell, silk-weaver, defunct.
„	22	Thomas Bromhall p. of Hugh Whickstead, glover.
„	22	Randle s. of John Leivesley, innholder, defunct, and p. of Hugh Whickstead.
„	22	John Bradley p. of Hugh Whickstead.
„	25	George Richardson, cooper, s. of William Richardson, defunct.
„	29	Thomas Higginson, mariner, ⎫ ss. of William Higgin-
„	29	John Higginson, glover, ⎭ son, butcher.
Aug.	18	John Cooke, cooper and fishmonger, s. of Geoffrey Cooke, fishmonger, defunct.
„	18	John Baugh, feltmaker, s. of Thomas Baugh, feltmaker.
„	31	William Gibbon p. of Richard Robinson, glover.
Sep.	4	Henry Jones, instrument maker.
„	4	John Cowles, yeoman.
„	13	Richard Harvie, gentleman, s. of Thomas Harvie, alderman, defunct.
„	13	John s. of William Coldocke, shoemaker.

* 1635-6 [11-12 C. i.] THOMAS KNOWLES, Mayor.

    Robert Looker, tallow-chandler.
    Thomas Bushell, tallow-chandler.
    Richard Throppe, stationer.
    Richard Hodgson, joiner.
    Henry Newport, shoemaker.
    John Harvey, ironmonger.
    Gilbert Vause, glasier.
    Thomas Townend, draper.
    Ralph Holmes, tanner.
    Thurstan Duggan, slater.
    James Smith, musician.
    Thomas Waynwright, clothworker.
    Geoffrey Malbon, apothecary.
    Thomas Snape, butcher.
    Peter Edwards, tanner.
    William Parry, ironmonger and merchant.
    Edward Bridge, glover.
    Richard Darwall, glover.
    John Griffith, clothier.
    David Humphreys.
    Thomas Humphreys, merchant.

Peter Fletcher, wetglover.
John Fletcher.
William Jackson, draper.
William Stirropp, shoemaker.
Richard Brett, merchant.
John Bennett, gentleman.
Anthony Dymocke, merchant.
Mark Bucksy.
Arthur Wilson, shoemaker.
Edward Millington, mercer.
Robert Lowe, baker.
John Conilow, beer-brewer.
Henry Yonge, ironmonger.
Thomas Jones, currier.
John Dod, merchant.
Richard Bradshaw, merchant.
Humphrey Lloyd, merchant.
John Massy, tanner.
Thomas Halewood, yeoman.
Robert Hughson the younger, ironmonger.
Hugh Higginson, tanner.
Richard Townend, ironmonger.
Robert Fletcher, haberdasher.
John Croftes, feltmaker.
Thomas Madocke, baker.

* This year is not complete.

1636-7 [12-13 C. i.] WILLIAM EDWARDS, Mayor.

Oct. 15 William s. of Peter Drinkwater, alderman, defunct.
,, 15 John Seddall, painter and barber, s. of John Seddall, ———.
,, 25 Dutton Bunbery p. of Thomas Wright, clockmaker.
,, 25 Thomas Aspinwall p. of William Lea, ironmonger.
Nov. 2 Robert Denwall, gentleman, s. of William Denwall, draper.
,, 22 Thomas Fitton, gentleman, s. of Charles Fitton, alderman, defunct.
,, 24 George Hiccocke p. of William Bradshaw, slater.
,, 29 John s. of Edward Allen, merchant, and p. of Thomas Crofts, feltmaker.
Dec. 26 Richard Harrison p. of John Ratcliffe, alderman and brewer, defunct.
,, 29 Thomas Pulford p. of John South, painter.
,, 29 Phillip Jackson p. of Stephen Albright, loriner.

Jan.	3	Thomas Wyat, gentleman, s. of Thomas Wyat, glasier.
„	16	Peter Hughes p. of William Sparke, alderman, merchant and ironmonger.
„	20	George Streete p. of Thomas Harrison, tailor.
„	23	Thomas Ryder, locksmith, s. of John Rider, locksmith.
„	29	Robert Fletcher, shoemaker, s. of Thomas Fletcher, shoemaker.
Feb.	4	Richard Rider, shoemaker, s. of Richard Rider, shoemaker.
„	11	Phillip Walker p. of John Fleete, tailor.
„	20	William s. of John Cowper, baker, and p. of John Brooke, beer-brewer.
„	20	Thomas Cartmell p. of John Brooke, beer-brewer.
„	20	John Hulton p. of John Brooke, beer-brewer.
„	21	Thomas Rollison p. of Thomas Aldersey, merchant.
Mar.	9	William Lewis p. of John Smith, pewterer.
„	23	George Pickavant, tallow-chandler, s. of John Pickavant, tallow-chandler.
Apr.	4	John Morrice p. of Thomas Morris, blacksmith.
„	12	Peter Price p. of Peter Snead, draper and hosier.
„	21	William Johnson p. of Gabriel Weaver, merchant, draper and hosier, defunct.
May	11	Robert Denson p. of Thomas Eaton, beer-brewer, defunct.
„	16	William Sutton p. of Charles Walley, alderman and innholder.
June	14	Peter Edwards p. of William Edwards, merchant and ironmonger.
„	17	Edward Hughes p. of John Edwards, clothworker.
„	21	Thomas Phillipps p. of Lawrence Yonge, glover.
„	28	Robert Gregory p. of William Horton, glover.
July	4	Thomas s. of John Gardner, smith, defunct, and p. of John Aldersey, ironmonger.
„	4	Hamlet s. of Phillip More, innholder, defunct, and p. of John Leckonby, ironmonger.
„	4	William s. of Edward Allen, merchant, defunct, and p. of Edward Harries, beer-brewer, defunct.
„	14	Richard Golborne, gentleman.
„	17	Humphrey Lloyd p. of John Hall, glover.
„	27	William Urian p. of Thomas Andrew, beer-brewer, defunct.
Aug.	1	Phillip s. of Ralph Wilson, and p. of Christopher Bernand, dyer.
„	1	William Jones p. of Richard Molleaux, weaver.
„	22	John Owen p. of Hugh Johnes, tailor.

THE ROLLS OF THE FREEMEN OF [1637-8

Sep. 5 Ralph Allen, gentleman, s. of John Allen of Chester, gentleman.
„ 8 John Bickerton.
„ 8 Evan Johnes, carpenter.
„ 8 George Morris.
Oct. 4 William Muchill p. of William Poynton, baker.

1637-8 [13-14 C. i.] THOMAS THROPPE, Mayor.

William Hilton, sherman.
Thomas Leivesley.
Robert Wareton, glover.
John Hilton, shoemaker.
Thomas Knowles.
William Gawne, tailor.
Lancelot Downes.
John Williams.
Hugh Whickstead, glover.
Robert Grice, glover.
John Prenton, dyer.
Randle Ball, glover.
John Finlow, glover.
Robert Pue, joiner.
David Pue.
George Tyrer.
William Heys, glover.
John Wynne, ironmonger.
Thomas Bruen, mercer.
Sampson Shelley, ironmonger.
Richard Wright, feltmaker.
John Whiteside, shoemaker.
Richard Calcott, turner.
Richard Lynniall, feltmaker.
Edward Tyrer, clockmaker.
Thomas ap Richard, barber.
William Ryder, yeoman.
Thomas Bavand, tanner.
Thomas Fletcher, glover.
George Bagot, glover.
John Modesley.
John Picke, mariner.
Percival Williams, merchant.
Samuel Ratcliffe, gentleman.
William Drinkwater, beer-brewer.
William Shurlocke, glover.

Robert Fezakerley, vintner.
Robert Couldocke.
Yuan Hulse, cook.

1638-9 [14-15 C. i.] ROBERT SPROSTON, Mayor.

William Davies, shoemaker.
William Davie, clothworker.
Richard Jones, clothworker.
Miles Bennet, clothworker.
John Sproston.
Randle Bridge, shoemaker.
Peter Cooke, feltmaker.
Richard Denson, baker.
William Kinley, beer-brewer.
Thomas Hiccocke, baker.
Thomas Hodgson, baker.
Peter Welchman, baker.
John Owffe, baker.
Thomas Kney, hatmaker.
John Beddow, feltmaker.
William Cronke, cardmaker.
John Fernall, dyer.
Francis Wade, butcher.
Richard Monkesfeild, butcher.
Edward Fisher, butcher.
John Barker, butcher.
Thomas Hanky, feltmaker.
John Wade, butcher.
Richard Price, butcher.
Robert Bore, feltmaker.
Ralph Morgan, shoemaker.
Thomas Deane.
John Wiatt, glasier.
Barnard Knee, shoemaker.
Nicholas Welch, cooper.
Thomas Lynnaker, fishmonger.
Edward Guest, ropier.
Thomas Thorneton, weaver.
Robert Dawson, mason.
William Bennett, feltmaker.
Arthur Walley, mercer.
Hamnett Bennett, glover.
Thomas Tilston, blacksmith.
John Guest.

John Stede, tanner.
James Hand, butcher.
Robert Robinson, slater.
Richard Wildinge.
John Seavell, shoemaker.
William Maxy.
Joseph Bruen, mercer.
Thomas Robinson, ironmonger.
John Taylor, shoemaker.
John Huet.
Richard Middleton, merchant.
David Lloyd, gentleman.

1639-40 [15-16 C. i.] ROBERT HARVY, Mayor.

William Granwall, chirurgeon.
Frederick Conway, ironmonger.
Thomas Gregory, shoemaker.
Edward Walker, tailor.
Richard Carden, innholder.
Andrew Ward, merchant.
Matthew Starkie, beer-brewer.
Hugh Crompe, baker.
Robert Rowland, yeoman.
Hugh Walton, yeoman.
Hugh Banks.
Peter Cotgreave.
Thomas Hicks.
Thomas Martin, glover.
Edward Fletcher, ironmonger.
Thomas Gibbons, feltmaker.
Thomas Broome, tailor.
John Scholefeild, feltmaker.
John Harrison, tailor.
Richard Eccleston, glover.
John Edwardes, smith.
William Lightbound, tailor.
Thomas Blease.
Robert Blease.
John Garfeild.
Richard Litherland.
Thomas Allen, vintner.
Hugh Ravenscroft, smith.
Thomas Harrison, glover.
Henry Evans, clothworker.

Robert Williams, feltmaker.
William Blanchard, linen-draper.
Robert Wright.
William Phillips, clockmaker.
John Lancaster, ironmonger.
Richard Minshull, ironmonger.
Thomas Dannald.
Daniel Kinge.
John Lache.
Thomas Browne, draper and hosier.
Paul Coulton.
John Jones, gentleman.
James Barrowe, tailor.
Richard Grice, glover.
Thomas Evans, pewterer.
Thomas Davies, weaver.
Richard Moreton.
Richard Johnson, apothecary.

1640-1 [16-17 C. i.] THOMAS ALDERSEY, Mayor.

Richard Cowper, shoemaker.
Hugh Hinde, tallow-chandler.
Robert Boydell, shoemaker.
Hugh Maddocke, tanner.
John Rathborne, tanner.
Edward Fitton, gentleman.
John Ball, smith.
George Fazakerley.
Randle Garratt.
Richard Gill, slater.
Randle Oulton, beer-brewer.
Richard Byrd, tanner.
John Skellerne.
John Johnson, joiner.
John Hill.
John Hanky.
Richard Streete, clothworker.
John Wood.
Thomas Warmincham, saddler.
Thomas Selsby, butcher.
Richard Edwards, butcher.
James Sheale, r——.
Richard Holme, tanner.
Urian Ryder, cutler.

Peter Price, plumber.
Francis Rodgers, cutler.
Robert Shurlock, shoemaker.
Thomas Higginson.
Randle Higginson.
Robert Worrall, carpenter.
Richard Hawkshawe.
William Maddocke.
William Croughton.
John Poole, feltmaker.
Thomas Muchell, feltmaker.
Robert Smith, feltmaker.
Richard Davenport, stationer.
Richard Croughton, barber.
John Looker, tallow-chandler.
John Oulton, ropier.
Robert Murrey, barber-chirurgeon.
James Alcocke.
Robert Edmundson, draper.
William Jackson, beer-brewer.

1641-2 [17-18 C. i.] THOMAS COWPER, Mayor.

Richard Annion, baker.
Daniel Gilbert, mercer.
John Davies, beer-brewer.
Joshua Taylor, chirurgeon.
John Taylor, chirurgeon.
Thomas Spencer, tanner.
Edward Bromley, shoemaker.
John Cracknel, tailor.
James Massey, turner.
John Caddocke, feltmaker.
William Bedward, clothworker.
John Calley.
John Coddington, tanner.
Richard Deane, baker.
Daniel Crofts, feltmaker.
Richard Gill, slater.
Robert King, clothworker.
Richard Bennett, saddler.
Randle Minshul, merchant.
William Hocknel, baker.
William Welshman, glover.

John Johnson, glover.
Randle Venables, glover.
Robert Taylor, glover.
Thomas Willolugh, beer-brewer.
Steven Owen, cutler.
John Bannion, cooper.
George Bunnel, beer-brewer.
John Hough, feltmaker.
Thomas Pemberton, shoemaker.
Thomas Bolland, joiner.
Thomas Kettell, joiner.
John Modesley, feltmaker.
John Leigh, clothier.
Henry Colley, tanner.
Edward Williams, feltmaker.
Edward Dolbie, glasier.
John Bird, ropemaker.
Thomas Bastwell, silkweaver.

1642-3 [18-19 C. i.] WILLIAM INCE, Mayor.

John Sproston, feltmaker.
William Litherland, tanner.
Daniel Radford, linen-draper.
George Swetnam, draper.
John Croughton, shoemaker.
Henry Bennet, merchant.
David Ince.
Robert Boothe, silkweaver.
John Lowe.
John Throppe, chirurgeon.
Thomas Calcott, feltmaker.
William Williames.
Randle Walker.
William Myddelton, tanner.
William Greene, shoemaker.
Thomas Eaton, beer-brewer.
William Hulton, draper.
John Markes, wine-cooper.
Samuel Walker, shoemaker.
William Bavand, tanner.
Francis Prince, blacksmith.
Robert Boothe, silkweaver.
John Rydley the younger, bricklayer.
William Throppe.

Henry Addison, shoemaker.
Peter Heywoode.
Michael Inglefield.
Randle Grosvenor.

1643-4 [19-20 C. i.] RANDLE HOLME THE YOUNGER, MAYOR.

Henry Mason, clothworker.
William Barton, feltmaker.
Richard Barker, shoemaker.
William Bedward, feltmaker.
Robert Fernall, butcher.
William Hayes, smith.
William Fisher, butcher.
Henry Wynstanley, cooper.
Peter Stringer.
Thomas Hollett, weaver.
George Leightfoote, baker.
William Welshman.
Robert Maddocke, tanner. .
Charles Weaver, draper.
Richard Broster, tanner.
Thomas Broster, tanner.
John Broster, tanner.
John Moulson, tanner.
Richard Wilson, tanner.
Robert Downham, webster.
Robert Farrington.
Theodore Prickett.
John Welsh, cooper.
Thomas Batha, baker.
Francis Jackson.
John Moores.
Hugh Amson.
John Williames.
Richard Corvell, feltmaker.

1644-5 [20-21 C. i.] CHARLES WALLEY, MAYOR.

Edward Morgan, shoemaker.
George Massey, beer-brewer.
John Knowles, ironmonger.
John Modesley, feltmaker.
Thomas Roberts, butcher.

Anthony Jones, butcher.
Paul Soones, butcher.
Francis Fornibie [? Formby], turner.
Timothy Buckley, tailor.
Richard Hiccocke, baker.
John Leonard, mercer.
Hugh Wiggen, butcher.

1646–7 [22–23 C. i.] WILLIAM EDWARDS, Mayor.

William Edwards, "Ilarchus."
Robert Whitbie, esquire.
William Wright, draper.
Jonathan Ridge, draper.
John Witter, apothecary.
John Whittell, ironmonger.
Henry Pemberton, ironmonger.
Thomas Pickeringe, ironmonger.
Adam Earle, ironmonger.
Richard Bridge, dyer.
Edward Burrowes, feltmaker.
Nathaniel Cooke, draper.
Jonathan Goldson, beer-brewer.
John Goldson, beer-brewer.
John Heskie, tailor.
Thomas Fernihughe, draper.
Anthony Hitchins, tanner.
William Huett, ironmonger.
Randle Jones, ironmonger.
Edward Bathowe, tanner.
William Grimsdiche, draper.
William Lloyd, feltmaker.
Thomas Ball, beer-brewer.
Thomas Younge, beer-brewer.
John Hilton, shoemaker.
John Ince, glover.
William Heifield, glover.
Jonathan Farrington, beer-brewer.
John Lingley, feltmaker.
Thomas Owlerhead, feltmaker.
Thomas Taylor, beer-brewer.
Richard Burowes, feltmaker.
John Johnson, feltmaker.
Thomas Kempe, baker.
Lawrence Fletcher, skinner.

James Hill, feltmaker.
John Saracold, merchant.
Richard Birchall, ironmonger.
Owen Roberts, carpenter.
James Appleton, carpenter.
Nathaniel Drinkwater, ironmonger.
Robert Wynne, ironmonger.
Samuel Vawdrey, ironmonger.
Moses Dolbye, glasier.
George Vause, feltmaker.
Adam Holmes, feltmaker.
Thomas Danald, linen-draper.
Humphrey Jones, linen-draper.
William Bridge, dyer.
William Richardson, innholder.
Thomas Duton, glover.
George Lloyd, gentleman.
John Annyon, innholder.
John Darwall, glover.
William Harvie, bricklayer and linen-draper.

1647-8 [23-24 C. i.] ROBERT WRIGHT, Mayor.

Mar. 18 William Streete, beer-brewer, s. of William Streete, of Chester, beer-brewer.
— Thomas Halliwell, yeoman, s. of —— ——.
— John Wildinge, yeoman, s. of —— ——.
— Thomas Ley, yeoman.
— Thomas Cony, draper, s. of —— Cony, clerk, and p. of Richard Bennet, merchant draper.
— Samuel Eyton, brewer.
— Daniel Bavand, gentleman, s. of ——.
— Adam Kempe, baker, [p. of] Ralph Leighe.
— Francis Fearnall, baker.
— Thomas Cowper, ironmonger, s. of Thomas ——.
— William Morris, fishmonger.
— William Glegge, clothworker.
Mar. 25 Thomas Morris, smith, s. of —— Morris, blacksmith.
„ 25 Thomas Annion, smith, p. of —— —— blacksmith.
„ 25 William Booth, smith, p. of Thomas Stockton, blacksmith.
— William Parsonage, feltmaker, s. of —— ——.
— Thomas Dodd, ironmonger, p. of —— ——.
— Daniel Crosse, ironmonger, p. of —— ——.
— Randle Halle, shoemaker, s. of —— ——.

—		Hamnet Kirkes, shoemaker, p. of —— ——.
—		William Leigh p. of —— Leigh, slater.
—		Ralph Ravenscroft p. of John Owen, tailor.
—		William Blundell p. of Edward Eaton, tailor.
Apr.	1	William Wright [p. of] Thomas Mottershead, merchant.
„	6	Hugh Bennett, draper, [s. of] John Bennett, ——.
—		Thomas Daggott, tallow-chandler, p. of —— ——.
—		Richard Pulford, baker.
Apr.	16	David Frances, tallow-chandler, p. of Ralph W——.
——	——	Edward Evans, mercer.
—		Richard Crane, currier.
May	11	Richard Dobbe p. of John Ireland, shoemaker.
„	11	Robert Finlowe, glover, s. of John Finlowe, glover.
„	16	Samuel Elcocke, tailor, s. of John Elcocke, tailor.
—		Richard Mercer, clothworker, - —— —— ——, clothworker.
—		William Harrison, webster, - —— —— ——, weaver.
—		John Davies, s. of —— ——, and p. of Richard Sproston, draper.
—		Humphrey Bridge, dyer, s. of —— ——.
—		Edward Higginson, butcher, s. of William ——.
—		Peter s. of Richard Rathbone, and p. of —— ——, baker, defunct.
June	7	John s. of Edward Griffeth, and p. of Jeffery Mal——, apothecary.
„	9	Edward Ledshame p. of William Crofts, clothworker, defunct.
„	10	Benjamin Johnson, draper, s. of John Johnson, draper, defunct.
„	30	Henry s. of Robert Woodcocke of Gilden Sutton, and p. of —— Kinsey, tailor.
—		John Locker, glover, s. of John ——.
——	5	Hamnet Taylor, saddler, p. of —— ——.
—		Thomas Nicholas, cooper, s. of Robert ——.
—		Thomas Hesketh, cooper, [s. or p. of] —— ——.
——	——	William Greggory, shoemaker.
July	13	Thomas Higginson, embroiderer, s. of Richard Higginson.
„	21	Richard Lucas, *alias* Goose [merchant, M.B.], tailor, s. of Thomas Lucas, *alias* Goose.
„	21	Thomas Watte p. of John Watte the younger, clothworker.
„	28	John Bushell p. of —— Hunt, beer-brewer.

1648 [24 C. i.] EDWARD BRADSHAW, Mayor.

— — Thomas Denson, shoemaker, [p. of] —— —gory, shoemaker.
— John Williames, hooper.
Sept. — Richard Gill, brewer.
— William Grice, yeoman.
— Charles Walley, merchant.
„ 15 Henry s. of William Hall, feltmaker, and p. of Miles Cooke, draper.
„ 20 John Phillippes, mercer, s. of Humphrey Phillippes, mercer.
Oct. 7 William Warrington, brewer, s. of George Warrington.
„ 7 Thomas Wright, brewer.
— Thomas Cotton, brewer, p. of —— ——.
— Thomas Dickenson, brewer, s. of [Ric ?] ——.
— Edward Wiatt, glasier, — of —— Wyatt, glazier, defunct.
— William Garrat, clothworker.
„ 13 Thomas Welsheman [chaunsler], s. of Thomas Welsheman, glover.
„ 13 Richard Bennett, shoemaker, s. of Randle Bennett, shoemaker.

1648-9 [24 C. i.- —] RICHARD BRADSHAWE, Mayor.

Richard Maddocke, feltmaker.
Richard Welshe, barber.
Edward Walker, shoemaker.
Peter Sproston, haberdasher.
Edward Powell, blacksmith.
Phillip Jackson, spurrier.
Richard Bennett, feltmaker.
John Blanchard, innholder.
Richard Greene, haberdasher.
Hugh Thorneley, blacksmith.
Ralph Almond, blacksmith.
Francis Phillippes, feltmaker.
William Edwardes, tailor.
John Williames, tanner.
Ralph Bathoe, tanner.
Francis Burges, tanner.
Thomas Heath, shoemaker.
Hugh Morris, butcher.
Thomas Owens, butcher.
Thomas Ireland, ironmonger.

William Ley, ironmonger.
Arthur Figes, ironmonger.
Joseph Witter, tailor.
Henry Meide, barber.
William Potter, feltmaker.
Edward Spanne, baker.
John Anderson, innholder.

1649–50. WILLIAM CROMPTON, Mayor.

Oct. 16   Edward Wilson, glover, s. of James Wilson, glover, defunct.
„ 18   George Harvie, millner [bricklayer, M.B.], s. of Thomas Harvie, millner, defunct.
Nov. 2   Matthew Anderton, innholder, s. of Hugh Anderton, innholder.
„ 6   William Betteley, barber, p. of Thomas Robinson, barber-chirurgeon, waxchandler, and painter.
„ 22   Nicholas Williames, clothier, s. of Richard Williames, clothier, and p. of Thomas Kettle, dyer, defunct.
„ 22   Richard Taylor p. of William Bromfeild, glasier.
„ 29   Daniel Leigh p. of John Owen, tailor.
Jan. 9   Edward Croughton, shoemaker, s. of William Croughton, shoemaker, defunct.
„ 10   William Turner p. of John Bridge, feltmaker.
Feb. 15   William Siddall, carpenter, s. of John Siddall, yeoman.
Oct. 22   Peter Coulton, butcher, s. of Paul Coulton, butcher.
Apr. 3   Peter Dewesberry, feltmaker, s. of Richard Dewesberry, feltmaker.
May 3   Edmund Mouldesworth p. of John Skellorne, ironmonger.
„ 3   John Trevers p. of Thomas Rowlandson, ironmonger.
July 1   William s. of —— Bennett, draper, and p. of Alexander Hinde, tallow-chandler.
„ 1   William Hinde, tallow-chandler, s. of Alexander Hinde, tallow-chandler.
„ 1   John Jones, feltmaker, s. of John Jones, feltmaker.
„ 1   William Meacocke, pewterer, s. of George Meacocke, pewterer.
„ 3   Edward s. of Christopher Dannold, glover, and p. of Thomas Lowe, baker.
„ 9   Ellis Lewis, silkweaver, s. of Ellis Lewis of Chester, silkweaver.
„ 9   William Ouslecroft p. of Thomas Warmincham, tailor.
„ 15   Randle Sargeant p. of Humphrey Jones, draper.
Sep. 12   Francis Goldson p. of Robert Harvie, bricklayer.

1650–1. RICHARD LEICESTER, Mayor.

William Prenton, dyer.
Richard Knowles, shoemaker.
George Inckle, shoemaker.
Richard Ledshame, tailor.
John Cotton, shoemaker.
Edward Walton, baker.
Edward Gray, clothier.
John Dawson, feltmaker.
Thomas Preece, clothworker.
John Halliwell, baker.
John Crumpe, baker.
Charles Hiccocke, baker.
Thomas Leigh, baker.
Randle Leicester, feltmaker.
Thomas Hancocke, tanner.
Christopher Brownet, cooper.
Richard Meacocke, pewterer.
Thomas Robinson, webster.
Urian Minshull, dyer.
Hugh Anckers, cooper.
Thomas Wainewright, cooper.
John Foster, feltmaker.
Christopher Tilston, feltmaker.
Richard Bridge, feltmaker.
John Ansteed, maltster.
John Hulton, shoemaker.
Thomas Allen, shoemaker.
Henry Bolton, feltmaker.
Thomas Cracknell, shoemaker.
John Johnson, blacksmith.
Humphrey Jackson, skinner.
William Whitehead, yeoman.
Samuel Fezakerley, yeoman.
Robert Fletcher, gentleman.
John Brocke, gentleman.
John Bannister.
John Gill, feltmaker.
Robert Heath, shoemaker.
Thomas Bridge, shoemaker.
John Fletcher, carpenter.
James Fletcher, glover.
Thomas Critchley, beer-brewer.
John Bradshawe, cutler.

Raphe Davenport, gentleman and clerk of the Pentice.
Nathaniel Watmoughe.
Richard Tottie.
Edward Walmesley, slater.
Richard Griffeth, glover.
Thomas Booth, slater.
Erasmus Price.
John Whitehead.
Tobias Parnell, apothecary.

1651. OWEN HUGHES [DIED; JOHN JOHNSON, SUCC.], MAYORS.

Oct. 28   Hugh Moulson, tanner, s. of Hugh Moulson, tanner.
„ 28   Peter Edwards, goldsmith, s. of Griffith Edwards, goldsmith.
„ 28   William s. of Edward Bromeley, tallow-chandler.
„ 28   Randle Bathoe, tanner, s. of David Bathoe, tanner.
„ 28   Peter Bennett p. of William Wilson, tanner.
„ 28   Nathaniell s. of Robert Radford, lynner, and p. of John Hulton, shoemaker.
Nov. 10   Captain Samuell Smyth, gentleman.
„ 13   William Lathe p. of Edward Wildinge, feltmaker.
„ 19   John Modesley p. of Edward Tompson, tailor.
„ 26   James Robinson, musician, s. of John Robinson, musician.

1651–2. JOHN JOHNSON, ESQUIRE, MAYOR.

Nov. 26   Thomas s. of Owen Ellis, vintner, and p. of Thomas Blessinge, barber.
„ 26   Thomas Bickerton, innholder, s. of John Bickerton of Chester, and p. of George Bennett of Chester, merchant.
Jan. 22   Humphrey Caddicke p. of Richard Grosvenor, feltmaker.
„ 27   Raphe s. of William Joynson, tanner.
„ 28   Richard Maddoc p. of John Williams, saddler.
„ 29   Nathaniel Basnett p. of Richard Johnson, apothecary.
Feb. 11   John Jones, baker, s. of John Jones, baker.
„ 14   Matthew Barkeley p. of Henry Yonge, ironmonger.
„ 20   Richard Moyle, clerk, s. of John Moyle, draper.
„ 25   Randle Jones, feltmaker, s. of John Jones, feltmaker.
„ 28   Thomas Ashton, innholder, s. of Richard Ashton, draper.

Feb. 28 Charles Alcocke, haberdasher, s. of Thomas Alcocke of London, haberdasher.
„ 28 Charles Leivesley, innholder, s. of John Leivesley, innholder.
„ 28 George Leendes, porter, s. of William Leendes, cooper.
Mar. 13 John Johnson p. of William Tapley, plasterer.
„ 13 Thomas Glegge, merchant, s. of William Glegge, merchant.
„ 16 John Barlowe, mason, s. of William Barlowe.
„ 16 Richard s. of William Higginson, butcher, and p. of William Streete, beer-brewer.
Apr. 5 Richard Taylor p. of Roger Liniall, feltmaker.
„ 5 Thomas Palyn p. of Thomas Crofts, feltmaker.
„ 5 John Annyon p. of Richard Hodgeson, joiner.
„ 29 Humphrey Dymocke, gentleman, s. of William Dymocke, gentleman.
„ 5 Reece Williames p. of Bryan Crosse, feltmaker.
„ 7 *Michael Hunt, cutler.
„ 7 Richard Yates p. of Hugh Shawe, carpenter, deceased.
„ 20 Thomas Gilbert, cutler, s. of Thomas Gilbert, cutler.
„ 29 John s. of John Annyon, slater.
„ 29 Francis Leivesley, barber, s. of John Leivesley, innholder.
June 17 Gowen Hudson, merchant, s. of Gowen Hudson, innholder.
„ 17 Randle Morgan, glover, s. of Randle Morgan, glover.
„ 22 Raphe Tompson, tailor, s. of Raphe Tompson, tailor.
July 1 Samuel s. of Thomas Welsheman, glover, and p. of John Harvie, ironmonger.
„ 14 Charles Hughes p. of John Wildinge, tailor, defunct.
Aug. 3 William Seale, butcher, s. of William Seale, butcher.
„ 3 George Starkey, brewer, s. of George Starkey, brewer.
Sep. 27 John s. of Richard Bridge, dyer.
„ 30 John Bradley, clerk, s. of Thomas Bradley, feltmaker.
Oct. 5 Richard Fisher, butcher, s. of Edward Fisher, butcher.
„ 6 William Broome p. of George Streete, tailor.

1652-3. WILLIAM BENNETT, Esquire, Mayor.

John Francis, tanner.
William Corbin, yeoman.
William Plumley.
Nathaniel Beavan, ironmonger.
John Ridge, draper.
Richard Francis, barber.

William Bryne, beer-brewer.
John Plumbe, carpenter.
Edward Griffith, slater.
Edward Walker, blacksmith.
Moyses Halliwell, tanner.
Richard Francis, feltmaker.
George Pemberton, feltmaker.
Robert Williamson, joiner.
John Kinge, baker.
Thomas Coppocke, tanner.
John Jones, baker.
Francis Higginson, embroiderer.
Christopher Bennett, beer-brewer.
Thomas Bennett, shoemaker.
Robert Bennett, beer-brewer.
Roger Lewis, clothworker.
John Lloyd, feltmaker.
Nathaniel Deane, ironmonger.
Samuel Deane, shoemaker.
William Stout, feltmaker.
Samuel Radford, linen-draper.
Robert Heywood, apothecary.
Christopher Sneyd, feltmaker.
Joseph Lingley, feltmaker.
Thomas Warminsham, shoemaker.
Nicholas Reece, feltmaker.
Barnett Throppe, feltmaker.
William Poole, barber.
William Bennett, mercer.
Randle Harrison, tailor.
John Asbrooke, shoemaker.

1653-4. EDWARD BRADSHAWE, Esquire, Mayor.

Oct. 28　Thomas Jones, barber, s. of Thomas Jones, baker.
Nov. 14　Richard Ley, shoemaker, s. of Thomas Ley, shoemaker.
„　17　John Lurtinge, yeoman, s. of William Lurtinge, feltmaker.
Dec. 6　Jonathan Maddocke, shoemaker, s. of John Maddocke, tanner.
„　6　Ralph Hughson [Huson, M.B.] p. of Robert Payne, shoemaker.
„　19　John Hiccocke p. of Edward Phillippes, tallow-chandler.
„　30　Charles Broster, chirurgeon, s. of Richard Broster, tanner.
„　30　Samuel Broster, tanner, s. of Richard Broster.

Jan.	9	Hugh Hands, milner, s. of Hugh Hands, dyer.
,,	9	William Cope, silkweaver, s. of Richard Cope, silkweaver.
,,	19	John s. of John Swinton, of Knutsford, co. Ches., mercer, and p. of Peter Leigh, ironmonger.
—		Thomas s. of James Crompton, tailor, and p. of Edward Roberts, beer-brewer.
Feb.	7	Robert s. of Richard Hill of Wallesey, and p. of John Ball, blacksmith.
Mar.	4	John s. of John Bastwell, glover.
,,	7	Marmaduke s. of Edward Lloyd, late of Newton, co. Salop, gentleman, and p. of Peter Leigh, ironmonger.
,,	7	Thomas Billington p. of John Whittle, ironmonger.
,,	7	Francis Skelherne p. of John Skelherne, ironmonger.
,,	7	Joseph Bradshawe p. of Samuel Bucke, ironmonger.
,,	7	Jonathan Whitbie, apothecary, p. of James Ravenscroft.
,,	7	Joseph [Samuel, M.B.] Witter p. of John Witter, apothecary.
,,	7	Timothy s. and p. of John Davies, draper.
,,	19	Robert Andrew, feltmaker, s. of William Andrew, feltmaker.
,,	17	Richard Cooke, yeoman, p. of Arthur Harvie, glover.
,,	27	William Selsby, butcher, s. of William Selsbie, butcher.
May	11	William Willoughbie servant and p. of Thomas Willoughbie, beer-brewer.
June	16	Phillip Standish p. of Thomas Hankie, feltmaker.
,,	30	Matthew Bingley p. of John Wilson, feltmaker.
July	18	Robert s. of George Chamberleine, and p. of Robert Denson, beer-brewer.
,,	18	Mathias Heys p. of John Croughton, shoemaker.
,,	18	Robert Mowson, tanner, s. of Robert Mowson, tanner.
,,	18	Myles Pemberton p. of Richard Fletcher, tanner.
,,	18	Robert Hey p. of Simon Ley, tanner.
Aug.	7	Thomas Mottershed, merchant, ⎫
,,	7	John Mottershed, merchant or ⎬ ss. of Thomas Mottershed, alderman and merchant.
,,	7	vintner, ⎪
,,	7	Albean Mottershed, vintner, ⎭
,,	7	Thomas Warminsham, tailor, s. of Thomas Warminsham, tailor.
,,	19	Samuel Cellars p. of William Heywood, shoemaker.
,,	19	Thomas Haslowe p. of William Richardson, butcher.
Oct.	1	Lawrence Leicester, shoemaker, s. of Lawrence Leicester, feltmaker.
,,	1	William Throppe p. of John Finlowe, glover.
,,	14	John Turner, yeoman, p. of William Higginson, innholder.

1654-5. RICHARD BYRD, Esquire, Mayor.

Thomas Lynikar, fishmonger.
John Smyth, baker.
Samuel Neild, skinner.
John Hinde, chandler.
Randle Bingley.
Raphe Bingley, tallow-chandler.
William Cappur, vintner.
Thomas Jones, yeoman.
Richard Huntington, feltmaker.
William Taylor, draper.
Gilbert Eyton, baker.
William Pike, baker.
John Nickoll, butcher.
Thomas Sympson, ironmonger.
Michael Bromley, tallow-chandler.
Randle Annyon, baker.
Robert Mosse, draper.
William Modesley, weaver.
John Callie, weaver.
Henry Lloyd, draper.
Samuel Collie, merchant.
John Calley, musician.
Richard Bruen, barber.
Owen Williams, beer-brewer.
William Dobson, yeoman or feltmaker.
Samuel Worrall, clothworker.
Samuel Cotton, feltmaker.
Thomas Thomasson, clothier.
William Halliwell, glover.
Samuel Morris, blacksmith.
Joseph Wells, glover.
George Revington, feltmaker.
Hugh Barkley, gentleman.
Robert Hewitt, ironmonger.
Robert Coddington, tanner.
Thomas Byrd, tanner.
Robert Owens, dyer.
John Owen, pewterer.
Humphrey Wright, beer-brewer.
William Throppe, stationer.
Thomas Drinkwater, merchant.
John Crosse of London, draper.
Peter Flecte, yeoman.

John Joynson, yeoman.
Thomas Pulford, yeoman.
Henry Trevis, draper.
Peter Nicholls, clothworker.
George Thomasson, tanner.
George Eyton, mariner.
William Eyton, mariner.
Thomas Singleton, merchant.
Nathaniel Eyton, beer-brewer.
Thomas Wilcocke, mercer.
Edward Hulton, merchant.

1655–6. WILLIAM WRIGHT, Esquire, Mayor.

Thomas Warminsham, shoemaker.
Isaac Hughes, tailor.
John Moreton, shoemaker.
Eliner Moreton, tailor.
Thomas Humphreys, stationer.
Nathaniel Clarke, beer-brewer.
Thomas Lache, shoemaker.
Thomas Edge, chandler.
Thomas Edwards, shoemaker.
William Bolland, joiner.
Richard Stockton, blacksmith.
George Cotton, baker.
Thomas Johnson, innholder.
Mathew Appleton, butcher.
James Bolland, turner.
Thomas Harrison, tailor.
Roger Jones, feltmaker.
Richard Dewsbury, feltmaker.
William Fletcher, shoemaker.
Samuel Gerrard, tailor.
Edward Croefoote, beer-brewer.
Randle Davies, feltmaker.
John Sparke, gentleman.
John Ashton, blacksmith.
Thomas Hancocke, blacksmith.
John Basford, innholder.
Hugh Dod, tailor.

1656–7. PETER LEIGH, Esquire, Mayor.

Richard Humpstone, tailor.
Henry Crosby, shoemaker.
William Roberts, carpenter.
Charles Moreton.
William Bathoe, tanner.
John Maddockes, tanner.
Joseph Wright, tanner.
William Thomason, baker.
Henry Johnson, joiner.
William Johnson, shoemaker.
Thomas Anion, innholder.
William Robinson, carpenter.
Thomas Crosse, clerk.
Jonathan Crosse, ironmonger.
Richard Heath, ironmonger.
Thomas Hassall, ironmonger.
Samuel Leigh, ironmonger.
Francis Weever, shoemaker.
John Malbone, blacksmith.
William Williamson, feltmaker.
Henry Bennett, beer-brewer.
Ralph Davies, innkeeper.
William Robinson, weaver.
John Davies, beer-brewer.
Robert Ridge, vintner.
John Brownet, cowper.
William Tunnar, tailor.
Richard Stringer, cutler.
Ralph Rutter, glover.
Richard Blinstone, butcher.
John Savage, gentleman.
John Richardson.
Nicholas Cowper, silkweaver.
Thomas Ball, feltmaker.
Thomas Wright, ironmonger.
Randle Wilson, dyer.
Thomas Cooxen, ironmonger.
Thomas Jenion, ironmonger.
Richard Dicus, tailor.
Samuel Potter, feltmaker.
Jonathan Edwards, ironmonger.
Edward Smith, fletcher.

Edward Williamson, linen-draper.
Randle Holme the younger, painter.
Vivian Davenport, mercer.

1657-8. RICHARD* MINSHULL, Esquire, Mayor.

Jonathan Cooke, linen-draper.
William Holme.
Mathew [Cowes ?], blacksmith.
William Bate, mercer.
William Dodd, ironmonger.
Raph Whitakers, ironmonger.
John Yong, shoemaker.
Joseph Cope, silkweaver.
John Heath, haberdasher.
Thomas Stringer, haberdasher.
John Queile the younger, tanner.
William Whittingham, gentleman.
Edward Taylor, barber.
Thomas Peeres, plumber.
John Hawkshaw, plumber.
Thomas Dalby, glazier.
William Snead, linen-draper.
James Knowsley, linen-draper.
John Rowlin, clothworker.
Jonathan Tapley, cowper.
—— Sparkes, labourer.
Thomas Hand, draper.
John Whittle, draper.
Benjamin Critchley, draper.
Thomas Millington, shoemaker.
Thomas Dawson, woollen-draper.
John Fletcher, barber.
John Boote, ironmonger.
John Holden, draper.
James Evans, silkweaver.
Thomas Davenport, barber.
John Adams, tallow-chandler.
William Bennett, saddler.
Robert Jones, dyer.
Thomas Smith, dyer.
George Orton, saddler.
William Reece, butcher.

* Ormerod gives this Mayor's name as Richard or Thomas; Hemingway as Thomas.

Thomas Hoose, shoemaker.
Raphe Downeham, mason.
John Ireland, cowper.
Nicholas Lawler, tailor.
William Fletcher, tanner.
Richard Doe, shoemaker.

1658–9. THOMAS HAND, Esquire, Mayor.

John Hiccocke, baker.
John Pemberton, glover.
Randle Bennyon, dyer.
William Bennett, saddler.
William Doley, ironmonger.
John Hughes, pewterer.
William Godfrey, innholder.
Peter Leighe, glover.
Richard Grosvenor, feltmaker.
Robert Cooke, baker.
Randle Baxter, joiner.
John Bennett, mercer.
William Smith, gentleman.
Thomas Totty, currier.
Robert Fletcher, skinner.
George Jackson, spurrier.
John Cranke, cardmaker.
Robert Parte, joiner.
Richard Tilston, bricklayer.
John Halwood, slater.
Kenricke Williams, ironmonger.
Thomas Walker, clothworker.
Samuel Rymer, clothworker.

1659. GERRARD JONES, Esquire, Mayor.

Roger Brereton, ironmonger.
Daniell Cornell, cooper.
Hugh Roberts, cooper.
William Cooper, ironmonger.
Thomas Parry, ironmonger.
William Basford.
Robert Basford.
John Parks, weaver.
Richard Leighe, feltmaker.
[Asah ?] Andrewe, carpenter.

Thomas Brereton, saddler.
Henry Aston, glover.
Edward Aston, glover.
Phillip Phillips, yeoman.
Phillip Brocke, pewterer.
John Gibbons, barber-chirurgeon.
Valentine Short, merchant.

1659–60 [— –12 C. ii.] JOHN JOHNSON, Esquire, Mayor.

William Cappar, ironmonger.
Thomas Holwood, glover.
John Partington, mercer.
Thomas Bruen, linen-draper.
John Fletcher, ironmonger.
Peter Bayly, beer-brewer.
William King, butcher.
Thomas Holliwell, baker.
Robert Hall, wine-cooper.
Thomas Davies, linen-draper.
George Bulkeley, gentleman.
John Meacocke, weaver.
Thomas Dutton, tallow-chandler.
John Griffith, beer-brewer.
John Kettle, joiner, carver, and turner.
Humphrey Lach, beer-brewer.
John Harvy, ironmonger.
Thomas Aspenwall, ironmonger.
James Mercer, apothecary.
Thomas Heath, apothecary.
Edward Oulton, beer-brewer.
Richard Maddocke, tanner.
George Warrington, shoemaker.
William Johnson, cook.
William Cooper, glazier.
John Cotgreave, baker.
Edward Starkie, beer-brewer.
William Higgnett, draper.
William Page, blacksmith.
William Kelsall, apothecary.
Thomas Hand, tailor.
Robert Morris, fishmonger.
Richard Bavand, tanner.
John Lewis, blacksmith.

Gilbert Reynolds, shoemaker.
Owen Marsh, ironmonger.
Raphe Bunnell, blacksmith.
Thomas Ledsham, tailor.
Isaac Clarke, tanner.
Richard Cope, silkweaver.
Henry Yong, beer-brewer.
John Yong, beer-brewer.
William Strett, tailor.
Robert Radford, linen-draper.
John Critchley, haberdasher.
Henry Darwell, glover.
Robert Cotgreave, clothworker.
William Darwell, glover.

1660-1 [12-13 C. ii.] ARTHUR WALLEY, Mayor.

Oct. 19   Henry Pickmore p. of Edward Higgenson, butcher.
„ 26   Thomas Fletcher, shoemaker, s. of John Fletcher of Chester, shoemaker.
„ 26   Luke Gillam, shoemaker, s. of Luke Gillam of Chester, shoemaker.
„ 26   William Wade p. of George Harvey of Chester, bricklayer.
„ 26   Daniel Leenes p. of William Younge, baker.
Nov. 7   William Wylme p. of William Grice, innholder.
—   Peter Taylor p. of —— ——, baker.
„ 20   Edward s. of ——t Knott of Chester, feltmaker, and p. of Thomas Bradley of Chester, feltmaker.
Dec. 17   Miles Pemberton p. of Thomas Willoughby, beer-brewer.
Jan. 22   Henry s. of Nicholas Williams of Conway, co. Carnarvon, tanner, and p. of John Skelhorne and Thomas Rowlandson, ironmongers.
Feb. 9   Robert s. of Robert Denteth of Orvenley, co. Ches., yeoman, and p. of John Johnson of Chester, merchant.
„ 20   Joseph Bennett, baker, s. of William Bennett of Elton, co. Ches., yeoman, and p. of Thomas Low of Chester, baker.
—   Peter Jones, brewer, s. of Griffith Williams [sic] of Qu——, and p. of Randle Oulton of Chester.
„ 25   William Owen, tailor, s. of John Owen of Chester, tailor.
„ 25   George Morris, innholder, s. of George Morris of Chester, innholder.

Feb.	25	George s. of William Saladine of Aston, co. Flint, yeoman, and p. of Thomas Heath the elder, of Chester, shoemaker.
,,	25	Samuel s. of Thomas Leenes of Woodchurch in Worral, co. Ches., yeoman, and p. of Thomas Bolland of Chester, joiner.
—		William s. of —— Starkey of Moore, and p. of Thomas Ash——, beer-brewer.
Apr.	1	Sir Thomas Smith, baronet, s. of Sir Thomas Smith of Chester, knight.
,,	5	Peter Stringer, linen-draper, s. of Peter Stringer of Chester, malster.
,,	13	John Worrall, feltmaker, s. of John Worrall, feltmaker.
,,	28	John Beforne, husbandman, s. of John Beforne of Handbridge, near Chester, husbandman, and p. of Robert Ashton of Chester, blacksmith.
May	1	Peter Wood, yeoman, s. of Thomas Wood of Little Peover, co. Ches., yeoman, and p. of Edward Wilding, feltmaker.
—		Thomas Moores, yeoman.
,,	6	William Jones, baker, s. of Hugh [Jones], and p. of Richard Hiccocke of Chester.
,,	6	Hugh Maddock, tanner, s. of Hugh Maddock of Chester, tanner.
,,	6	Thomas s. of Anne Ellis of Tarvin, widow, and p. of Hugh Maddock of Chester, tanner.
,,	7	William Williamson, linen-draper, s. of Thomas Williamson of Chester, linen-draper and milliner, defunct, and p. of William Williams, linen-draper and milliner.
,,	9	Morgan s. of John Evans of "The nuth len," chapman, and p. of Richard Mercer, clothworker.
,,	18	Thomas Taylor, draper, s. of Richard Taylor, draper.
,,	18	Henry Jannion, shoemaker.
June	5	John Harrison the younger, tailor, s. of John Harrison of Chester, tailor.
,,	14	Ellis s. of Robert Reice of Boughton, and p. of Roger Lyneall of Chester, feltmaker.
,,	26	William Woods, mason, s. of John Woods, mason.
,,	28	Thomas s. of William Carrington of Elton, co. Ches., yeoman, and p. of John Owen, tailor.
,,	29	John Goughe, blacksmith, s. of John Goughe, blacksmith.
July	10	John Hull, joiner, s. of Thomas Hull of Chester, joiner.

1661-2] THE CITY OF CHESTER 145

		Thomas Croxton, upholsterer.
Sep.	23	Edmund Mathewes p. of John Ridley, bricklayer.
Oct.	2	William s. of William Girdler of Birmingham, co. Warwick, long cutler, and p. of Urian Ryder of Chester, cutler.
,,	9	Benjamin Deane, shoemaker, s. of Thomas Deane of Chester, shoemaker.
,,	9	Henry s. of William Crompton of Hillcott, co. Staffs., gentleman, and p. of William Crompton of Chester, merchant.
,,	9	John s. of John Pemberton of Cauldy, yeoman, defunct, and p. of William Heywod, shoemaker.
,,	9	William s. of William Ashton of Chaulton, co. Ches., yeoman, and p. of Edward Morgell, shoemaker.
		Thomas Jackson, glover.

1661-2 [13-14 C. ii.] THOMAS THROPPE, Esquire, Mayor.

Oct.	14	Thomas Jackson, brother of John Jackson, and p. of Randle Venables of Chester, glover.
,,	22	John Buck, ironmonger, s. of Samuel Buck of Chester, ironmonger.
,,	22	Robert Johnson, shoemaker, s. of John Johnson of Chester, shoemaker.
,,	29	Richard Ormes, baker, s. of Richard Ormes of Chester, baker.
,,	30	John s. of Robert Rogers of Calcott, co. Ches., husbandman, and p. of Thomas Morris the younger, blacksmith.
Nov.	19	John s. of Richard Carden of Chester, maltmaker, and p. of William Blundell, tailor.
Dec.	5	Robert s. of Robert Cotton of Willaston, co. Ches., blacksmith, and p. of Robert Hill, blacksmith.
,,	27	Ralph s. of John Dutton of Bidston, co. Ches., gentleman, and p. of Thomas Watt, clothworker.
Jan.	3	Owen s. of Owen Ellis, late of Chester, vintner, and p. of Arthur Walley, mercer.
,,	7	John Hough, ironmonger, s. of Anne Hough of Oxton, co. Ches., widow, and p. of Peter Leigh, alderman.
,,	21	Richard s. of Thomas Davies of Vale, co. Ches., husbandman, and p. of Hugh Shaw, carpenter.
,,	27	William s. of John Barkley of Chester, gentleman, defunct, and p. of John Hulton, shoemaker.
Feb.	1	Hugh Maddock, tanner, s. of Richard Maddock of Lea Newbold, co. Chester, gentleman, and p. of Richard Broster, alderman.

Feb.	5	William Browne, draper [gentleman, M.B.], p. of William Hulton, draper.
,,	5	Thomas Chapman p. of Gerrard Jones, goldsmith.
,,	5	Michael Lench, barber-chirurgeon, p. of John Taylor.
,,	5	Richard Ordes, tallow-chandler, p. of Edward Mercer.
,,	21	William King, butcher, s. of William King of Chester, butcher.
,,	21	Robert s. of Thomas Roberts and p. of William Higginet, butcher.
,,	21	John Lambskin p. of William Richardson, butcher.
Mar.	8	William Ince the younger, merchant, s. of William Ince, alderman.
,,	17	John Johnson p. of John Annion of Chester, slater.
,,	26	John s. of William Taylor of Rabie and p. of Randle Bingley, baker.
Apr.	24	Ralph Bellin, fishmonger, s. of Thomas Bellin of "Thorneton de Hough," co. Ches., yeoman, and p. of William Morris of Chester, cooper and fishmonger.
,,	25	Robert Mercer, merchant, s. of Robert Mercer of Edge Lane in West Derbie, co. Lanc., gentleman, and p. of John Johnson, alderman and merchant.
May	2	William Greatbach, ironmonger, s. of Daniel Greatbach, alderman.
,,	2	Thomas s. of Thomas Bavand, esquire, and p. of William Hewitt of Chester, ironmonger.
,,	3	George s. of Elizabeth Bedson of Neston, co. Ches., widow, and p. of Hugh Mouson the elder, tanner.
June	10	Thomas Mason, weaver, s. of Robert Mason of Shotwicke, co. Ches., husbandman, and p. of Peire Davies, weaver and linen-draper.
,,	16	John Parry of Chester, carpenter.
,,	16	Laurence s. of John Gwalter of Great Mortin, co. Lanc., husbandman, and p. of John Annion of Chester, joiner.
,,	16	Thomas s. of Henry Carter of Greeneaugh, co. Lanc., yeoman, and p. of John Johnson of Chester, joiner.
,,	16	Randle Bridge, innholder, s. of Randle Bridge of Chester, innholder, defunct.
,,	30	John s. of John Williams of Abbergelly, co. Denbigh, gentleman, and p. of Richard Brett of Chester, merchant.
,,	30	Thomas Cosson, barber-chirurgeon, s. of Richard Cosson of Chester, labourer, and p. of Richard Francis, barber-chirurgeon and wax-chandler.

July	28	William Minshull, shoemaker, s. of Ralph Minshull of Chester, shoemaker.
Sep.	2	John Fletcher, wetglover, s. of Peter Fletcher of Chester, wetglover.
,,	3	Luke s. of Hugh Jones of Kilkin, co. Flint, yeoman, and p. of John Poole of Chester, haberdasher.
,,	11	Thomas s. of Thomas Tottie of Childer Thornton, co. Ches., husbandman, and p. of Edward Dannold of Chester, baker.
,,	15	John s. of Richard Coason of Chester, labourer, and p. of Hugh Mowson of Chester, tanner.
,,	18	William s. of John Aldcroft of Knottesford, co. Ches., innholder, and p. of John Griffith, apothecary.
Oct.	1	Richard Leving, esquire.
,,	1	John Phillipps, gentleman.
,,	1	John Maughan, gentleman.
,,	1	Robert Meacock, upholsterer.
,,	6	John Urmeston, baker, s. of Richard Urmeston of Chester, baker.
,,	8	Robert Barnes, tailor, s. of Edward Barnes of Chester, tailor, defunct.

1662-3 [14-15 C. ii.] RICHARD BROSTER, Esquire, Mayor.

Thomas Minshull, ironmonger.
Richard Throppe, stationer.
Joshua Leene, beer-brewer.
Peter Woodworth, ironmonger.
John Roberts, ironmonger.
William Wilson, tanner.
Thomas Maddock, tanner.
Richard Jones, weaver.
Richard Burroughes, baker.
Richard Lurting, feltmaker.
Robert Fletcher, shoemaker.
Robert Leivesley, innholder.
William Partridge, blacksmith.
Roger Thomason, feltmaker.
James Palin, barber-chirurgeon.
Hugh Stringer, barber-chirurgeon.
William Bristow, tanner.
Richard Wright, ironmonger.
Richard Smith, tanner.
John Kirks, tanner.

Samuel Kelsall, dyer.
John Thomason, beer-brewer.
Simon Lea, tanner.
Daniel Hutchins, tanner.
William Baguley, turner.
Richard Coulson, tanner.
Robert Warmingham, goldsmith.
Ralph Burroughes, ironmonger.
John Booth, silkweaver.
Richard Potter, turner.
Roger Gorse, carpenter.
Robert Sproston, gentleman.
Robert Hatton, butcher.
Robert Sproston, feltmaker.
Richard Davies, feltmaker.
William Harrison, cooper.
Thomas Bannion, cooper and fishmonger.
Richard Thomason, currier.
Richard Savage, esquire.
Peter Bellard, brewer.
Obadiah Eaton, draper.
Samuel Revington, feltmaker.
Robert Hankey, feltmaker.
John Maddock, tanner.
Thomas Perrey, tanner.
Adam Bettie, tallow-chandler.
Thomas Adney, innholder.
Richard Deane, baker.

1663-4 [15-16 C. ii.] JOHN POOLE, Esquire, Mayor.

Oct. 27   Brian Bolland, joiner, s. of Richard Bolland of Chester, joiner.

„ 29   Thomas Dewsbury, feltmaker, s. of Richard Dewsbury of Chester, feltmaker.

Nov. 13   William Bennett, shoemaker, } ss. of Randle Bennett
„ 13   Randle Bennett the younger, } of Chester, alderman.

Dec. 29   John Hawkart, butcher, s. of Thomas Hawkart of Hope, co. Derby, and p. of Richard Price, butcher.

„ 29   Reginald Woods p. of Ralph Almond, blacksmith.

„ 29   John Deane p. of William King, butcher.

„ 30   John Yong, mercer, s. of Henry Yong of Chester, ironmonger.

„ 30   Thomas Buck, ironmonger, s. of Samuel Buck of Chester, ironmonger.

Dec. 30		William Thrallfell p. of Richard Townesend of Chester, ironmonger.
Jan. 16		Randle s. of Charles Tomblinson of Clive, co. Ches., yeoman, and p. of John Croughton of Chester, shoemaker.
Feb. 13		William Ireland, shoemaker, s. of John Ireland of Chester, shoemaker.
,,	13	Richard Evans p. of George Bunnell, beer-brewer.
Mar. 13		Robert Wayne, butcher, s. of Richard Wayne of Chester, butcher, defunct.
,,	17	George Nickson, husbandman, s. of John Nickson of Chester, feltmaker.
,,	26	Richard Preece [Price, M.B.], butcher, s. of Richard Price, butcher.
,,	29	Edward Edge p. of Urian Minshull, dyer.
Apr. 16		Samuel Hawshaw, plumber, s. of Thomas Hawshaw, plumber, defunct.
,,	16	John Lewis p. of Thomas Welshman, glover.
,,	16	Edward Gill, slater, s. of Richard Gill of Chester, slater, defunct.
,,	16	William Jackson p. of John Johnson, plasterer, defunct.
May 12		Bradford Throppe, shoemaker, s. of Richard Throppe, shoemaker.
,,	12	William Heald, baker, s. of William Heald, baker.
,,	12	John Rymmer, silkweaver, s. of William Rymmer, clothworker.
,,	26	Richard Bushell ⎫
,,	26	William Smith ⎬ pp. of John Caddick, feltmaker.
June 4		John s. of Robert Hughes of Hendre befay, co. Flint, yeoman, and p. of Hugh Harvey of Chester, glover.
,,	14	Thomas Baker, gentleman.
,,	22	John Ledsham, feltmaker, s. of Randle Ledsham, defunct.
July 15		Francis Snead, glover, s. of Richard Snead of Chester, glover, defunct.
,,	16	Robert Ince, gentleman, s. of Robert Ince of Chester, shoemaker, defunct.
,,	22	Robert s. of John Martine of Eastham, co. Ches., yeoman, and p. of Robert Chamberlaine of Chester, brewer.
,,	16	Peter Griffith, husbandman, p. of William Ince of Chester, alderman.
Aug. 13		William Alcock, tailor, s. of James Alcock of Chester, tailor.
,,	16	John s. of John Page of Whixa, co. Salop, husbandman, and p. of Thomas Dickenson of Chester, beer-brewer.

Sep. 10 Thomas Ireland, shoemaker, s. of John Ireland of Chester, shoemaker.
„ 10 George Harvie, linen-draper, s. of George Harvie of Chester, linen-draper.
„ 23 Thomas Morrice, bricklayer and linen-draper, s. of Richard Morris of Chester, butcher, defunct, and p. of Robert Harvie of Chester, bricklayer and linen-draper.
„ 23 George Wilson, gentleman.
„ 26 Richard Breeze, tanner, s. of Robert Breese of Pulton, co. Ches., yeoman, and p. of William Wilson of Chester, tanner.
Oct. 11 Henry Gardner, yeoman, s. of Thomas Gardner of Chester, ironmonger, defunct.
„ 11 Edward Lloyd p. of Richard Bridge of Chester, dyer.

1664-5 [16-17 C. ii.] RICHARD TAYLOR, Esquire, Mayor.

Silvan Witter, tailor.
Richard Bird, tanner.
Charles Moulson, tanner.
Thomas Throppe, vintner.
Richard Adams, draper.
Henry Hughes, gentleman.
Richard Machell, blacksmith.
William Browne, mercer.
Ralph Hockenhall, ironmonger.
Sir Richard Grosvenor, baronet.
John Higginbothom, mercer.
William Ouldham, gentleman.
Thomas Bulkeley, cooper.
Nathaniel Weld, shoemaker.
Ralph Hilton, gentleman.
Robert Fletcher, brewer.
Robert Oreton, tallow-chandler.
Charles Ravenscroft, apothecary.
John Meols, ironmonger.
William Welshman, baker.
John Kettle, joiner.
Richard Williamson, barber-chirurgeon.
George Turner, shoemaker.
Thomas Ball, wetglover.
Mathew Browne, bricklayer.
Randle Richardson, linen-draper.

Thomas Bealey, body-maker.
John Bannyon, feltmaker.
Hugh Starkey, barber-chirurgeon.
William Robinson, feltmaker.
William Jennyon, bricklayer.
William Hughes, bricklayer.
William Patton, draper.
Richard Jennings, mercer.
Richard Hiccocke the younger, baker.
Stephen Smith, esquire.
William Bird, merchant.
John Lloyd, mason.
John Hunt, barber-chirurgeon.
Abraham Heathley, slater.
John Taylor, draper.
John Taylor, shoemaker.
William Billington, ironmonger.

1665-6 [17-18 C. ii.] RANDLE OULTON, Esquire, Mayor.

Dec. 18 Richard Jackson, vintner, s. of Francis Jackson of Chester, tailor.
Jan. 13 John Jones p. of Ralph Ravenscroft of Chester, tailor.
„ 29 Samuel Jones, goldsmith, s. of Gerrard Jones of Chester, goldsmith, defunct.
„ 29 William s. of John Hibbert of Little Mancott, co. Flint, gentleman, and p. of Hamnet Kerks of Chester, shoemaker.
„ 31 Richard Massey p. of John Hulton of Chester, shoemaker, lately alderman of the city.
Feb. 13 Joseph Maddock p. of William Blundell of Chester, tailor.
„ 22 Thomas s. of Thomas Gibbons of Chester, feltmaker, and p. of William Potter of Chester, feltmaker.
Mar. 26 Samuel Robinson, draper, s. of Edward Robinson of Chester, weaver.
„ 26 Nathaniel Williamson, mercer, p. of William Bate and afterwards of John Leonard, mercer, defunct.
„ 26 John Sudlow p. of John Witter, apothecary.
„ 26 Phillip Williams p. of Thomas Dannatt, linen-draper.
„ 26 Richard Reece, linen-draper, p. of William Sneyd.
„ 26 Robert Gillam, corviser, s. of Luke Gillam of Chester, corviser.
„ 29 Owen Jones p. of Thomas Roberts of Chester, butcher.

152 THE ROLLS OF THE FREEMEN OF [1665-6

May 3 John Cally the younger, chapman, s. of John Cally the elder, chapman.
" 3 Henry Watt p. of Ralph Minshull of Chester, shoemaker, defunct.
" 19 Robert Evans p. of William Twiss of Chester, blacksmith.
June 13 Ottiwell Shawcrosse p. of John Harrison of Chester, tailor.
July 16 Charles s. of William Christian of the Isle of Man, esquire, and p. of Samuel Buck of Chester, ironmonger.
" 16 Thomas s. of Ellen Wrench of Leftwich, co. Ches., widow, and p. of Thomas Hassall of Chester, ironmonger.
" 16 John Rughe s. of Hugh Williams [sic] of Llanegrin, co. Merioneth, gentleman, defunct, and p. of Thomas Cowper of Chester, ironmonger.
Aug. 3 John Johnson, shoemaker, s. of William Johnson of Chester, draper, defunct.
" 14 John Harpur, glover, } ss. of John Harpur of Chester, Henry Harpur, glover, } glover.
" 25 Samuel Ratcliffe p. of Thomas Billington of Chester, ironmonger.
" 25 Samuel Gerrard p. of John Travers of Chester, ironmonger.
" 25 Samuel Johnson p. of Hugh Anderton of Chester, innholder.
" 25 Bartholomew Johnson, blacksmith, s. of Robert Johnson of Chester, blacksmith.
Sep. 3 John Knight p. of George Harvie of Chester, bricklayer.
" 4 Thomas Hutchins, tailor, s. of Thomas Hutchins of Chester, tailor, defunct.
" 6 William Ratcliffe, gentleman, s. of John Ratcliffe of Chester, esquire.
" 6 George Meredith p. of Randle Morgan of Chester, glover.
Oct. 6 John Grimsditch, tallow-chandler, s. of William Grimsditch of Chester, defunct.
" 6 Richard Sourton p. of Robert Ridge of Chester, vintner.
" 11 William Hine p. of Henry Winstanley of Chester, cooper.
" 15 ‡Hugh Stringer p. of Thomas Darwell, glover, defunct.

1666-7 [18-19 C. ii.] WILLIAM STREET, Esquire,
MAYOR.

Oct. 15 William Allen of Chester, merchant, s. of William Allen of Chester, beer-brewer, defunct [duplicate entry in M.B. for preceding year].
Dec. 14 William Tompson of Chester, clerk.
Jan. 12 William Jannion p. of Thomas Bolland of Chester, joiner.
„ 14 Thomas Street of Chester, beer-brewer.
„ 14 Samuel s. of Henry Yong of Chester, ironmonger, and p. of Thomas Hand of Chester, draper.
„ 14 William Dutton of Chester, glover.
Mar. 15 Richard King of Chester, tallow-chandler, s. of William King of Chester, butcher.
„ 15 Thomas Yong p. of Richard Key of Chester, beer-brewer.
„ 15 John Roberts p. of Richard Trafford of Chester, tallow-chandler.
„ 15 Hugh Wynn p. of Urian Mynshull of Chester, dyer.
„ 25 Randle s. of Randle Sherrington of Netherley, co. Ches., yeoman, and p. of Thomas Denson of Chester, shoemaker.
„ 28 John Cotgreave, maltster, s. of Reece Cotgreave of Chester, clothworker.
Apr. 4 Robert Murray p. of Thomas Parnell of Chester, ironmonger.
„ 4 William Nicholls, clothworker, s. of Thomas Nickolls of Chester, clothworker.
„ 8 Raphe s. of William Boulton of Liverland, co. Lanc., yeoman, and p. of Henry Boulton of Chester, feltmaker.
„ 10 Thomas Griffith, yeoman.
„ 10 John Roe of Tarvin, co. Ches., p. of Thomas Jones of Chester, currier.
May 24 William s. of William Davies of Chester, shoemaker, and p. of Robert Heath of Chester, shoemaker.
July 11 William Edwards p. of Thomas Cowper the younger, ironmonger.
„ 11 John Saint John p. of Thomas Parnell, ironmonger, defunct.
„ 18 Lewis Williams p. of Thomas Cowper of Chester, alderman, and Thomas Cowper the younger of Chester, ironmongers.
„ 18 Peter Williams p. of Henry Williams of Chester, ironmonger.

Aug. 7　Thomas s. of Thomas Adams of Chester, shoemaker, defunct, and p. of Robert Shurlock of Chester, shoemaker.
July 16　William Williams, esquire, *in lege eruditus*.
Sep. 17　George Malbon, barber-chirurgeon, s. of Henry Malbon of Wollerts Hall, co. Ches., gentleman, and p. of John Wright of Chester, barber-chirurgeon, wax-chandler, and painter.
„ 26　John Woodward, late of Crowton, co. Ches., yeoman.
Oct. 7　Thomas Harrison p. of Edward Williamson, linen-draper.
„ 7　Owen Shone, barber-chirurgeon, p. of Thomas Davenport, barber-chirurgeon, wax-chandler, and painter.
„ 10　John Palin p. of Robert Ridge of Chester, vintner.
„ 10　Samuel Smith p. of Hugh Roberts of Chester, cooper.
Jan. 4　William Dodd p. of William Page of Chester, blacksmith.

1667-8 [19-20 C. ii.] RICHARD HARRISON, Esquire, Mayor.

— 　John Bridge, scrivener.
Oct. 23　Thomas Bridge, feltmaker, — of Edward Bridge of Chester.
„ 26　Jonathan s. of John Cotgreave of Christleton, co. Ches., yeoman, and p. of Randle Oulton of Chester, beer-brewer.
„ 26　Richard Denson, feltmaker, s. of Robert Denson of Chester, beer-brewer, defunct.
„ 26　Robert s. of Richard Ashton, yeoman, defunct, and p. of John Owen of Chester, tailor.
„ 26　John s. of John Denson, late of Whitby, co. Ches., yeoman, and p. of Richard Denson of Chester, baker.
— —　Thomas Bostocke, apothecary, p. of Natha— —— ——
——ecary.
— 12　Isaac Warminsham, tailor, — —— —— Warminsham, late of Chester, ——.
Nov. 29　Moses Wirrall, clothworker, s. of John Wirrall, clothworker, ——, defunct.
Dec. 5　Richard s. of Thomas Adams, late of Chester, shoemaker, and p. of William Blundell of Chester, tailor.
„ 7　Francis Bennett, feltmaker, s. of Hamnet Bennett of Chester, wetglover.
„ 7　William Ball, wetglover, s. of William Ball, late of Chester, wetglover.

Benjamin Willcocke, beer-brewer.
Richard Bennett, innholder.
Hugh Arthur, clothworker.
William Brandrett, innholder.
William Forshall, shoemaker.
Richard Yates, slater.
Charles Jackson, blacksmith.
William Fovell, barber-chirurgeon.
William Gamull, gentleman.
Thomas Gamull, ironmonger.
Valentine Gamull, haberdasher.
William Hale, butcher.
John Hankie, tallow-chandler.
Samuel Higgenson, clerk.
Edward Moreton, glover.
John Fletcher, shoemaker.
John Johnson, glover.
William Richardson the younger, butcher.
William Crewe, ironmonger.
William Wilson, shoemaker.
Francis Wade, butcher.
John Salmon, haberdasher.
Peter Barker, gentleman.
George Bennett, saddler.
Thomas Lyneall, feltmaker.
John Calcott, turner.
William Grice, merchant.
Robert Parkes, clothier.
William Heyley, cooper.
Nicholas Locker, linen-draper.
Thomas Walley, feltmaker.
George Mainwaring, merchant.
Peter Bodvell, bookseller.
Thomas Clerke, gentleman.
David Edwards, carpenter.
Randle Aston, glover.
Robert Price, innholder.
Isaac Crosse, joiner.
John Handcock, saddler.
Griffith Tregorne, saddler.
Randle Walker, linen-draper.
Lewis Parry, ironmonger.
Samuel Fletcher, tanner.
Samuel Selby, baker.

1668-9 [20-21 C. ii.] CHARLES, Earl of Derby, Mayor.

Francis Fearnall, baker.
Nathaniel Drinkwater, barber.
Peter Downeham, mason.
William Mosse, butcher.
Christopher Harrison, innholder.
Miles Pemberton, glover.
Thomas Coe, shoemaker.
Timothy Smith, tailor.
Samuel Finlow, glover.
Francis Stringer, yeoman.
Raphe Bulkeley, tailor.
William Newport, tailor.
Jonas Haywarde, shoemaker.
John Smith, brewer.
Peter Starkie, brewer.
Richard Poole, haberdasher.
John Burrowes, draper.
Henry Leaconby, ironmonger.
Thomas Dannold, linen-draper.
John Shelley, ironmonger.
John Robinson, ironmonger.
John Adams, ironmonger.
William Bennett, ironmonger.
John Golborne, apothecary.
James Hutchinson, ironmonger.
Henry Rathborne, joiner, &c.
Randle Faulke, clothworker.
Thomas Haukshaw.
William Heys, blacksmith.
William Caddocke, feltmaker.
Henry Cowen, shoemaker.
Thomas Hankie.
Cadwallader Jones, ironmonger.
John Smalshaw, brewer.
Thomas Davies, brewer.
Thomas Partridge, silkweaver.
John Lounds, baker.
William Briscoe, blacksmith.
Thomas Bourne, gentleman.
William Wilbraham, tallow-chandler.
Nathaniel Bullen, goldsmith.
Samuel Heath, confectioner.

1669–70 [21–22 C. ii.] ROBERT MORREY, Esquire, Mayor.

Humphrey Ball, glover.
Joseph Billington, clockmaker.
Raphe Finchett, baker.
Edward Wainwright, cooper.
Richard Oulton, beer-brewer.
James Gualter, joiner.
Humfrey Lewis, tanner.
John Fox, butcher.
Richard Lewis, shoemaker.
John Ward, instrument maker.
Jonathan Colly, tanner.
Arthur Bolland, beer-brewer.
Thomas Bolland, beer-brewer.
James Pares, mercer.
William Rosingreave, brewer.
Richard Dyerson, tanner.
Thomas Trafforde, tanner.
John Prince, maltster.
John Bennett, yeoman.
James Lemm, distiller.
Joseph Pritchard, blacksmith.
John Bevan, butcher.
Randle Pickmeire, butcher.
Richard Briscoe, linen-draper.
John Ince, gentleman.
Jame[s] Cottingham, tailor.
Thomas Fisher, butcher.

1670–1 [22–23 C. ii.] THOMAS WILLCOCK, Esquire, Mayor.

Oct. 22 Thomas Whittle, shoemaker, s. of John Whittle, shoemaker.
„ 30 Michael Johnson, soap-boiler.
Nov. 4 Edward, s. of —— Litherland of Chester, tanner, and p. of Edward Kinsey of Chester, tailor.
„ 10 Randle Willcocke, picture drawer, s. of William Willcocke, late of Chester, gentleman.
„ 10 Henry Hall the younger, tanner, s. of Henry Hall the elder of Chester, innholder.
„ 10 Charles Gamull p. of John Bennett, mercer, defunct.

Dec. 3 Thomas Skellington, shoemaker, s. of William Skellington of Chester, shoemaker.
" 15 John Fearnall of Chester, button-maker.
" 19 John Potter p. of Richard Dycas, tailor.
" 21 Thomas Wade, gentleman.
" 21 George Hewett, gentleman.
" 21 Raphe Hulton, watchmaker.
Jan. 11 Edward Bennett of Chester, draper.
" 11 Randle Minshull, innholder, s. of Randle Minshull of Chester, innholder.
" 11 Samuel Maddock, baker.
" 11 Richard Holland p. of Richard Brett of Chester, vintner.
" 11 Sir John Arderne, knight.
" 11 John Barker p. of Edward Robinson of Chester, weaver.
" 25 Henry Bennett, merchant, s. of Henry Bennett, late of Chester, merchant.
" 25 Puleston Partington, watchmaker.
" 25 John Gwynn, button-maker.
" 28 Matthew Ellis, upholsterer.
Feb. 2 Raph Whittley, gentleman.
" 3 John Allenson, p. of John Twa——, ironmonger.
Mar. 15 Nathan Bradburne p. of John Lancaster, ironmonger.
" 15 Jonathan Price p. of Francis Jackson, tailor.
" 27 William Ball, wetglover, s. of Randle Ball of Chester, wetglover.
Apr. 4 Thomas Watt, clothworker, s. of Thomas Watt of Chester, clothworker, defunct.
" 21 Benjamin Bleas of Chester, apothecary.
May 9 John s. of William Throppe of Chester, wetglover, and p. of John Finlow of Chester, wetglover.
" 9 Joseph Moseley, feltmaker, s. of Joseph Moseley of Chester, feltmaker.
" 9 William Hampton p. of John Joynston of Chester, shoemaker.
—— 22 Robert Werden, esquire.
June 22 Alexander Rigbye, esquire.
July 18 Thomas s. of Egidius Reece and p. of William Reece of Chester, hornbreaker.
Aug. 1 Timothy Deane, ironmonger.
" 1 Robert Rea p. of John Hough of Chester, ironmonger.
" 1 George Dycas p. of Sara Dod, ironmonger.
July 3 William Mercer, tallow-chandler.
Sep. 1 Samuel Bannion, baker, s. of John Bannion, cooper, defunct.

| 1671–2] | THE CITY OF CHESTER | 159 |

Sep. 1 Thomas Gill p. of William Bradshaw, slater.
Oct. 12 Raphe Hulton, shoemaker.
„ 12 Gerard Jordan p. of Edward Wilson, glover.
„ 12 Christopher Dannott of Chester, baker.
„ 12 Daniel Browne p. of Hugh Han—— of Chester, glover.
„ 12 William Plumton p. of Nicholas Knowles, shoemaker.

1671–2 [23–24 C. ii.] WILLIAM WILSON, Esquire, Mayor.

Dec. 11 William s. of Ralph Hickson of Chester, labourer, and p. of Phillip Walker of Chester, tailor.
„ 16 Robert Burroughes, feltmaker, s. of Robert Burroughes of Chester, feltmaker.
„ 22 Raphe Wilson p. of Richard Meacocke of Chester, pewterer.
„ 26 Samuel Kirkes, upholsterer.
„ 26 William Stacye [Stacey, M.B.] p. of Matthew Appleton, butcher.
Jan. 12 Samuel Pike p. of William Aldcroft of Chester, tailor.
„ 18 John Harrison the younger, p. of William Blundell, tailor.
„ 18 John Shepherd p. of Richard Portor, turner.
„ 26 John Tompson p. of John Dawson, feltmaker.
„ 26 Phillip Tompson p. of Thomas Morris, bricklayer.
Feb. 12 Seth Hulton p. of Ralph Downeham of Chester, mason.
„ 16 Daniell Colson, plasterer, p. of Edward Gray of Chester, bricklayer.
Mar. 11 John Bulkeley, cooper, s. and p. of Thomas Bulkeley of Chester, cooper.
„ 26 William Martin, barber-chirurgeon, s. of John Martin of Chester, shoemaker.
„ 26 Owen Hughes, linen-draper, s. of Owen Hughes, late of Chester, alderman.
„ 26 William Plumley, vintner, s. of William Plumley of Chester, vintner, defunct.
„ 26 William Crane, barber-chirurgeon, s. of Richard Crane of Chester, currier.
„ 26 Joseph Gill p. of Samuel Leigh, ironmonger.
„ 26 Thomas Shaw p. of Charles Ravenscroft of Chester, apothecary.
Apr. 26 Robert Carter, gentleman.
May 2 Joseph Basnet p. of Henry Williams, ironmonger.
„ 2 Daniel Taylor p. of Robert Townesend, ironmonger.

June 11 George Wright, yeoman.
„ 11 Thomas Bibby, labourer.
„ 27 John Lewis, bricklayer.
July 2 William Gowen, tailor, s. of William Gowen of Chester, tailor, defunct.
„ 19 Thomas Halliwell p. of William Alcocke of Chester, tailor.
Aug. 1 Roger Cumberbach, barber-chirurgeon, p. of Robert Morrey, alderman.
„ 17 Thomas s. of Richard Yates of Chester, feltmaker, and p. of William Hughes of Chester, bricklayer.
„ 17 Peter Platt, bricklayer, p. of John Ridley the younger, of Chester, bricklayer and linen-draper.
„ 17 Joseph Hincks, silkweaver, s. of Edward Hincks of Chester, innholder.
„ 17 Richard Rutter p. of Ralph Dutton, clothworker.
Oct. 8 Francis Shepherd p. of Thomas Ashton, innholder.
„ 9 Adam Kemp the younger, baker, s. of Thomas Kemp, baker, defunct.
„ 9 Randle Hanley p. of William Thomason, baker, defunct.
„ 9 Richard Taylor, glazier, s. of Richard Taylor, glazier.
„ 9 Edward Burroughes, barber-chirurgeon, s. of Edward Burroughes, innholder, defunct.
„ 9 Joseph Maddock, tanner, s. of John Maddock, alderman.
„ 9 Thomas Bolland the younger, joiner, s. of Thomas Bolland, joiner.
Mar. 10 ‡Christopher Back p. of John Jones of Chester, tailor.

1672-3 [24-25 C. ii.] GAWEN HUDSON, Esquire, Mayor.

Oct. 11 Charles Jones.
„ 24 John Hancock, tailor, s. of Thomas Hancock of Chester, tanner.
Nov. 12 Robert Williamson, linen-draper.
„ 12 Thomas Finchett p. of John Caddock, feltmaker.
„ 29 John Poole, yeoman.
Dec. 21 Thomas Throppe, painter, s. of Bernard Throppe of Chester, feltmaker.
„ 24 William Johnson, blacksmith, s. of John Johnson of Chester, blacksmith.
„ 24 Joseph Adams p. of Richard Stockton of Chester, blacksmith.
Jan. 13 John Sproston, feltmaker, s. of John Sproston of Chester, feltmaker, defunct.

Jan.	11	James Bradshaw, esquire, s. of Edward Bradshaw of Chester, esquire, defunct.
,,	22	Richard Ratcliffe, gentleman, s. of John Ratcliffe of Chester, esquire, defunct.
,,	22	Daniel Standish p. of Thomas Hanke of Chester, feltmaker, defunct.
,,	22	Thomas Walton, baker, s. of Edward Walton.
,,	31	Thomas Dodd, gentleman.
Feb.	5	Nathaniel Batho p. of Thomas Morrice, bricklayer.
,,	5	William Jackson p. of Anthony Hutchins, tanner.
,,	5	Charles Darwell, glover.
,,	6	John Bingley, tallow-chandler, s. of Randle Bingley, baker.
,,	6	Matthew Anderton the younger, innholder, s. of Matthew Anderton of Chester, innholder.
,,	6	Isaac Warmincham, saddler, s. of Thomas Warmincham, saddler.
,,	6	Peter Joynson, shoemaker, s. of John Joynson, shoemaker.
,,	6	Edward Welshman, baker, s. of William Welshman, baker.
,,	6	Benjamin Hall, tallow-chandler, s. of Henry Hall, innholder.
,,	6	John Johnson, tallow-chandler, s. of John Johnson, joiner.
,,	6	Thomas Barton p. of Nicholas Cowper of Chester, silkweaver.
,,	6	Edward Bridge, bricklayer, s. of William Bridge, brewer, defunct.
,,	8	George Browne p. of John Meoles, ironmonger.
,,	8	Robert Sands p. of Peter Leighe of Chester, glover.
,,	8	William Fletcher, glover, s. of Richard Fletcher, wetglover, defunct.
,,	8	William Wicherley p. of Edward Aston, glover.
,,	8	Richard s. of William Betteley of Chester, barber, defunct.
,,	10	Francis Crancke, cardmaker, s. of Edward Crancke, cardmaker.
,,	8	Robert Bennett, shoemaker, s. of Randle Bennett, alderman.
,,	10	Robert Goughe, slater, s. of John Goughe, blacksmith.
,,	8	Theodore Hughes, shoemaker.
,,	10	Edward Tompson, pipemaker.
,,	10	Peter Niccholl, mason.
,,	10	Henry Seale, butcher, s. of W. Seale, butcher.

Feb.	10	John Fletcher, pipemaker, s. of John Fletcher, feltmaker.
,,	10	Thomas Cowdocke p. of William Robinson, slater.
,,	10	Alban Gray, bricklayer, s. of Edward Gray, bricklayer.
,,	10	John Davies p. of John Hughes, slater.
,,	10	Abel Andrew, carpenter, s. of Asa Andrew, carpenter.
,,	10	Ralph Foster p. of Edward Bridge, innholder.
,,	10	Daniel Woods, plasterer, } ss. of John Woods of
,,	10	John Woods, plasterer, } Chester, feltmaker.
,,	ult.	Thomas Wyatt, glasier, s. of John Wyatt of Chester, glasier, defunct.
,,	10	George Hunt p. of John Fox, tailor.
Mar.	24	Raphe Davies p. of Thomas Knowles of Chester, baker.
Apr.	4	James Baguley, turner, s. of William Baguley, turner, defunct.
,,	7	Richard Stubbs p. of William Wilson, tanner.
Mar.	24	Edward Partington, mercer, p. of Thomas Wilcocke, alderman.
May	3	William Hewett p. of William Hewett, ironmonger.
,,	31	John Walley p. of Thomas Billington, ironmonger.
June	12	John Parsonage, feltmaker, s. of William Parsonage, feltmaker.
,,	17	Peter Bostock, mason.
,,	27	Thomas Thornley, wetglover, p. of Thomas Jackson, glover.
July	11	Richard Tyddar [or Tedder], yeoman.
,,	11	William Johnson p. of Thomas Hulse, shoemaker.
,,	29	Hughe Conway p. of John Booth, silkweaver.
Sep.	2	John Griffith, glover, s. of Richard Griffith of Chester, glover, defunct.
,,	22	William Barnes p. of John Williams, plasterer.
,,	26	Thomas Kettle, dyer, s. of Edward Kettle, dyer, defunct.
,,	27	David Evans p. of William Ince, alderman.
,,	30	Joseph Twemlow p. of Randle Richardson of Chester, linen-draper, defunct.
Oct.	6	Lawrence Roberts, wine-cooper, s. of Thomas Roberts of Chester, butcher, defunct.
,,	6	Thomas s. of Hugh Moulson of Chester, alderman, defunct, and p. of Thomas Davenport of Chester, barber-chirurgeon.
,,	6	James Johnson, brewer, p. of Edward Oulton of Chester, beer-brewer.
,,	6	Charles Banner, beer-brewer, p. of Randle Oulton of Chester, alderman.

1673-5]   THE CITY OF CHESTER   163

Oct. 6 Richard Parsons p. of Robert Denteth of Chester, merchant.
„ 9 Peter Yong, brewer, s. of Thomas Yong of Chester, beer-brewer.

1673-4 [25-26 C. ii.] THOMAS SIMPSON, Esquire, Mayor.

    Jonathan Pemberton, silkweaver.
    Christopher Brownett, tailor.
    William Witter, ironmonger.
    Peter Bennett, ironmonger.
    Thomas Haddock, dyer.
    George Hinckley, vintner.
    John Penketh, innholder.
    Robert Higginson, innholder.
    Richard Grundy, blacksmith.
    Charles Leche, mercer.
    John Kelsall, ironmonger.
    Thomas Jannion, currier.
    Daniel Crosse, joiner.
    Phillip Brock the younger, brazier.
    Daniel Batho, tanner.
    Thomas Browne, bricklayer.
    William Ellcock, ironmonger.
    William Bradshaw, cutler.
    Henry Lewis, ironmonger.
    Samuel Pownall, blacksmith.
    John Bristow, tanner.
    Joseph Yong, brewer.
    Edward Eaton, cooper.
    Richard Steele, butcher.
    Roger Ewde, clothworker.
    John Delamaine, gentleman.
    Samuel Leadbeater, ironmonger.
    Abraham Swift, merchant.
    Thomas Sadler, ironmonger.
    Andrew Browne, barber-chirurgeon.
    Samuel Welshman, tallow-chandler.
    David Mason, shoemaker.

1674-5 [26-27 C. ii.] RICHARD WRIGHT, Esquire, Mayor.

    Nathaniel King, ironmonger.
    Raphe Poole, draper.
    Richard Bavand, gentleman.

Charles Bavand, gentleman.
John Williams, cooper.
Isaac Croughton, tailor.
John Owfe the younger, baker.
Job Twemlow, blacksmith.
Ambrose Edwards, draper.
Thomas Adams, yeoman.
Thomas Shocklache, tailor.
Thomas Ryder, yeoman.
William Ryder, tailor.
Richard Rhodes, shoemaker.
John Hale, brewer.
Henry Roughley, ironmonger.
Griffith Knowles, shoemaker.
William Warmingham, shoemaker.
Edward Dodd, shoemaker.
Thomas Winington, plasterer.
Francis Gamul, linen-draper.
Edward Walmsley, slater.
Thomas Wakefield, plasterer.
James Leighe, apothecary.
Thomas Cudworth, innholder.
Peter Leicester, gentleman.
Samuel Sudlow, dyer.
Samuel Aspenwall, ironmonger.
Richard Whickstead, wetglover.
William Turner the younger, feltmaker.
Samuel Turner, feltmaker.
Robert Williams, glover.
Richard Wright, gentleman.
Richard Minshull, gentleman.
Richard Streete, gentleman.
Joseph Witter, gentleman.
Jonathan Whitby, barber-chirurgeon.
Edward Burroughes, feltmaker.
Joseph Taylor, feltmaker.
William Moreton, glover.
John Cotgreave, brewer.
Foulke Patton, tanner.
William Croughton, shoemaker.
John Croughton, shoemaker.
William Higginson, butcher.
Samuel Lawton, dyer.
Benjamin Jones, merchant.
Robert Taylor, weaver.
Francis Barton, wood-comber.

Samuel Bulkeley.
John Sutton, shoemaker.
Thomas Sefton, mariner.
Peter Lloyd, feltmaker.
John Kerison, feltmaker.
William Newton, tailor.

1675-6 [27-28 C. ii.] HENRY LLOYD, Esquire, Mayor.

Henry Yong, ironmonger.
Hughe Knowles, ironmonger.
Thomas Holland, barber.
Peter Venables, glover.
John Willme, innholder.
George Halliwell, tailor.
Thomas Pemberton, tailor.
George Finlow, skinner.
Samuel Weston, brewer.
Samuel Walley, wetglover.
Richard Brereton, ironmonger.
John Minshull, stationer.
Thomas Dannold, baker.
John Salmon the younger, silkweaver.
John Finchett, brewer.
Ellis Lloyd, ironmonger.
John Mostyn, joiner.
Randle Vause, linen-draper.
Thomas Bavand, turner.
Samuel Dycus, brewer.
Robert Sparke, linen-draper.
Richard Clues, clothworker.
Thomas Yong, brewer.
William Hewett, gentleman.
Robert Drew, clockmaker.
John Tilston, blacksmith.
William Crosse, cooper.
Richard Fisher, fishmonger.
Richard Bulkeley, cooper.

1676-7 [28-29 C. ii.] JOHN YONGE and JOHN MADDOCKE, Esquires, Mayors.

John Palin p. of Samuel Walker of Chester, shoemaker.
William King, baker, s. of John King of Chester, baker.

John Holland p. of Robert Mosse, draper.
Thomas s. of Richard Golborne of Chester, gentleman, and p. of Thomas Pickering of Chester, mercer.
Henry Yates p. of Richard Yates of Chester, slater.
Charles Broster, gentleman, s. of Charles Broster of Chester, gentleman, defunct.
Robert Harvey of London, haberdasher, s. of Richard Harvey of Chester, gentleman, defunct.
John Thorneley, blacksmith, s. of Hugh Thorneley of Chester, smith, defunct, and p. of Richard Formeby of Chester, smith.
Roger Lewis p. of Robert Moulson of Chester, tanner.
Nathaniel Batho, tanner, s. of William Batho of Chester, tanner.
Randle Oulton of Chester, mercer, s. of Randle Oulton of Chester, alderman.
Richard Harrison, gentleman, s. of Richard Harrison of Chester, alderman.
Thomas Saunderson p. of Lawrence Gualter of Chester, joiner.
William Litherland p. of Henry Johnson of Chester, joiner.
John Hulse, tailor, s. of Huen Hulse of Chester, cook, defunct.
Thomas Urmeston, pipemaker, s. of Richard Urmeston of Chester, labourer.
Thomas Walmesley p. of Nathan Jolly, ironmonger.
John Adshead p. of Nathaniel Weld of Chester, shoemaker.
John Hankey p. of William Gregory, defunct, and afterwards of Edward Croughton, shoemaker.
John Saunders p. of Nathaniel Basnett of Chester, apothecary.
Randle s. of William Dicas, yeoman, and p. of Thomas Dannold, linen-draper.
Hugh Hine, tallow-chandler, s. of William Hine, tallow-chandler, defunct.
Richard Wilbraham p. of Ralph Edge of Chester, tallow-chandler.
Sir Thomas Grosvenor, baronet.
John Kinnaston, mercer, p. of Owen Ellis, alderman.
Peter Pemberton p. of Nathaniel Bunnell, goldsmith.
Edward Roby p. of James Knowsley of Chester, linen-draper.
David Williams p. of Thomas Ashton of Chester, brewer, defunct.

1677–8] THE CITY OF CHESTER 167

    Ephraim Bennett, brewer, s. of Robert Bennett of Chester, brewer, defunct.
    Raphe Edge p. of Thomas Hassall, ironmonger.
    William Moore, cooper, s. of William —— of Chester, cooper.
    Thomas Rogers p. of John Lloyd, mason.
    John Annyon, joiner.
    John Poole, haberdasher, s. of John Poole of Chester, alderman, defunct.
    Joseph Wright, tanner. [M.B. reads Jonathan Dawson p. of Joseph Wright, tanner.]
    Charles Williams, tanner, s. of John Williams, tanner.
    Richard Niccholls, clothworker, s. of Peter Niccholls, clothworker.
    William Venables p. of Thomas N——, clothworker.
    Samuel Bingley, baker, s. of Randle Bingley, baker.
    Richard s. of Richard Shone of Chester, glover, defunct, and p. of Robert Shone of Chester, tallow-chandler.

1677–8 [29–30 C. ii.] WILLIAM INCE, Esquire, Mayor.

Nov. 6 Joseph Whittle, clerk, s. of John Whittle of Chester, ironmonger, defunct.
„ 6 William Harrison p. of Richard Dobbs, shoemaker.
Dec. 3 Thomas s. of Randle Jones of Scondur, co. Flint, gentleman, defunct, and p. of Hugh Moulson of Chester, tanner, defunct.
„ 4 Elias Lewis, merchant draper, s. of Ellis Lewis of Chester, silkweaver, and p. of John Moyle of Chester, merchant draper and hosier.
„ 14 Thomas s. of Richard Bennett, feltmaker, and p. of Richard Yates of Chester, carpenter.
„ 14 Joseph Roylands p. of Robert Booth, silkweaver.
„ 19 Thomas s. of William Turner, feltmaker, and p. of Randle Bingley, baker.
„ 29 Raphe Wright p. of Francis Skellerne of Chester, ironmonger.
Jan. 16 David Jones p. of Lewis Williams of Chester, ironmonger.
„ 19 Thomas Yong, brewer, s. of Thomas Yong, brewer.
„ 19 Nathaniel s. of Robert Kirks of Dunham on the Hill, co. Ches., yeoman, and p. of William Jennyons of Chester, joiner.
„ 31 Michael Croughton, joiner, s. of William Croughton, shoemaker, defunct.

Jan.	31	Charles Croughton, silkweaver, s. of John Croughton, shoemaker, defunct.
,,	31	John Millington p. of Thomas Jones, currier.
Feb.	5	Jonathan Ridge, gentleman, s. of Jonathan Ridge, late of Chester, draper.
,,	5	John King p. of John Crumpe of Chester, baker.
,,	11	George Fearnall p. of Nicholas Cooper, silkweaver.
,,	25	John Worrall, clothworker, s. of Samuel Worrall, clothworker, defunct.
,,	28	John Whitby, apothecary, s. of Jonathan Whitby, apothecary, defunct.
,,	28	John Sudlow p. of John Golborne, apothecary.
,,	28	Thomas Moores p. of Thomas Coe, shoemaker.
Mar.	22	John Ensdale p. of George Malbon, barber-chirurgeon, defunct.
Apr.	13	Roger Jackson, yeoman.
,,	20	George Atkinson, bookseller.
,,	22	Hugh Croxton ⎫
,,	22	Joseph Fisher ⎬ pp. of John Skellerne, ironmonger.
,,	22	Thomas Price, butcher, s. of Richard Price the elder, butcher.
May	3	Thomas Fletcher p. of Francis Skellerne of Chester, ironmonger.
,,	13	Samuel Deane s. of Samuel Deane, shoemaker, defunct.
June	8	Francis Jackson the younger, tailor, s. of Francis Jackson, tailor.
,,	12	Michael Bromley, tallow-chandler, s. of Michael Bromley of Chester, tallow-chandler.
July	8	Edward s. of William Bromley, maltster, and p. of John Crump, baker, lately defunct.
,,	17	Robert Key p. of Richard Higginson of Chester, brewer.
,,	20	William Wright, merchant, ⎫ ss. of William Wright of
,,	20	Peter Wright, merchant, ⎬ Chester, merchant.
,,	20	John Shard p. of John Witter of Chester, apothecary.
Aug.	9	William Billinge p. of Thomas Wally of Chester, feltmaker.
,,	19	Robert Cowdocke, blacksmith.
Sep.	2	William Rathbone p. of Henry Pemberton, baker.
,,	16	George Oulton, goldsmith, s. of Randle Oulton of Chester, alderman.
,,	16	Richard Holding p. of John Knight of Chester, bricklayer.
Oct.	4	William Sproston, feltmaker, s. of John Sproston, feltmaker, defunct.
,,	4	Reignold Woods, blacksmith. [William Hughes p. of Reignold Woods, blacksmith, M.B.]

| 1678-9] | THE CITY OF CHESTER | 169 |

Oct. 7 Samuel Dannatt, baker, s. of Edward Dannatt of Chester, baker, and p. of John Fletcher of Chester, barber, defunct.
„ 10 Joseph Denson p. of John Denson, baker.
„ 10 Thomas Taylor, barber, } ss. of Joshua Taylor,
„ 10 Joshua Taylor, shoemaker. } barber.

1678-9 [30-31 C. ii.] WILLIAM HARVEY, Esquire, Mayor.

Thomas Cotton, shoemaker.
George Barlow, turner.
Thomas Knowles, tanner.
Thomas Meoles, ironmonger.
William Wright, ironmonger.
John Thomas, saddler.
Sir Peter Pindar, baronet.
Thomas Jones, ironmonger.
John Partridge, linen-draper.
David Partridge, silkweaver.
Samuel Eaton, brewer.
Laurence Fletcher, feltmaker.
John Higginson, tailor.
Richard Taylor, feltmaker.
George Taylor, feltmaker.
Randle Sargeant, draper.
Thomas Ley, shoemaker.
George Brock, pewterer.
Isaac Willoughby, brewer.
John Hatton, skinner.
William Poynton, ironmonger.
Thomas Booth, shoemaker.
Richard Leighe, husbandman.
George Quick, blacksmith.
John Stringer, gentleman.
Charles Bennett, gentleman.
William Throppe, shoemaker.
George Shurlock.
Benjamin Hull, joiner.
William Gualter, joiner.
Edward Bennett, shoemaker.
Paul Maddock, shoemaker.
Thomas Taylor, shoemaker.
Thomas Jones, carpenter.
John Davies, clothworker.

Peter Kelley, shoemaker.
Joseph Owfe, baker.
Henry Salusbury, barber-chirurgeon.
Joseph Crowfoot.
John Larden, feltmaker.
William Layton, shoemaker.
William Selby, butcher.
John Johnson, joiner.
John Whitehead, silkweaver.
Richard Whitehead, silkweaver.
Thomas Whitehead, maltster.
Edward Brereton, saddler.
Samuel Dobb, tailor.
Moses Dannatt, beer-brewer.
John Jordan, bricklayer.
Randle Leicester, button-maker.
James Allcocke, tailor.
Thomas Fletcher, tanner.
Thomas Gile, baker.
Simon Harrison, shoemaker.
John Hands, shoemaker.
Thomas Plumley, carpenter.
John Williamson, ironmonger.
John Bennett, shoemaker.
Thomas Jones, pipemaker.
Thomas Hulton, shoemaker.
Joseph Leadbeater, carpenter.
John Fletcher, carpenter.
George Reece, feltmaker.
John Dewsbury, feltmaker.
Randle Moseley, labourer.
Mathew Moseley, labourer.
Phillip Bore.
Robert Wright, tanner.
William Throppe, glover.
Thomas Wright, tanner.
William Reece the younger, hornbreaker.
William Yong, bricklayer.
John Powell, tailor.
Samuel Hiccock, clockmaker.
Robert Ellis, glover.
Samuel Burrowes, feltmaker.
Stephen Page, feltmaker.
Richard Johnson, feltmaker.
Thomas Dutton, glover.
James Williams, blacksmith.

John Crank, cardmaker.
Charles Broster, tanner.
Joseph Meacock, pewterer.
Thomas Fearnall, butcher.
Thomas Malbon, blacksmith.
Richard Shoar, butcher.
Benjamin Ashton, beer-brewer.
John Hay, yeoman.
William Bennett, yeoman.
James Goulding, bricklayer.
Robert Rowlands, bricklayer.
Jonathan Kirks, silkweaver.
——nett Kirks, drawer and upholsterer.
—— —venscroft, tailor.
—— ——treet, glover.
—— ——er, butcher.
—— ——, blacksmith.

[NOTE.—The above blank spaces are caused by the termination of this roll being torn, and a portion of it missing. It is possible a few additional entries may have been on the roll when entire.]

Thomas Platt, bricklayer.
Samuel Leighe, feltmaker.
Raphe Blagge, innholder.
Raphe Leicester, gentleman.
John Percivall, yeoman.
Charles Boswell, pavier.
Henry Harpur, apothecary.
Evan Jones, haberdasher.
George Booth, esquire.
Thomas Gray, turner.
William Maddock, feltmaker.
Jonathan Couldson, feltmaker.
William Mather, saddler.
Hughe Dodd, glover.
Benjamin Cotgreave, tallow-chandler.
John Hine, haberdasher.
William Bulkeley, tanner.
John Moulson, tanner.
Thomas Hesketh, esquire.
Josiah Whittle, vintner.
Randle Tunnea, brewer.
Henry Bafron, weaver.
John Whitehead, yeoman.
Thomas Wattmouth, barber-chirurgeon.
James Mort, mason.

John ap Ellis the younger.
John Chritchley, upholsterer.
Thomas Bradshaw, cutler.

1679–80 [31–32 C. ii.] WILLIAM WILLME, Esquire, Mayor.

Oct. 27   Nathan Eddowes p. of Ralph Bunnell, bricklayer.
„   29   William Cokaine [Cookayne, M.B.] p. of Thomas Hassall, ironmonger.
„   29   Joseph Clarke p. of John Buck, watchmaker.
Dec. 5   William Croxton p. of Hugh Starkey, barber-chirurgeon.
„   5   Richard Eaton p. of George Vause, barber-chirurgeon.
Jan. 13   Stephen Garland p. of John Hunt, barber-chirurgeon.
Feb. 9   Thomas Arthur p. of Lewis Williams, ironmonger.
Mar. 27   William Adgett p. of George Palyn, shoemaker.
Apr. 13   Thomas Shurlock p. of Jonathan Price, tailor.
„   13   Samuel Brandrett [Brandred, M.B.] p. of John Fox, tailor.
„   21   Robert Robinson p. of Samuel Fletcher, tanner.
„   24   John Manwaring, esquire, s. of Sir Thomas Maunwaring of Peover, co. Ches., baronet.
„   24   Thomas Whitley, esquire, s. of Roger Whitley of Peele, co. Ches., esquire.
May 4   Benjamin Ratcliffe, ironmonger, s. of John Ratcliffe, esquire.
„   4   John Bannion p. of Peter Starkey, brewer.
„   4   John Kirkes p. of Richard Adams, tailor.
„   4   Henry Harpur p. of Richard Bridge, dyer.
July 22   Peter Edwards the younger, goldsmith, s. of Peter Edwardes of Chester, alderman.
„   22   Mathew Wright of Chester, ironmonger, s. of Thomas Wright of Chester, ironmonger.
„   22   Samuel Radford the younger, linen-draper, s. of Samuel Wright [sic], linen-draper.
„   22   Thomas Fernihaugh, draper, s. of Thomas Fernihaugh, draper.
„   21   Robert Farrington p. of William Plumbley, vintner and merchant.
„   27   John Poynton p. of Edward Oulton of Chester, beer-brewer.
Aug. 2   Thomas Macklin p. of William Eyton, mariner.
„   14   Richard Leving, esquire, s. of Richard Levinge, esquire, lately Recorder of Chester, defunct.

Sep. 8 John Richardson p. of John Hulton of Chester, shoemaker.
„ 25 Peter Whitley, esquire.
Oct. 14 Nathaniel Eaton, brewer [tailor, M.B.], s. of Nathaniel Eaton, brewer.

1680–1 [32–33 C. ii.] JOHN ANDERTON, Esquire, Mayor.

John Barlow, apothecary.
Francis Corbishall, ironmonger.
Thomas Chamberlaine, weaver.
Josiah Parkes, clothier.
Samuel Parkes, clothier.
Thomas Howell, goldsmith.
Nicholas Williams, tailor.
John Johnson, shoemaker.
Charles Griffith, innholder.
Edward Davies, clothworker.
Humphrey Walley, mercer.
William Proby, goldsmith.
Thomas Critchley, draper.
Robert Millington, joiner, carver, and turner.
Josiah Dawson, barber-chirurgeon.
John Basnett, apothecary.
Robert Anderson, apothecary.
Samuel Cooke, ironmonger.
Richard Plumley, linen-draper.
William Fletcher, mason.
Thomas Brownett, cooper.
Daniel Dycas, tailor.
John Darlington, shoemaker.
Raph Morgell, merchant draper.
Edward Williamson, innholder.
John Roberts, ironmonger.
Daniel Leenes, turner.
Mathew Twemlow, tallow-chandler.
Joseph Pemberton, blacksmith.
Robert Moulson, tanner.
John Dobb, wetglover.
John Hancock, joiner.
James Evans, silkweaver.
Moses Marsh, upholsterer.
Urian Moulson, tailor.
Joshua Wrench, linen-draper.

John Maddock, tanner.
William Fernihaugh, ironmonger.
Thomas Higginson, brewer.
Phillip Wilson, dyer.
Thomas Hassall, gentleman.
William Hulton, grocer.
John Farrar, shoemaker.
John Key, slater.
Peter Williams, slater.
John Coulson, plasterer.
John Whitehead, tailor.
William Pulford, carpenter.
Henry Jones, saddler.
Edward Lloyd, linen-draper.
Thomas Moulson, tanner.
Thomas Hughes, tanner.
Francis Touchett, apothecary.
Randle Turner, merchant.
Henry Jackson, gentleman.
Randle Edge, shoemaker.

1681-2 [33-34 C. ii.] GEORGE MAINWARING, Esquire, Mayor.

Robert Bromley, brewer.
James Whitney, combmaker.
Edward Fox, tanner.
John Robinson, brewer.
Josiah Gorse, butcher.
Richard Vernon.
Thomas Ascough.
William Finlow, glover.
Thomas Robinson, goldsmith.
Robert Bellin, cooper and fishmonger.
John Davies.
William Smith, baker.
Thomas Foulkes, carpenter.
Peter Meredith, brewer.
Edward Wright, skinner.
Thomas Price, plumber.
Edward Croughton, tanner.
George Byrd, ironmonger.
Edward Butler, ironmonger.
Zacchary Wright, ironmonger.
John Banner, brewer.

John Wilkinson, barber-chirurgeon.
Daniel Wilson, shoemaker.
William Halliwell, tobacconist.
Hugh Halliwell, baker.
Thomas Wrench, carpenter.
Theodore Aldcrofte, merchant.

1682-3 [34-35 C. ii.] PETER EDWARDS, Esquire, Mayor.

Nicholas Cowper, silkweaver.
John Meacock the younger, weaver.
Joseph Buckley, blacksmith.
John Griffith, turner.
Randle Ince, smith.
Thomas Fox, baker.
Richard Fox, turner.
Thomas Davies, carver.
Humphrey Hewitt, ironmonger.
Raphe Walley, goldsmith.
Samuel Throppe, cooper.
Charles Jellicoe, baker.
Ephraim Bardsley, baker.
Owen Maddock, glasier.
Charles Walley, fishmonger.
Thomas Walley, brewer.
Richard Eaton, mariner.
Samuel Gervice, silkweaver.
John Pemberton, linen-draper.
Calcott Aldersey, ironmonger.
Charles Ashton, watchmaker.
Samuel Taylor, barber-chirurgeon.
Humphrey Owen, ironmonger.
Thomas Challoner, barber-chirurgeon.
John Warrington, brewer.
Richard Snead, fletcher.
Peter Bennett, woollen draper, hosier, innholder, merchant, ———.
John Billinge, wetglover.
John Oulton, merchant.
Robert Hine, brewer.
David Bulkeley, linen-draper.
Rowland Parry, ironmonger.
William Hadock, innholder.

1683-4 [35-36 C. ii.] WILLIAM STREETE, Esquire, Mayor.

Peter Humphreyes, barber-chirurgeon, &c.
Thomas Ludman, pewterer.
Randle Bannion, soapmaker.
Isaac Thomas, carpenter.
Robert Lounds, mercer.
John Halliwell, glasier.
Robert Morris, glasier.
Rowland Eakin, clothworker.

1684-5 [36-37 C. ii.–1 J. ii.] Sir THOMAS GROSVENOR, Baronet, Mayor.

Powell Williams, gentleman, macebearer.
Richard Parker, gentleman.
Charles Anderton, gentleman.
Charles Warmingham, barber-chirurgeon.
John Hulton.
William Swift, merchant.
Samuel Colson, barber-chirurgeon.
"Jebus" Bathoe.
John Harrison, beer-brewer.
Joseph Prestburie, wetglover.
Thomas Williams, wetglover.
Peter Leigh, wetglover.
Josiah Cooke, dyer.
William Warmingham, tailor.
Samuel Horton, beer-brewer.
Henry Young, silkweaver.
Samuel Nicholl.
William Moores, shoemaker.
John Nicholls, shoemaker.
George Carman, spurrier.
Francis Leech, doctor of phisicke.
Charles Seladine, barber.
Samuel Joynson, shoemaker.
Epham Elcocke, mercer.
Thomas Leigh, baker.
Joseph Brotherston, butcher.
Humphrey Page, bookseller.
Joseph Pemberton.
Benjamin Maddock, tailor.

	Thomas Stringer, turner.
	Thomas Pate, butcher.
	Richard Totty, joiner.
	Thomas Edwards, linen-draper.
	Richard Broster, saddler.
	William Jones, cordiner.
Sep. 21	Thomas Partington, mercer.
	Joseph Massie, mercer.
	Thomas Biggens, tailor.
,, 26	Robert Hulse, brewer.
Oct. 3	Morrice Wynne, ironmonger.

1685-6 [1-2 J. ii.] WILLIAM WILSON, Esquire, Mayor.

	Joseph Wigh, tanner.
	Thomas Minshull, silkweaver.
	John Williams, beer-brewer.
Dec. 24	Thomas Ward, silkweaver.
,, 24	Thomas Wood, feltmaker.
Jan. 23	Richard Steevenson, apothecary.
,, 23	Roger Wilbraham, tallow-chandler.
,, 23	William Quicke, blacksmith.
	Peter Alcocke, blacksmith.
Feb. 6	Charles Sheale, butcher.
Mar. 12	Thomas Skellerne, ironmonger.
,, 12	Henry Edwards, ironmonger.
,, 12	Thomas Parnell, ironmonger.
,, 19	John Sudlowe, maltster.
,, 29	Richard Reece, linen-draper.
,, 30	Richard Blaze, shoemaker.
Apr. 3	John Hinton, haberdasher.
,, 3	George Eaton, mariner.
,, 10	Francis Minshull, linen-draper.
,, 10	Peter Dunbaben, glasier.
,, 10	William Lancelot, joiner.
,, 10	Thomas Crosse, joiner.
,, 16	Phebian Billingham, cordiner.
June 12	Timothy Gardiner, goldsmith.
,, 12	John Broster, pewterer.
,, 12	John Jackson, skinner.
,, 18	Thomas Weston, innholder.
July 3	John Dobbe, cordiner.
,, 10	Peter Leadbeater, brewer.
,, 10	Edward Leadbeater, ironmonger.
,, 10	William Bellis, ironmonger.

M

July 20 John Gregorie, gentleman.
„ 28 Samuel Hawborne, sugar baker.
„ 28 Randle Dannold, barber.
Sep. 4 Hugh Maddock, tanner.
„ 25 Thomas Bromeley, saddler.
„ 25 Hugh Rhodes, shoemaker.
Oct. 4 Jonathan Wrenchall, joiner.
„ 8 Richard Bevan, blacksmith.
„ 10 Charles Pindar, esquire.
„ 10 Henry Williamson, *in Medicin doctor*.
„ 10 Peter Bell, cordiner.
„ 12 Thomas Warmingham, cordiner.
„ 12 John Warmingham, silkweaver.
„ 12 John Deane, cordiner.

1686-7 [2-3 J. ii.] EDWARD OULTON, Esquire, Mayor.

Oct. 20 Thomas Ellis, innholder.
Nov. 6 Charles Browne, draper.
„ 10 George Meacocke, beer-brewer.
„ 10 John Dawson, beer-brewer.
„ 10 John Cartwright, tailor.
Dec. 13 Robert Bulkeley, grocer.
„ 13 John Yeomans, grocer.
„ 13 John Rothwell, cordwainer.
„ 21 Thomas Jones, tanner.
„ 29 George Bingley, feltmaker.
Jan. 10 Mathew Jones, beer-brewer.
„ 15 Thomas Simpson, gentleman.
„ 15 Henry Lloyd, draper.
Feb. ult. John Wright, carpenter.
Mar. 16 Samuel Farrington, maltster.
„ 28 William Wade, mason.
Apr. 11 William Croxton, upholsterer.
„ 11 George Woodes.
May 2 Edward Nickson, mason.
„ 7 John Williams, currier.
„ 16 Robert Crosbie, shoemaker.
„ 16 Randle Pemberton, shoemaker.
June 11 Richard Dewsbury, barber.
„ 11 John Jennions, feltmaker.
„ 15 Abraham Jones, saddler.
„ 15 Thomas Darwell, glover.
„ 18 John Brereton, barber-chirurgeon.
„ 27 Peter Leigh, brazier.

1687–8]   THE CITY OF CHESTER   179

June 29 Ephraim Welshman, tallow-chandler.
July 2 Richard Fletcher, tallow-chandler.
  „ 19 Joseph Sefton, dyer.
  „ 30 James Rushton, bricklayer.
Aug. 3 John Royle, innholder.
  „ 29 William Williams, esquire.
Sep. 5 William Jackson, bricklayer.
  „   6 Edward Puleston, woollen-draper.
  „   6 John Stringer, haberdasher.
  „ 17 John s. of Hugh Bennett of Willaston.
Oct. 13 Ralph Davenport, barber-chirurgeon.
  „ 13 Francis Edgesly, brewer.
  „ 14 Hugh Starkey, alderman.

1687–8 [3–4 J. ii.] HUGH STARKEY, Esquire, Mayor.

Oct. 26 Puleston Partington, watchmaker.
  „ 26 John Golbornes, apothecary.
  „ 26 Richard Taylor the younger, glasier.
  „ 26 Joseph Dyson, tinplate worker.
  „ 26 John Minshull, stationer.
  „ 26 John Critchley, upholsterer.
  „ 26 Joseph Stout, butcher.
  „ 29 John Conway, slater.
Nov. 9 Joseph Dod, wetglover.
Dec. 5 Richard Levinge, esquire, Recorder of Chester.
  „   5 Sir Thomas Grosvenor, baronet.
  „   9 Edward Starkey, sheriff.
  „   9 Jonathan Whitby, sheriff. [Note here attached to roll:—"Starky and Whitby sworn Sheriffs 9 Dec. 1687."]
  „ 20 Richard Taylor, merchant.
Jan. 9 Joseph Lingley, gentleman.
  „   9 John Williamson, gentleman.
  „   9 Robert Warmingham, tailor.
  „   9 John Younge, cordiner.
  „   9 Thomas Coe, cordiner.
  „   9 Thomas Bridge, cordiner.
  „   9 Richard Colson, tanner.
  „   9 Thomas French, tailor.
  „   9 William Reece, hornbreaker.
  „ 14 Samuel Carden, innholder.
Feb. 2 Abner Shcoles, upholsterer.
Apr. 2 William Maxfeild, innholder.
  „   2 John Bentley, innholder.

May	28	Richard Carden, brewer.
June	27	Peter Potter, skinner.
„	27	Mathias Buckley, linen-draper.
		Richard Ordes, barber.
July	7	William Brumbley, joiner.
„	9	George Calcen, chirurgeon.
„	16	Paul Wilcocke, ——.
„	16	Robert Parsons, fishmonger.
„	23	John Fox, tailor.
„	23	William Rider, tailor.
„	23	John Millington, currier.
„	23	John Banner, beer-brewer.
„	23	Isaac Warmingham, tailor.
„	23	Mathew Twemlow, chandler.
„	23	William Hinde, baker.
„	23	Thomas Wright, tailor.
„	23	Hugh Conway, silkweaver.
Aug.	4	Samuel Fletcher, brewer.
„	4	Thomas Cottingham, chirurgeon.
„	29	Henry Crosbie, cordwainer.
„	29	James Hutchinson, leavelooker.
„	29	Randle Vause, leavelooker.
„	29	Caldecott Aldersey, ironmonger.
„	29	Charles Leech, mercer.
„	28	Thomas Whiteof, carpenter.

1688-9 [4 J. ii.-1 W. & M.] WILLIAM STREET, Esquire, Mayor.

Dec.	22	Thomas Jackson, yeoman, p. of Thomas Wright of Chester, grocer.
„	22	Samuel s. of Samuel Revington of Chester.
„	22	John s. of John Richardson, late of Chester.
„	22	Elias Massey p. of George Hunt of Chester, pipemaker.
„	22	John s. of Huth—— Henthorne of Chester, sugar baker.
„	24	Richard Brock p. of George Mainwaring of Chester, merchant.
Jan.	9	(B) Robert Livesley.
„	9	(B) John Wright, esquire.
„	9	(B) Egidius Reece.
„	9	(B) Thomas French.
„	9	(B) Thomas Wright.
„	9	(B) Thomas Hall.
„	9	(B) John Hall.

Jan.	9	(I) Thomas Henthorne.
,,	9	(I) Thomas Whitside.
,,	10	(B) Robert Davies.
,,	10	(B) William Farrington.
,,	10	(B) Samuel Rymmer.
,,	10	(I) John Brandwood.
,,	10	(I) John Davies.
,,	10	(B) William Hiccock.
,,	10	(B) Richard Bradshaw.
,,	10	(I) Richard Muchell.
,,	10	(B) Roger Maddockes.
,,	10	(I) Nathaniel Cokayne.
,,	10	(I) Samuel Done.
,,	10	(B) Henry Haslow.
,,	10	(B) William Farshaw.
,,	10	(I) Thomas Edwards.
,,	10	(B) Samuel Partridge.
,,	10	(B) Richard Williamson.
,,	10	(I) John Bulkley.
,,	10	(B) John Salusbury.
,,	10	(B) John Bromley.
,,	10	(B) John Ellis.
,,	10	(B) Richard Higginson.
,,	11	(B) Richard Warmingham.
,,	11	(B) John Foulkes.
,,	11	(B) Samuel Bennett.
,,	11	(B) Thomas Annion.
,,	11	(B) Richard Ledsam.
,,	11	(I) Benjamin Pemberton.
,,	11	(B) Charles Warrington.
,,	11	(B) Thomas Morris.
,,	11	(B) Josiah Young.
,,	11	(I) John Hunt.
,,	11	(B) William Ravenscroft.
,,	11	(B) George Revington.
,,	11	(B) John Johnson.
,,	11	(B) Francis Johnson.
,,	11	(B) Nathaniel Smith.
,,	11	(B) Samuel Harrison.
,,	11	(B) Evan Evans.
,,	11	(B) Robert Davies.
,,	11	(I) Robert Gervis.
,,	11	(B) William Bolton.
,,	9	†Edward Wynne, esquire.
,,	11	(B) Jonathan Cope.
,,	11	(I) Robert Martyn.

Jan. 11 (B) Nicholas Reece.
„ 11 (I) John Kelsall.
„ 11 (I) Ralph Done.
„ 11 (B) John Dunbavin.
„ 16 John Clayton p. of Isaac Warmingham.
„ 14 (I) Thomas Battridge.
Feb. 16 (B) Robert Jones.
„ 18 (B) Richard Thomason.
„ 18 (B) Joseph Welsh.
„ 18 (B) Thomas Thomason.
„ 19 David Parry.
„ 21 (B) Edmund Mathews.
„ 22 Richard Wynne p. of William Wilson, tanner.
„ 29 Roger Comberbach, gentleman.
Mar. 27 John Fernihaugh s. of Thomas Fernihaugh of Chester, woollen-draper.
„ 27 Robert s. of Robert Radford of Chester, linen-draper.
„ 27 Robert Carrington p. of John Shard of Chester, apothecary.
Apr. 17 Thomas s. of William Bennett of Chester, ironmonger.
Jan. 5 Thomas Bannion p. of Thomas Young, brewer.
July 4 Richard s. of Henry Haslow.
Aug. 14 Hugh } ss. of Henry Hand.
„ 14 Stephen
„ 17 Richard Clerkson, carpenter.
Sep. 18 Samuel } ss. of John Trevers [Travers, M.B.].
„ 18 Tryall
†Geoffrey Malbone.

1689-90 [1-2 W. & M.] FRANCIS SKELLORNE, Esquire, Mayor.

Nov. 16 (I) John Redrope.
„ 23 (I) Henry Rutter.
„ 30 (I) Offley Wilkinson.
„ 30 (I) Thomas Denson.
„ 30 (I) John Shawe.
Dec. 21 John s. of Peter Bostocke.
Jan. 25 Owen s. of Owen Ellis, late of Chester, mercer.
Feb. 15 John Hale, gentleman.
„ 15 Thomas Stoppord.
„ 15 Thomas Pemberton p. of Peter Pemberton, goldsmith.
„ 19 (B) Randle Venables.
„ 19 John s. of Owen Jones, butcher.
„ 22 Arthur s. of William Wilson, alderman.

Feb.	22	Robert s. of Hugh Starkey, alderman.
”	22	(B) James Tompson.
”	22	(B) Thomas Throppe.
”	22	(B) George Throppe.
”	22	(I) William Sellars.
”	22	(B) Thomas Dunbavin.
”	22	(B) Nathaniel Fearnall.
”	22	(I) Thomas Gill.
”	26	(B) George Johnson.
”	26	(B) Thomas Johnson.
”	26	(B) Robert Johnson.
”	26	(B) John Cotgreave.
”	26	(B) Henry Crosby.
”	26	(B) Charles Hughes.
”	26	(I) Thomas Whawell.
Mar.	1	(B) John Gibbons.
”	1	(B) Thomas Gardiner.
”	1	(B) Samuel Hayes.
”	8	(B) Thomas Williamson.
”	8	(B) Thomas Hankey.
”	8	(I) John Woodworth.
”	8	(I) William Page.
”	8	(B) Thomas Gibbons.
”	8	(B) John Moulson.
”	8	(B) Joseph Wright.
”	8	(B) Richard Young.
”	8	(B) Thomas Ledsam.
”	8	(B) Bradford Tonna.
”	8	(B) George Tonna.
”	8	(B) Charles Morrys [Morris, M.B.].
”	8	(B) Thomas Pattridge.
”	8	(I) Richard Sherlock.
”	8	(I) William Colson.
”	8	(I) Thomas Shridgley.
”	13	(B) Samuel Jones, gentleman.
”	13	(B) Thomas Hancocke.
”	13	(B) John Moreton, cordwainer.
”	13	(B) Charles Johnson.
”	13	(I) Thomas Hatfeild.
”	13	(B) Samuel Jennings.
”	13	(B) Thomas Wilson.
”	13	(B) William Mosse.
”	13	(B) Daniel Colson.
”	13	Thomas s. of John Fletcher.
”	13	(B) Peter Taylor.
”	13	(B) John Thomason.

Mar.	13	(B) Edward Kelly.
,,	13	(B) John Annion.
,,	13	(B) Thomas Ball.
,,	13	(B) Hugh Cowdocke.
,,	13	(I) John Strettall.
,,	13	(B) Edward Tompson.
,,	13	(B) Thomas Harvey.
,,	13	(I) Richard Bennett.
,,	13	(B) Richard Davies.
,,	13	(B) William Skellington.
,,	13	(B) Robert Dobbe.
,,	13	(B) Titus Dewsbury.
,,	13	(I) George Bannion.
,,	13	(B) John Gaulter.
,,	13	(B) Richard Porter.
,,	13	(B) Thomas Stocton.
,,	13	(B) John Bolland.
,,	13	(B) John Ireland.
,,	13	(B) John Fletcher.
,,	13	(I) James Held.
,,	13	(I) John Serratt.
,,	13	(I) Thomas Halmarke.
,,	13	(B) John Davies.
,,	13	(B) Samuel Kelsall.
,,	13	(I) William Gough.
,,	15	Cornelius s. of Ralph Phillips, gent., and p. of Thomas Ireland.
,,	15	John Palin p. of Daniel Batho, tanner.
,,	15	Henry s. of John Pemberton, cordwainer.
,,	15	Thomas Rylands p. of Griffin Knowles, cordwainer.
,,	15	William Goodaker p. of Mathew Anderton, merchant.
,,	15	John s. of John Cotgreave, baker.
,,	15	Joseph Jordan p. of William Hughes, bricklayer.
,,	15	Thomas s. of John Kerkes, tanner.
,,	15	Thomas s. of Thomas Young, brewer.
,,	15	John s. of Samuel Fletcher, tanner.
,,	15	William s. of Hugh Moulson, tanner.
,,	15	William s. of John Sudlow, apothecary.
,,	15	John s. of William Hale, butcher.
,,	15	William s. of William Willoughby, brewer.
,,	15	Samuel Hinton p. of Robert Anderson, apothecary.
,,	15	John Houlford p. of Daniel Crosse, joiner.
,,	15	Nathaniel } ss. of William Selby, butcher.
,,	15	Thomas
,,	15	Peter s. of Robert Hatton, butcher.
,,	15	Robert s. of Jonathan Cotgreave, brewer.

Mar. 15	John s. of William Briscowe, skinner.
,, 15	Esau s. of Esau Andrew, carpenter.
,, 15	Robert s. of William Richardson, butcher.
,, 15	Henry s. of John Turner, tailor.
,, 15	Ralph s. of Ralph Hilton, cordwainer.
,, 15	Thomas s. of Richard Bavand, smith.
,, 15	John s. of William Richardson, butcher.
,, 15	Symon s. of Edward Broster, tanner.
,, 15	John s. of Richard Ormes, yeoman.
,, 15	Thomas Whithead p. of Abraham Heathley, slater.
,, 15	Aaron Esalls [Asalls, M.B.] p. of Richard Dicas, tailor.
,, 15	Ralph s. of Ralph Hulton [Hilton, M.B.], gentleman.
,, 15	Thomas Manning p. of John Jenson, cordwainer.
,, 15	Mathew s. of Henry Johnson, joiner.
,, 15	John s. of Edward Powell, blacksmith.
,, 15	Humphrey Sharpe p. of Thomas Ormes, pipemaker.
,, 15	William s. of Edward Powell, blacksmith.
,, 15	John Meredith p. of William Woods, mason.
,, 15	Peter s. of Richard Bennett, innholder.
,, 15	Francis s. of William Woods, mason.
,, 15	John Moreton p. of William Adshead, cordwainer.
,, 15	Joseph Richardson p. of William Robinson, plasterer.
,, 15	John s. of Thomas Ball, brewer.
,, 15	Samuel Davies p. of " Jac " Mort, mason.
,, 15	Alexander Rowdon p. of William Hughes, bricklayer.
,, 15	John Simcocke p. of Edward Tompson, pipemaker.
,, 15	Samuel Broughall p. of Charles Jackson, smith.
,, 15	Thomas Walley p. of Thomas Walley, feltmaker.
,, 15	Richard Scott p. of Abel Andrew, carpenter.
,, 15	Thomas Griffith p. of Robert Farrington, innholder.
,, 15	Nicholas s. of William Ince, alderman.
Apr. 12	William Richards p. of Thomas Deane, cordwainer.
,, 17	Peter Wrench.
,, 17	Robert Young.
,, 17	Lawrence Harvey.
June 4	Henry Gill p. of Thomas Holland, barber.
,, 6	Hugh Phitheon.
July 12	Richard s. of Francis Skellerne, mayor of the city.
,, 23	Thomas Orme p. of John Pemberton, merchant.
Aug. 4	Joseph Wright p. of William Buckley, tanner.
Sep. 24	John Wrench, watchmaker.
,, 24	Ralph Massie of Chester, cordwainer.
,, 24	John Reade, mercer.
,, 24	William Ingam, cabinetmaker.
Oct. 4	Joseph Williams.

Oct. 8 John Leenes p. of —— Leenes, joiner.
„ 9 Griffith Williams, esquire, Deputy Recorder of Chester.
„ 9 Alexander Pulford p. of Peter Edwards, goldsmith.

1690–1 [2–3 W. & M.] NATHANIEL WILLIAMSON, Esquire, Mayor.

Oct. 18 Reginald Whittaker p. of Thomas Roberts of Chester, butcher, defunct.
Dec. 13 Robert Griffith p. of Thomas Ashton of Chester, brewer, defunct.
„ 20 *William Wills of Chester, merchant.
Apr. 18 John Hiccocke, baker, s. of John Hiccocke of Chester, baker.
Nov. 15 John Kelsall p. of Richard Reece of Chester, linen-draper.
„ 15 Benjamin s. of Joseph Maddocke of Chester, tailor.
„ 22 Richard Shaw p. of William Davies of Chester, cord-wainer.
„ 22 Thomas Walworth p. of Randle Batho of Chester, tanner.
„ 29 John Simmons, barber, p. of John Ensdale.
May 19 William Gamul p. of William Hynde of Chester, baker, defunct.
„ 19 Richard Gamul, chandler, p. of John Bingley of Chester, tallow-chandler.
June 6 Ebenezer s. of John Trevers of Chester, ironmonger.
„ 13 John s. of William Turner of Chester, feltmaker.
„ 23 *Peter Shakerley, esquire.
July 1 John s. of Hugh Conway of Chester, silkweaver.
„ 4 Thomas s. of Thomas Davenport of Chester, barber-chirurgeon.
„ 7 Richard s. of Richard Adams of Chester, draper.
„ 18 *Thomas Stapleton.
Aug. 4 Charles Hostage [Hostich, M.B.] p. of John Higginson, tailor.
„ 4 Peter Mort p. of Thomas Walmesley of Chester, ironmonger.
Sep. 5 Jonathan Brewer p. of James Mort of Chester, mason, defunct.
„ 12 Samuel Ashbrooke p. of Christopher Packe of Chester, tailor.
Oct. 5 Thomas Bowker p. of Thomas Minshall of Chester, ironmonger, defunct.

Oct.	5	Joseph Hodgson p. of John Minshall of Chester, stationer.
„	5	Nathan Maddocke p. of Anthony Nicholls of Chester, blacksmith.
„	10	Andrew Boswell p. of Owen Shone of Chester, chirurgeon.
„	10	Peter s. of Thomas Jackson of Chester, wetglover.
„	12	John s. of Richard Massey of Chester, cordwainer.
„	13	James Doe p. of Richard Doe of Chester, cordwainer.
„	31	Andrew Hall p. of George Palin of Chester, cordwainer.

1691–2 [3–4 W. & M.] HENRY, EARL OF WARRINGTON, MAYOR.

Jan.	16	Randle s. of Randle Aston of Chester, skinner.
„	16	Benjamin Cockaine p. of Thomas Heath of Chester, apothecary.
„	16	James Walley p. of John Dewsbury of Chester, feltmaker.
„	16	Isaac Sharp of Chester, gentleman.
„	16	*Thomas Ogden, gentleman.
—		Moses Worrall p. of Christopher Eakin, clothworker.
Apr.	11	Thomas Hiccocke p. of Hugh Moulson of Chester, tanner.
„	11	James Litler p. of William Throp of Chester, cordwainer.
„	11	Richard Sconce p. of George Finlow of Chester, drawer in Dee.
May	9	Richard Maddocke p. of Ralph Blag of Chester, innholder.
„	9	Samuel Taylor, gentleman, s. of Richard Taylor of Chester, alderman, defunct.
July	5	Giles [Egidius] Reece p. of Thomas Holland, barber.

1692–3 [4–5 W. & M.] ROGER WHITLEY, ESQUIRE, MAYOR.

Oct.	15	James Mainwaring, merchant, s. of George Mainwaring of Chester, alderman.
„	15	Ralph Burroughs, draper, s. of John Burroughs of Chester, draper.
„	15	Charles Gerrard, linen-draper, s. of Samuel Gerrard of Chester, tailor.

Oct.	26	John Gaulter, joiner, s. of James Gaulter of Chester, joiner, defunct.
„	26	Richard Wirrell [Werrall, M.B.] p. of —— Halliwel of Chester, tailor.
Nov.	4	William Bolland, joiner, s. of William Bolland of Chester, joiner.
Jan.	2	James Dewsbury, feltmaker, s. of Thomas Dewsbury of Chester, feltmaker.
„	6	William Smith p. of John Dannold of Chester, chandler, defunct.
„	14	Robert Wrench p. of Michael Croughton of Chester, joiner, defunct.
„	14	Robert Breck [Brock, M.B.] p. of Thomas Wrench of Chester, carpenter, defunct.
„	21	Henry Grantham, yeoman, s. of Geoffrey Grantham of [Wervin ?], co. Ches., yeoman, and p. of Jonathan Cotgreave of Chester, [brewer ?].
Feb.	11	Thomas Phillips, yeoman, s. of John Phillips of Chester, gentleman, defunct.
„	11	John Chaddick [Chadwicke, M.B.], barber-chirurgeon, p. of Owen Shone of Chester, barber-chirurgeon, defunct.
Mar.	4	John Cleaton [Clayton, M.B.], feltmaker, p. of Thomas Bridge of Chester, haberdasher.
„	11	George Johnson p. of Richard Taylor of Chester, glasier.
„	25	William s. of Jane Wynne of " Kanufud," co. Denbigh, widow, and p. of John Pugh of Chester, ironmonger.
Apr.	8	John Catherall, glasier, s. of John Catherall of Foulke Stapleford, co. Ches., blacksmith, defunct, and p. of Robert Morris of Chester, glasier and fishmonger.
„	22	William s. of Francis Sheaphard of Chester, innholder, and p. of John Parks of Chester, linen-draper.
„	29	Uriah s. of Randle Bingley of Chester, baker, and p. of John Bingley of Chester, chandler.
„	29	Randle s. of Randle Bingley, and p. of Nathan Bradbourne of Chester, ironmonger.
May	6	George s. of George Taylor, late of Chester, yeoman, and p. of William Woodfin of Chester, slater.
„	11	Thomas s. of William Patton, late of Chester and now of Warrington, co. Lanc., draper.
„	11	John s. of John Pemberton, late of Chester and now of Liverpool, co. Lanc., apothecary.
„	20	Randle Greene p. of Thomas Dannald of Chester, baker, defunct.

June 23		Thomas s. of Robert Mosse, late of Chester and now of London, draper.
July	5	John s. of William Page of Chester, blacksmith, defunct.
,,	5	Josiah Jackson, glover, s. of Thomas Jackson of Chester, glover.
,,	5	Joseph Annyon, barber, s. of John Annion of Chester, joiner, defunct.
,,	5	John Swinton, ironmonger, s. of John Swinton of Chester, ironmonger, defunct.
,,	8	Henry Birkenhead p. of Thomas Dannald of Chester, linen-draper, defunct.
,,	24	Samuel Sefton p. of William Hughes of Chester, tailor, defunct.
,,	24	Thomas s. and p. of Thomas Biggins of Chester, tailor.
Sep.	30	William Hall of London, needleman, s. of Henry Hall of Chester, innholder, defunct.
Oct.	7	William Thompson, gentleman, s. of William Thompson of Chester, clerk.
,,	7	George Crooke p. of James Alcock of Chester, tailor.
,,	7	Henry s. of Daniel Coulson [Colson, M.B.] of Chester, plasterer, and p. of Samuel Colson of Chester, barber.
,,	7	William Critchley, feltmaker, s. of Thomas Critchley of Chester, innholder, defunct.
,,	12	Samuel Bolland, brewer, s. of Arthur Bolland of Chester, brewer.
,,	12	Henry Salisbury, wigmaker, s. of Henry Salisbury of Chester, wigmaker.
,,	12	Thomas s. of John Hughes of Chester.
,,	12	John Basfeild, gardiner, s. of William Basfeild of Chester, gardiner.

1693-4 [5-6 W. & M.] ROGER WHITLEY, Esquire, Mayor.

Nov.	25	John s. of Richard Taylor, button-maker, and p. of Nicholas Cowper of Chester, silkweaver.
Dec.	2	Thomas Mottershead, glover, p. of Thomas Jackson, wetglover.
,,	6	Ralph s. of Ralph Boulton of Chester, feltmaker, defunct, and p. of George Vause, barber.
,,	9	*Francis Sayer, plumber.

Dec. 13		Nathaniel s. of Nathaniel Deane of Chester, ironmonger, defunct, and p. of Nathaniel Weld of Chester, shoemaker.
Jan. 27		Robert Welch p. of Richard Harrison of Chester, brewer, defunct.
,, 27		Peter Starkey, brewer, s. of Peter Starkey of Chester, brewer, defunct.
Feb. 17		*William Coker, cheese factor.
,, 17		*Thomas Pickmore.
Mar. 10		Peter Shaw p. of William Bennet, feltmaker.
Apr. 21		Benjamin Dod, barber-chirurgeon, p. of Hugh Starkey, alderman.
,, 24		Adam Alcock, apothecary, p. of John Golborn.
May 2		James s. of John Bealy of Gloverstone, yeoman, and p. of Edward Leadbeater, ironmonger.
,, 8		Charles s. of Phillip Brock, pewterer, and p. of Samuel Dannald, barber.
June 27		*Benjamin Lownds, tailor.
July 7		Richard Wright p. of Thomas Weston of Chester, innholder, defunct.
,, 21		John Williams, esquire, s. of Sir William Williams, knight and baronet, recorder of Chester.
,, 21		Thomas Kennion p. of Abel Andrew, late of Chester, carpenter.
Aug. 25		*Richard Leigh.
Sep. 1		George Bennion p. of William Fernihaugh of Chester, ironmonger.
,, 15		John s. of John Taylor, shoemaker, defunct, and p. of Edward Butler of Chester, ironmonger.
,, 15		Richard Booth p. of George Harvey of Chester, bricklayer.
,, 22		Thomas Thorton of Lower Kinnerton, co. Ches., p. of Thomas Lynnaker of Chester, cooper and fishmonger, by indenture dated 25th Dec. 1655.
,, 22		Gerrard s. of John Jones of Chester, tailor, and p. of Robert Fletcher, late of Chester, furrier.
,, 24		Richard Brock, beam maker, s. of Phillip Brock of Chester, pewterer.
,, 29		George s. of John Martin of Chester, husbandman, and p. of Thomas Hassell of Chester, ironmonger, defunct.
Oct. 6		Samuel Edwards, goldsmith, s. of Peter Edwards of Chester, alderman and goldsmith.
,, 6		John s. of John Sparrow of Little Heath in the parish of "Auldem," co. Ches., gentleman, and p. of Hugh Starkey of Chester, alderman and chirurgeon.

1694-5] THE CITY OF CHESTER 191

Oct. 6 Griffith s. of Anthony Harrison, late of Beaumaris, co. Anglesey, grocer, and p. of John Pugh of Chester, ironmonger.
,, 6 John s. and p. of Robert Murray of Chester, ironmonger.
,, 6 Samuel s. of John Tilston, defunct, and p. of Robert Murrey of Chester, ironmonger.
,, 6 Thomas s. of Thomas Cragge of Chester, labourer, and p. of Thomas King of Chester, shoemaker.
,, 6 John s. of Richard Bridge of Chester, dyer.
,, 6 Samuel Bennet, maltster, s. of Henry Bennet of Chester, brewer, defunct.
,, 6 Vaughan s. of Thomas Solden [Soden, M.B.] of the Grange, co. Letrim, gentleman, and p. of John Pugh of Chester, ironmonger.
,, 6 William Woodfin, slater, s. of William Woodfin of Chester, slater.
,, 9 Richard s. of Mary Golding of Chester, widow, and p. of Thomas Jones of Chester, pipemaker.

1694-5 [6 W. & M.-7 W. iii.] ROGER WHITLEY, Esquire, Mayor.

Oct. 13 Francis Burges, silkweaver, s. of Francis Burges of Chester, tanner.
,, 13 Josiah s. of Thomas Moores of Chester, ironmonger, defunct.
,, 27 Stephen Wilkinson p. of Edward Morgan of Chester, shoemaker.
Dec. 1 James s. of Joshua Gerrard of Werneth, co. Ches., gentleman, and p. of William Fernihaugh of Chester, ironmonger.
,, 1 Benjamin s. of William Barrow of Churton, co. Ches., webster, and p. of Thomas Hankey of Chester, feltmaker.
,, 31 Nicholas s. of Nichol Wilson, late of Coolane, co. Salop, yeoman, and p. of William Litherland of Chester, joiner.
,, 31 William Hale, butcher, s. of William Hale of Chester, butcher, defunct.
Jan. 5 John Locket p. of Thomas Booth of Chester, shoemaker.
,, 19 *John Houseman, gentleman.
,, 19 Edward s. of Richard Hiccock of Chester, innholder, defunct.

192   THE ROLLS OF THE FREEMEN OF   [1694-5

Feb. 16   Robert s. of Roger Comberbach, late of Chester, barber-chirurgeon, and p. of Thomas Parnell of Chester, ironmonger.
„ 16   Thomas Mercer, chandler, s. of William Mercer of Chester, chandler.
Mar. 9   Alexander s. of Alexander Denton of Leighton, co. Ches., gentleman, and p. of John Holland of Chester, draper.
„ 30   Samuel s. of Thomas Sadler of Chester, ironmonger, defunct, and p. of Nathaniel Bevan of Chester, ironmonger.
„ 30   William s. of Samuel Rimmer of Chester, clothworker, and p. of John Shard of Chester, apothecary.
„ 30   Henry Jennings, barber, s. of Henry Jennings of Chester, cordwainer, defunct, and p. of Samuel Taylor of Chester, barber-chirurgeon.
Apr. 6   Thomas s. of John Billinge the elder of Chester, dry-glover, and p. of John Billinge of Chester, wet-glover.
„ 6   *William Minshull, esquire.
„ 9   Daniel Potter, tailor, s. of John Potter of Chester, tailor, defunct.
July 2   William Minshull, ironmonger, s. of Thomas Minshull of Chester, ironmonger, defunct.
„ 2   Lawrence s. of Lawrence Gaulter of Chester, joiner, and p. of John Roberts of Chester, ironmonger.
„ 6   *George Hastings, carpenter.
„ 6   *William Hughes, yeoman.
„ 13   Joseph s. of Jonathan Cotgreave of Chester, brewer, and p. of John Halliwell of Chester, baker.
„ 20   Charles Chesway p. of William Selby the younger of Chester, butcher.
Aug. 19   *Roger Whitley the younger, esquire.
„ 19   *Morgan Whitley, esquire.
„ 19   *Edward Partington of Chester, tobacco-cutter.
„ 19   Thomas Hiccock of Chester, baker, s. of Richard Hiccock of Chester, *in medicin doctor*, defunct.
Sep. 21   William Gamul, dyer, s. of Thomas Gamul of Chester, ironmonger, defunct.
„ 21   William s. of Elizabeth Whittle of Worthenbury, co. Flint., widow, and p. of William Mercer of Chester, chandler.
„ 28   Robert Ridge s. of Robert Ridge of Chester, vintner, defunct.
„ 28   Joseph s. of Thomas Pike of Frankby, co. Ches., yeoman, and p. of Henry Young of Chester, ironmonger.

Sep. 28		William s. of William Basfeild of Chester, gardener, and p. of Robert Bellin of Chester, cooper.
Oct.	2	Francis s. of John Bostock of Macefen, co. Ches., yeoman, and p. of Thomas Moulson of Chester, barber-chirurgeon.
,,	2	John Tilston, joiner, s. of Modland Tilston of Gresford, co. Denbigh, and p. of Thomas Davies of Chester, joiner carver.
,,	5	John Hanley p. of Randle Dannold of Chester, barber-chirurgeon, defunct.
,,	5	John Bennet p. of John Colson of Chester, plasterer.
,,	5	Thomas s. of Randle Crue of Holt, co. Denbigh, gentleman, and p. of Edward Starkey of Chester, brewer.
,,	5	Charles Soreton p. of Richard Streete of Chester, brewer, defunct.
,,	5	Thomas s. of William Richardson of Chester, butcher, defunct.
	—	John Peever [Peover, M.B.], merchant, s. of Robert Peover of Chester, yeoman, and p. of George Mainwaring of Chester, alderman, defunct.

1695-6 [7-8 W. iii.] ROGER WHITLEY, Esquire, Mayor.

Oct.	26	Richard Taylor, gentleman, } ss. of John Taylor of Chester, innholder, defunct.
,,	26	William Taylor }
Nov.	2	Ellis Foulkes of Hope, yeoman, s. of David Foulkes of Chester, tailor, defunct.
,,	9	John s. of Edward Johnson of Chester, feltmaker, and p. of Edward Burroughs of Chester, feltmaker.
,,	9	Robert s. of Margerie Crosse of Burton, co. Lanc., widow, and p. of Isaac Crosse of Chester, joiner, defunct.
,,	9	Solomon s. of John Davies of Chester, brewer, defunct.
,,	13	Thomas Ley p. of Bradford Throp of Chester, cordwainer.
,,	13	Richard Wilkinson p. of Richard Dicas of Chester, tailor.
,,	13	Joseph s. of Ralph Bellin of Chester, cooper and fishmonger, defunct.
,,	13	Ralph Suthorn } pp. of William Lloyd of Chester, feltmaker.
,,	13	William Leigh }
,,	13	Edward Powell, yeoman, s. of Edward Powell of Chester, blacksmith, defunct.
,,	13	Henry s. and p. of Jonathan Tapley of Chester, wine-cooper.

Nov. 16	Thomas Burroughs, gentleman,	ss. of Ralph Burroughs of Chester, ironmonger, defunct.
,, 16	Ralph Burroughs, ironmonger,	
,, 16	Samuel Kirkes the younger, upholsterer, s.	of Samuel Kirkes of Chester, upholsterer.
,, 16	Peter Harefinch p.	

,, 16 William s. of William Robinson of Chester, slater, defunct, and p. of Phebean Billingham of Chester, cordwainer.

,, 16 William s. of John Calley of Chester, husbandman, defunct, and p. of John Anderson of Chester, innholder.

,, 16 John s. of Thomas Moyle of Kinnerton, co. Flint., draper, and p. of John Davies of Chester, brewer.

,, 16 John Smith p. of Samuel Gervis of Chester, silkweaver.

,, 16 William s. of Daniel Woods of Chester, plasterer.

,, 16 Richard Humphreys p. of Thomas Reece of Chester, hornbreaker, defunct.

,, 16 William Gibbons, feltmaker, s. of Thomas Gibbons of Chester, feltmaker.

,, 16 Hugh Calveley p. of Daniel Crosse of Chester, joiner.

,, 23 *John Deane, watchmaker.

,, 27 George s. of Henry Crosby of Chester, cordwainer, defunct.

,, 27 *William Blackmore, plumber.

,, 30 Andrew Armstrong p. of Peter Bennet of Chester, innholder, defunct.

,, 30 Peter Percival p. of Thomas Fearnall of Chester, butcher.

Dec. 7 Robert Crompton, gentleman, s. of Robert Crompton of Chester, gentleman, defunct.

,, 7 *Samuel How of Chester, sivemaker.

,, 7 *Andrew Middleton of Chester, distiller.

,, 14 Richard s. of Richard Bushell of Chester, feltmaker, and p. of William Harrison of Chester, shoemaker.

,, 21 Thomas s. and p. of Thomas Ward of Chester, silkweaver.

,, 23	Thomas Cowper, gentleman,	ss. of Thomas Cowper of Chester, gentleman, defunct.
,, 23	John Cowper, gentleman,	
,, 23	William Parry, merchant,	ss. of Lewis Parry of Chester, ironmonger.
,, 23	John Parry, ironmonger,	

Jan. 4 Rowland s. of Rowland Batrich of Barrow, co. Ches., gentleman, and p. of Arthur Bolland of Chester, brewer.

1696–7] THE CITY OF CHESTER 195

Jan. 25   Robert s. of Thomas Warmingham of Chester, tailor, and p. of Isaac Warmingham of Chester, tailor.
May 23   Robert s. of John Kirkes of Chester, tanner, defunct, and p. of William Cokayne, ironmonger.
June 13 *Henry Standish of Chester, mariner.
July 13 Richard s. of Thomas Penket of Great Neston, co. Ches., yeoman, and p. of Joseph Bennet of Chester, ironmonger, defunct.
„ 18   *Daniel [Samuel crossed out] Large, printer of cloth.
Aug. 28 Thomas Chapman, barber, s. of John Chapman, gentleman, and p. of Richard Dewsbury of Chester, feltmaker.
„ 28   Owen s. of Owen Meredith of Belgreave, and p. of Roger Wilbraham of Chester, chandler.
„ 28   Ralph s. of Edward Deane of Ledsham, yeoman, and p. of Ralph Blag of Chester, innholder, defunct.
Oct. 3   Griffith p. of Humphrey Owen of the parish of Dolgethly, co. Merioneth, yeoman, and p. of Abraham Jones, late of Chester, saddler.

1696–7 [8–9 W. iii.] PETER BENNET, Esquire, Mayor.

Nov. 11 William s. of Thomas Calley of Neston, co. Ches., yeoman, and p. of Christopher Pack of Chester, tailor.
„ 11   Hugh s. of Robert Smith of Morley, co. Ches., and p. of John Wilkinson of Chester, barber-chirurgeon.
„ 14   William s. of John Kelsall of Pickton, co. Ches., yeoman, and p. of William Rider of Chester, tailor, defunct.
„ 21   John Maddock, tanner, s. of Thomas Maddock of Chester, tanner.
Dec. 2   Samuel Grindley, smith, s. of Richard Grindley of Chester, smith.
Jan. 13 Thomas s. of Richard Dod of Burland Green, co. Ches., yeoman, defunct, and p. of John Thomason of Chester, brewer.
Feb. 3   Thomas s. of Henry Ridley, late of Namptwich, co. Ches., innholder, and p. of Robert Carrington of Chester, apothecary.
„ 3   John Burroughs, mercer, s. of John Burroughs of Chester, alderman, defunct, and p. of John Kynaston of Chester, alderman.
„ 3   John Thomason of Middlewich, co. Ches., s. of William Thomason of Chester, baker, defunct.

Feb.	13	Ralph s. of Thomas Brown of Chester, yeoman, and p. of Francis Touchet of Chester, apothecary.
,,	24	John s. of John Kelley of Chester, musician, defunct, and p. of Thomas Holliwell of Chester, tailor.
May	15	Arthur s. of Arthur Becket of Soond, co. Ches., and p. of John Shand of Chester, apothecary.
June	5	Henry Pemberton, citizen and apothecary of London, and s. of Henry Pemberton of Chester, baker.
,,	5	John Pemberton, ropier, s. of Henry Pemberton, baker.
,,	21	Thomas s. of Richard Reece of Chester, linen-draper, defunct.
July	12	Thomas s. of William Helley of Upton, co. Ches., yeoman, and p. of Theodore Aldcroft of Chester, merchant, defunct.
,,	22	Randle Holme the younger, herald painter, s. of Randle Holme of Chester, herald painter.
July	10	Hugh s. of —— Colley, clerk, and p. of Henry Bennet of Chester, merchant.
,,	24	William s. of —— Knot of Chester, ——, and p. of Alban Gray of Chester, bricklayer.
Aug.	7	William s. of William Rothwell of Chester, cordwainer, and p. of John Rothwell of Chester, lastmaker.
,,	28	*Peter Weston, esquire.
Sep.	25	Owen Hughes, barber, s. of Owen Hughes of Chester, linen-draper, and p. of Thomas Holland of Chester, barber-chirurgeon.
Oct.	4	Charles s. of Richard Hiccock of Chester, innholder, defunct, and p. of William Poynton of Chester, ironmonger.
—		William Woods the younger, mason, s. of William Woods of Chester, mason.
,,	6	John s. of John Davyes of Chester, slater, defunct, and p. of Richard Parsons, mariner.
,,	6	Moses s. of Randle Bingley of Chester, baker, and p. of John Catherall of Chester, barber-chirurgeon.
,,	9	Charles s. of George Bird of Broxton, co. Chester, gentleman, and p. of Thomas Robinson of Chester, goldsmith.
,,	9	Evan s. of Evan Bythell of Lloynegrine, co. Flint, defunct, and p. of Edward Partington of Chester, mercer.
,,	9	Thomas Taylor p. of Thomas Taylor of Chester, barber-chirurgeon, defunct.
,,	9	John s. of Lawrence Browne of Chester, yeoman, and p. of Samuel Jennings of Chester, joiner.

[1696–7]   THE CITY OF CHESTER

Oct. 12 Randle Oulton, brewer, s. of Randle Oulton of Chester, alderman, defunct.
„ 12 Richard s. and p. of Thomas Ward of Chester, silkweaver.
„ 12 Thomas s. and p. of Thomas Bridge of Chester, feltmaker.
„ 12 Charles s. and p. of Charles Boswell of Chester, pavier,
„ 12 Thomas Litler p. of Richard Blease of Chester, shoemaker.
„ 12 *Thomas Birkenhead, gentleman.
„ 12 *Thomas Holmark.
„ 13 John s. of John Johnson of Chester, innholder, defunct.
„ 13 Joseph s. of Joseph Maddock, "portator," and p. of Henry Pemberton of Chester, ropier.
„ 13 Thomas Barton, silkweaver, s. of Thomas Barton of Chester, silkweaver.
„ 13 Ralph Leigh the younger, skinner, s. of Ralph Leigh of Chester, skinner, defunct.
„ 14 Edward Bennet, ironmonger, s. of William Bennet of Chester, ironmonger, defunct.
„ 14 Thomas Brock, pewterer, s. of Philip Brock of Chester, pewterer.
„ 14 Richard Swift, gentleman, s. of Isaac Swift of Chester, merchant, defunct.
„ 14 John Rogers, mason, s. of Thomas Rogers of Chester, mason.
„ 14 Edward s. of Edward Williams of Chester, feltmaker, defunct.
„ 14 John s. of Peter Nichols of Chester, mason.
„ 14 Charles Conway, silkweaver, s. of Hugh Conway of Chester, silkweaver.
„ 14 Edward Starkey, brewer, s. of Edward Starkey of Chester, brewer.
„ 14 John Chapman p. of Richard Shone of Chester, chandler.
„ 14 Henry Burroughs, feltmaker, s. of Richard Burroughs of Chester, feltmaker, defunct.
„ 14 James Wright, ironmonger, s. of Thomas Wright of Chester, ironmonger, defunct.
„ 14 Robert Cotgreave, baker, s. of John Cotgreave of Chester, baker.
„ 14 John s. of Joseph Pritchard of Chester, blacksmith, defunct.
„ 14 William s. of Joshua Taylor of Chester, shoemaker.
„ 14 Robert s. of Randle Handley of Chester, baker, defunct.

Oct.	14	Richard s. of Thomas Ormes of Chester, pipemaker.
,,	14	William s. of William Martyn of Chester, barber-chirurgeon, defunct.
,,	14	Ralph Sudlow, apothecary, s. of John Sudlow of Chester, apothecary, defunct.
—		John s. of Thomas Walley of Chester, feltmaker.
,,	14	John Rowland p. of Edward Walmesley of Chester, slater.
,,	14	Joseph Kelsall p. of William Croughton of Chester, shoemaker, defunct.
,,	14	William Kelsall p. of Thomas Orms of Chester, tobacconist.
,,	14	John s. of Edward Litherland of Chester, tailor.
,,	14	John Sharp p. of William Maddock of Chester, bricklayer.
,,	14	Joseph s. of John Harrison of Chester, tailor, defunct.
,,	14	David Davyes p. of Richard Plumb of Chester, vintner, defunct.
,,	14	William s. of Richard Jones of Chester, clothier.
,,	14	John s. of John Fearnall of Chester, button-maker.
,,	14	John s. of George Palin of Chester, shoemaker, defunct.
,,	14	William s. of William Wilson of Chester, cordwainer, defunct.
,,	14	Richard s. of Edward Thompson of Chester, pipemaker.
,,	14	Thomas s. of Thomas Wakefeld of Chester, plasterer.
,,	14	Hugh s. of Thomas Davenport of Chester, barber-chirurgeon, defunct.
,,	14	Daniel s. of Daniel Woods of Chester, plasterer.
,,	14	William s. of William Johnson of Chester, cordwainer.
,,	14	Thomas Skellern p. of Thomas Stoppord of Chester, tobacco-cutter.
,,	14	Richard Parrat p. of John Holland of Chester, draper.
,,	14	Edward Hincks, linen-draper, s. of Joseph Hincks, late of Chester, silkweaver.
,,	14	Edward Hallwood, glover, s. of Thomas Hallwood of Chester, glover, defunct.
,,	14	Richard Wettenhall p. of William Woods of Chester, mason.
,,	14	Uriah Woodfin, slater, s. of William Woodfin of Chester, slater.
,,	14	John s. of William Johnson of Chester, smith, defunct.
,,	14	Joseph Bennet the younger, baker,⎫
,,	14	William Bennet ⎬ ss. of Joseph Bennet of Chester, baker.
,,	14	John Bennet ⎭

Oct.	14	Samuel Davyes p. of Thomas Davyes of Chester, carver.
,,	14	Benjamin s. of Randle Thomason of Chester, cordwainer, defunct.
,,	14	Humphrey s. of William Caddock of Chester, feltmaker.
,,	14	William Wettenhall p. of Jonathan Goldson of Chester, feltmaker.
,,	14	Richard s. of William Hind of Chester, cooper.
,,	14	George s. of David Mason of Chester, cordwainer, defunct.
,,	14	William s. of William Hughes of Chester, bricklayer, defunct.
,,	14	Thomas s. of Thomas Cowdock of Chester, slater, defunct.
,,	14	Thomas s. of Thomas Pemberton of Chester, cordwainer, defunct.
,,	14	George s. of George Vause of Chester, barber.
,,	14	Joseph Lightfoot p. of Thomas Fox, late of Chester, and now of Hawarden, baker.
,,	14	Thomas s. of John Davyes of Chester, clothworker.
,,	14	William s. of George Harvey of Chester, bricklayer.
,,	14	Charles s. of Reginald Woods of Chester, smith, defunct.
,,	14	George Mainwaring p. of John Johnson of Chester, cordwainer.
,,	14	John s. of Thomas Bruen of Chester, linen-draper, defunct.
,,	14	Charles Woods, baker, s. of William Woods of Chester, mason.
,,	14	Richard s. of John Maddock of Chester, tanner, defunct.
,,	14	Peter Stringer the younger, gentleman, s. of Peter Stringer of Chester, linen-draper.
,,	14	John Sproston, cooper, s. of John Sproston of Chester, castor-maker, defunct.
,,	14	Joseph s. of William Harrison of Chester, cooper.
,,	14	Thomas Sherrard p. of Jonathan Wrenchall, joiner.
,,	14	Lawrence Griffith p. of Thomas Deane of Chester, cordwainer.
,,	14	William s. of William Harrison of Chester, cooper.
,,	14	George Smith p. of Samuel Smith of Chester, cooper.
,,	14	John s. of Thomas Bennion of Chester, feltmaker, defunct.
,,	14	James Key p. of John Hallwood of Chester, slater, defunct.

Oct.	14	John Davyes, cordwainer, s. of Richard Davyes of Chester, feltmaker, defunct.
,,	14	William Dob p. of Henry Yates of Chester, slater.
,,	14	Nathaniel s. of William Harrison of Chester, cooper.
,,	14	Robert s. of Robert Williamson of Chester, linen-draper, defunct.
,,	14	Henry Haythorn p. of John Hunt of Chester, cordwainer, defunct.
,,	14	Gilbert s. of John Hough of Chester, ironmonger.
,,	14	Henry Milner p. of Samuel Walmsley of Chester, slater.
,,	14	Francis s. of Ralph Bulkley of Chester, tailor, defunct.
,,	14	Thomas Stubs, slater, s. of Richard Stubs of Chester, tanner, defunct.
,,	14	John s. of Samuel Venables, and p. of William Ireland of Chester, cordwainer.
,,	14	John Allenson the younger, ironmonger, s. of John Allenson of Chester, ironmonger.
,,	15	John Starkey, barber-chirurgeon, s. of Hugh Starkey of Chester, alderman.
,,	15	John Skellern, ironmonger, s. of Francis Skellern of Chester, alderman.
,,	15	Edward Davyes p. of Thomas Bavand of Chester, tanner.
,,	15	John Usher p. of Bradford Throp of Chester, shoemaker.
,,	15	John Bolland, brewer, s. of Thomas Bolland of Chester, brewer.
,,	15	Peter Plat, bricklayer, s. of Peter Plat of Chester, bricklayer.
,,	15	Richard s. of Joseph Denson of Chester, baker, defunct.
,,	15	William s. of William Johnson of Chester, smith, defunct.
,,	15	Richard s. of Thomas Yates of Chester, bricklayer.
,,	15	Mathias s. of Mathias Heyes of Chester, cordwainer, defunct.
,,	15	Thomas s. of Edward Thompson of Chester, papermaker.
,,	15	John Stot p. of John Tilston of Chester, smith, defunct.
,,	15	Thomas s. of John Fearnall of Chester, dyer, defunct.
,,	15	Thomas s. of John Tilston of Chester, smith, defunct.
,,	15	John s. of John Kelley of Chester, " portator."
,,	15	Evan s. of John Fearnall of Chester, dyer, defunct.
,,	15	John s. of George Mainwaring of Chester, alderman, defunct.

Oct.	15	John Hickson, tailor, s. of William Hickson of Chester, tailor.
,,	15	Thomas s. of John Coulson of Chester, plasterer.
,,	15	William s. of William Mores of Chester, cooper.

1697-8 [9-10 W. iii.] WILLIAM ALLEN, Esquire, Mayor.

Nov. 27		Owen s. of Edward Burroughs of Chester, barber-chirurgeon, defunct.
Dec. 10		John Parker, mercer, s. of John Parker of Chester, mercer.
,,	10	Maurice Briscoe, smith, s. of William Briscoe of Chester, blacksmith.
Jan.	5	Thomas s. of Thomas Urian of Stoke, co. Ches., defunct, and p. of Ellis Lewis, draper.
,,	6	Robert s. of Owen Ellis of Chester, mercer, defunct.
,,	11	Joseph s. of John Hatton, of Charlton, co. Ches., yeoman, defunct, and p. of John Bingley, chandler.
Feb.	7	Jonathan Bostock p. of William Crue of Chester, ironmonger.
,,	19	*John Poughtin [alias Poughin, M.B.], musician.
,,	26	*Robert Piggott, gentleman.
Mar. 12		John s. of Samuel Revington of Chester, feltmaker, and p. of John Jones of Chester, tailor.
,,	24	Griffith Malbone, smith, s. of John Malbone of Chester, smith.
,,	25	Joseph s. of Robert Philpott of Chester, mariner, defunct, and p. of Charles Croughton of Chester, silkweaver.
Apr.	9	John s. of John Dutton of Frodsham, co. Ches., yeoman, defunct, and p. of William Gaulter of Chester, joiner.
,,	16	John s. of William Owlerhead of Foulk Stapleford, co. Chester, yeoman, and p. of Jabez Bathoe of Chester, tanner.
,,	25	Randle Moyle p. of Owen Ellis of Chester, mercer.
May 21		John s. of Samuel Williams of Handbridge, labourer, and p. of Thomas Leigh of Chester, baker.
June 23		John s. of John Davies of Chester, brewer, and p. of Daniel Crosse, joiner.
,,	25	John s. of Edward Daxon of Coddington, co. Ches., clerk, and p. of Robert Carrington, apothecary.
,,	25	William s. of James Alcock of Chester, tailor, defunct, and p. of his brother, James Alcock, tailor, defunct.
. July	9	John s. of Richard Tudor of Chester, innholder.

July 12 Charles Malbone, gunsmith, s. of John Malbone of Chester, gunsmith, defunct.
„ 14 Thomas Goulborn, apothecary, s. of John Goulborn of Chester, alderman, defunct.
„ 18 Joseph Bennet p. of John Catherall of Chester, barber-chirurgeon.
„ 23 Edward s. of Edward Burrowes of Chester, barber-chirurgeon, defunct.
„ 25 William Ince, gentleman, s. of Robert Ince of Dublin, and late of Chester, haberdasher.
„ 28 *Francis Gell, esquire.
Aug. 6 Joseph s. of John Rylands of Parkgate, co. Ches., carpenter, and p. of Thomas Davyes, carver.
„ 20 *Thomas Haughton, gentleman.
Sep. 3 *Thomas Bowers, gentleman.
„ 3 Richard Wright, gentleman, s. of Thomas Wright of Chester, ironmonger, defunct.
„ 3 *David Griffith, inkhorn-turner.
Oct. 8 *Ellis Hughes, brazier and pewterer.
„ 8 Joseph Soreton, skinner, s. of Thomas Soreton of "Hunpsterston," co. Ches., gentleman, and p. of Randle Aston of Chester, glover.
„ 10 William Ireland, cordwainer, } ss. of William Ireland of
„ 10 Francis Ireland, cordwainer, } Chester, cordwainer.
„ 12 *Lawrence Swarbreck, mariner.
„ 12 Thomas Prince p. of John Bradshaw of Chester, innholder.
„ 12 Richard White p. of Joseph Brotherstone of Chester, butcher, defunct.
„ 13 William Allen, merchant, s. of William Allen, esquire, mayor of the city.
„ 13 Samuel s. of Edward Davies, late of Wrexham, co. Denbigh, mercer, and p. of Thomas Bowker of Chester, ironmonger.
„ 13 Samuel Maddock, baker, s. of Samuel Maddock of Chester, baker.
„ 13 Richard s. of John Holliwell, late of Chester, baker.
„ 13 Randle s. of John Bingley of Chester, chandler, and p. of Abner Scoles of Chester, upholsterer.
„ 13 John s. of John Bingley of Chester, chandler, and p. of Timothy Gardner of Chester, goldsmith.
„ 13 St John Jones p. of Edward Partington of Chester, mercer.
„ 13 William Fernihaugh p. of Evan Jones of Chester, haberdasher.
„ 13 Thomas s. of Adam Kemp of Chester, baker, and p. of John Bingley of Chester, chandler.

Oct. 13   Thomas Bedson p. of Thomas Deane of Chester, cordwainer.
„   13   Thomas s. of Thomas Morris of Chester, smith.

1698–9 [10–11 W. iii.]. HENRY BENNET, Esquire, Mayor.

Nov. 12   John s. of William Brock of Chester, esquire and mercer, and p. of William Cokayn of Chester, ironmonger.
Dec. 8   John Thomason, brewer, s. of John Thomason of Chester, brewer.
Jan. 23   William Moyle, merchant, p. of Michael Johnson of Chester, alderman.
Feb. 9   Humphrey Collinge p. of Richard Taylor of Chester, glasier.
„   18   Robert s. of Ottiwell Shawcrosse of Chester, tailor, and p. of Isaac Warmingham of Chester, tailor.
„   18   John Mathews p. of Adam Kemp of Chester, baker.
Mar. 4   Thomas s. of Robert Higginson of Chester, innholder, defunct.
„   6   Jonathan s. of Jonathan Pickering of Mickle Trafford, co. Ches., husbandman, and p. of Thomas Whitaffe of Chester, carpenter.
„   31   Edward s. of Edward Twanbrook, late of Wallbank juxta Daresbury, co. Ches., gentleman, and p. of William Ingham of Chester, cabinetmaker.
Apr. 1   *Joseph Eaton, vintner.
„   1   *William Lammas, mariner.
„   1   *William Sharman, cabinetmaker.
„   1   *Samuel s. of Richard Dyason of Chester, tanner.
„   8   George s. of John Smith of Chester, baker, defunct, and p. of Richard Totty of Chester, joiner.
„   29   Thomas s. of John Walley of Chester, ironmonger.
June 17   Richard Oulton, haberdasher, s. of Edward Oulton of Chester, alderman, defunct.
Aug. 14   Richard Ashton, periwig-maker, s. of Richard Ashton of Chester, innholder, defunct.
Sep. 12   Thomas s. of Charles Croughton of Chester, silkweaver, and p. of Robert Radford, linen-draper.
Oct. 17   William Dicas p. of Peter Venables of Chester, glover.
„   12   Simon Lloyd p. of Lewis Parry of Chester, ironmonger.
„   12   Edward Ellis p. of Edward Butler of Chester, ironmonger.
„   13   *Samuel Hughson, gentleman.
„   13   *Richard Worger, mariner.

Oct. 13 *Thomas Maddock, mariner.
„ 13 *John Cappur.
„ 13 William Prince p. of Thomas Bromley of Chester, saddler, defunct.
„ 13 Jonathan Dutton p. of Ephraim Bardsley of Chester, baker.

1699–1700 [11–12 W. iii.]. WILLIAM BENNET, Esquire, Mayor.

Nov. 4 *Robert Brerewood, gentleman.
„ 4 *John Lloyd, esquire.
„ 4 *James Cropper, mariner.
„ 4 Edward Johnson, merchant, p. of Michael Johnson of Chester, alderman.
„ 4 Joseph Dannald, barber, s. of Christopher Dannald of Chester, baker, defunct.
Dec. 23 Thomas Dannald, baker, s. of Thomas Dannald of Chester, baker, defunct.
Jan. 6 Thomas Hammond p. of James Gilbert of Chester, chandler, defunct.
Feb. 2 Joseph s. and p. of John Meredith of Chester, mason, defunct.
„ 5 Hugh s. of Hugh Wooley of Mickle Trafford, co. Ches., yeoman, and p. of Thomas Cottingham of Chester, barber.
„ 5 Nathaniel s. of John Kelsey of Pickton, defunct, and p. of Peter Taylor of Chester, baker.
„ 8 Peter s. of Mary Gerrard of Tarvin, co. Ches., widow, and p. of Robert Spark of Chester, linen-draper.
„ 10 John s. of John Whawell, labourer, and p. of Randle Handley of Chester, baker.
Mar. 23 Nathaniel s. and p. of Henry Hall of Chester, ——.
„ 23 Thomas s. of John Hiccock of Chester, baker, defunct, and p. of Edward Croughton of Chester, tanner.
„ 23 Edward s. of Joseph Wright and p. of Ralph Davyes of Chester, baker.
Apr. 5 Peter s. of T—— Parry of Hope, co. Flint, yeoman, and p. of Thomas Bridge of Chester, feltmaker.
„ 3 Samuel s. of —— Hill of Warrington, co. Lanc., and p. of —— Batho, tanner, defunct.
„ 27 Richard Townsend p. of Alban Gray of Chester.
„ 27 John s. of John Shone of Chester, husbandman, and p. of Edward Calley, weaver.
„ 29 *Charles s. of Charles Hurleston of Newton, co. Ches., esquire.

May 25		*Daniel Pickance, mariner.
June	1	Lancaster s. of Thomas Roughley of Sutton, co. Lanc., gentleman, and p. of Joseph Basnet of Chester, ironmonger, defunct.
„	14	John Bruen p. of Gilbert Eaton of Chester, baker, defunct.
Sep.	19	Thomas s. of William Hale of Chester, butcher, defunct, and p. of William Hale of Chester, butcher.
„	21	*John Newton, yeoman.
Oct.	6	Edward Bulkley, smith, — of Joseph Bulkley of Chester, smith.
„	6	John Totty s. of Edw—— —— of Greenfield, co. Flint, yeoman, and p. of the said Jo—— Bulkley.
„	7	Gerrard Townsend, merchant, s. of Robert Townsend of Chester, defunct.

THE RECORD SOCIETY

FOR THE

PUBLICATION OF ORIGINAL DOCUMENTS

RELATING TO

LANCASHIRE AND CHESHIRE

COUNCIL, 1905-6

Sir GEORGE J. ARMYTAGE, Bart., F.S.A., Kirklees Park, Brighouse, *President*.

G. E. COKAYNE, M.A., F.S.A., Clarenceux King of Arms, Heralds' College, London, E.C., *Vice-President*.

Lieut.-Col. HENRY FISHWICK, F.S.A., The Heights, Rochdale, *Vice-President*.

JOHN PAUL RYLANDS, F.S.A., 2 Charlesville, Birkenhead, *Vice-President*.

HENRY BRIERLEY, Mab's Cross, Wigan.

THOMAS H. DAVIES-COLLEY, M.A., Newbold, near Chester.

WILLIAM FARRER, Hall Garth, Carnforth.

Colonel PARKER, Browsholme, Clitheroe.

R. D. RADCLIFFE, M.A., F.S.A., Old Swan, Liverpool.

The Rev. Canon STANNING, M.A., The Vicarage, Leigh, Lancashire.

CHARLES W. SUTTON, M.A., Free Reference Library, Manchester.

WM. ASHETON TONGE, Staneclyffe, Disley.

HONORARY TREASURER

JOHN PAUL RYLANDS, F.S.A., 2 Charlesville, Birkenhead.

HONORARY SECRETARY

WM. FERGUSSON IRVINE, F.S.A., 56 Park Road South, Birkenhead.

RULES

1. That the Society shall be called the RECORD SOCIETY, and shall have for its object the transcribing and publishing of Original Documents relating to the Counties of Lancaster and Chester.

2. That the affairs of the Society shall be governed by a Council consisting of a President and twelve Members, the former of whom shall be *annually* elected by the Council.

3. That three Members of the Council shall form a quorum.

4. That the subscription of Members of the Society shall be £1, 1s. per annum, which shall entitle them to the publications for the year; but any Member whose subscription shall be two years in arrear shall thereupon be removed from the Society, and shall not be re-admitted until all arrears have been paid. The number of Members is limited to 350.

5. That the subscriptions shall be due in advance on the 30th of June in each year, and that no work shall be issued to any Member whose subscription is in arrear.

6. That an Annual Meeting of the Society shall be held in the month of October, of which due notice shall be sent to all the Members. At this meeting a Report of the work of the Society, with a Statement of the Income and Expenditure, shall be presented. These shall be annually published, together with a List of Members and the Rules of the Society.

7. That so long as the funds of the Society permit, two volumes at least shall be issued to the Members in each year.

8. That no copies of the publications of the Society shall be sold to non-members, except at an increased price to be fixed by the Council.

9. That no payment shall be made to any person for editing any work for the Society, but that the Editor of each Volume shall be entitled to twenty copies of the work so edited by him.

10. That the Treasurer's Accounts shall be audited by two Members of the Society, who shall be elected at the Annual Meeting.

11. No alteration shall be made in any of the above Rules except at the Annual General Meeting. Notice of any proposed alterations must be sent to the Hon. Secretary a month before such General Meeting.

12. That a meeting of the Council of the Society shall be called by the Hon. Secretary at least once in every three months.

The Annual Subscription of £1, 1s., entitling the Members to all the Volumes issued for that year, may be paid to the Hon. Treasurer, or to the credit of the Society at their Bankers, the Manchester and Liverpool District Banking Company, Limited, at any of their branches.

RECORD SOCIETY—LANCASHIRE AND CHESHIRE

REPORT FOR THE YEAR 1904-5

Read at the Annual Meeting held in the Audit Room of Chetham's Hospital, Manchester, 24th October 1905.

SINCE the Annual Meeting, held on the 24th October 1904, two volumes have been issued to the Members. The first of these, Volume 49, is in continuation of Volume 47, being Part II. of the Lancashire Assize Rolls, including the two Rolls of Assize for the years 1284 and 1285. To these have been added two Appendices. The first is a schedule of Lancashire Assizes for which special Justices had been assigned, extracted from the Patent Rolls 1-57 Henry III.; the second includes the fines and amercements before the Justices in Eyre in Lancashire recorded on the Pipe Rolls of Henry III., and the third is a schedule of the Assize Rolls for Lancashire. This volume was edited by Colonel Parker, to whom the Society is also indebted for a present of the transcript of the volume.

The second volume issued to Members during the year is a collection of the Final Concords for Lancashire from 1377 to 1509. This makes the third volume of Fines edited by Mr. William Farrer. The transcripts are also a gift from the Editor.

The Council wish again to record their appreciation of the generosity of both Colonel Parker and Mr. Farrer in presenting these valuable transcripts.

For the current year there are two volumes already in the press. The first is a Miscellaneous volume, which will include (*a*) an Index to the Wills relating to Lancashire and Cheshire for the period 1595–1665, recently found at the Probate Registry at Chester, (*b*) an Index to the Wills and Inventories remaining in the Bishop's Registry at Chester, 1701–1800, and (*c*) the Hearth Tax Returns for a portion of the County of Chester for the year 1663. The second volume, now in the press, is the first part of the Rolls of Admission to the Freedom of the City of Chester (1392–1805). It is hoped that this volume will include all the entries down to the year 1700, leaving the eighteenth century to be dealt with in a subsequent volume. As stated in the last Annual Report, the Society is indebted to Mr. J. H. E. Bennett of Chester for the present of this transcript, which he has collated where possible with the original entries in the Mayor's Books.

Mr. Farrer has also very kindly offered a further volume of Fines or a second volume of Lancashire Inquests and Feudal Aids, and it is hoped that one of these will be put in hand immediately. It is not necessary to repeat again this year the large list of documents ready for the printers as soon as funds permit.

A few sets of the Society's *Proceedings* are still on hand. Members can obtain the price of sets or of single volumes by applying to the Honorary Secretary.

The following is a complete list of the Society's publications already printed up to the present time:—

1878–79.
I. Commonwealth Church Survey.
II. Index to the Wills at Chester, 1545 to 1620.

1879–80.
III. Lancashire Inquisitions. Stuart Period. Part I. 1603 to 1613.

1880–81.
IV. Index to the Wills at Chester, 1621 to 1650.
V. The Register of Prestbury, co. Chester, 1560 to 1636.

1881–82.
VI. Cheshire and Lancashire Funeral Certificates. 1600 to 1678.
VII. Lancashire and Cheshire Records. Part I.

1882–83. VIII. Lancashire and Cheshire Records. Part II.

1883–84.
IX. Preston Guild Rolls, 1397 to 1682.
X. Index to the Lancashire Wills proved at Richmond, 1457 to 1680.

1884–85.
XI. Exchequer Depositions, 1558 to 1702.
XII. Miscellanies, Lancashire and Cheshire. Vol. I.

REPORT OF THE SOCIETY

1885–86.
- XIII. Index to the Lancashire Wills proved at Richmond, 1680 to 1748.
- XIV. Annales Cestrienses.

1886–87.
- XV. Index to the Wills at Chester, 1660–1680.
- XVI. Lancashire Inquisitions. Stuart Period. Part II. 1614 to 1622.

1887–88.
- XVII. Lancashire Inquisitions. Stuart Period. Part III. 1622 to 1625.
- XVIII. Index to the Wills at Chester, 1681 to 1700.

1888–89.
- XIX. Civil War in Cheshire.
- XX. Index to the Wills at Chester, 1701 to 1720.

1889–90.
- XXI. The Register of Leyland, co. Lancaster. 1653 to 1715.
- XXII. Index to the Wills at Chester, 1721 to 1740.

1890–91.
- XXIII. Index to the Lancashire Wills proved at Richmond, 1748 to 1792.
- XXIV. The Royalist Composition Papers relating to Lancashire. Vol. I. A and B.

1891–92.
- XXV. Index to the Wills at Chester, 1741 to 1760.
- XXVI. The Royalist Composition Papers relating to Lancashire. Vol. II. C to F.

1892–93.
- XXVII. Lancashire Lay Subsidies, Henry III. to Edward I.
- XXVIII. Plundered Minister's Accounts, Lancashire and Cheshire. Part I. 1643–1654.

1893–94.
- XXIX. The Royalist Composition Papers relating to Lancashire. Vol. III. G and H.

1894–95.
- XXX. A Collection of Lancashire and Cheshire Wills.
- XXXI. Miscellanies, Lancashire and Cheshire. Vol. II.

1895–96.
- XXXII. Pleadings and Depositions in the Duchy Court of Lancaster. Part I.
- XXXIII. Miscellanies, Lancashire and Cheshire. Vol. III.

1896–97.
- XXXIV. Plundered Minister's Accounts, Lancashire and Cheshire. Part II. 1654–1660.
- XXXV. Pleadings and Depositions in the Duchy Court of Lancaster. Part II.

1897–98.
- XXXVI. The Royalist Composition Papers relating to Lancashire. Vol. IV. I to O.
- XXXVII. Index to the Wills at Chester, 1761 to 1780. A to M.

1898–99.	XXXVIII. Index to the Wills at Chester, 1761 to 1780. N to Z.
	XXXIX. Lancashire Final Concords. Part I. 1196 to 1307.
1899–1900.	XL. Pleadings and Depositions in the Duchy Court of Lancaster. Part III.
	XLI. Lancashire Court Rolls, 1323–1324.
1900–01.	XLII. Manchester Quarter Sessions Records. Part I.
	XLIII. Miscellanies, Lancashire and Cheshire. Vol. IV.
1901–02.	XLIV. Index to the Wills at Chester, 1781–1790.
	XLV. Index to the Wills at Chester, 1791–1800.
1902–03.	XLVI. Lancashire Final Concords. Part II. 1308 to 1377.
	XLVII. Lancashire Assize Rolls. Part I. 1202–1281.
1903–04.	XLVIII. Lancashire Inquests, Extents, &c. Part I. 1205–1307.
1904–05.	XLIX. Lancashire Assize Rolls. Part II. 1284–1285.
	L. Lancashire Final Concords. Part III. 1377–1509.

☞ The Council must again refer to Rule 5, under which no volume can be delivered to any Member whose Subscription is in arrear.

THE RECORD SOCIETY—LANCASHIRE AND CHESHIRE

Receipts and Expenditure from 1st July 1904 to 30th June 1905.

Dr.

	£	s.	d.
Balance (Bank-book) 30th June 1904	244	18	1
Subscriptions paid, July to December 1904	133	7	0
Subscriptions paid, January to June 1905	27	6	0
Books sold	1	15	0
Bank Interest	3	3	2
	£410	**9**	**3**

Cr.

				£	s.	d.
TRANSCRIPTS, &c.—						
Miss Walford, Visitation of Cheshire	£5	0	0			
Mr. Price, Index to Wills at the Bishop's Registry, 1701–1800	5	0	0			
Mr. Gamon, Marriage Licence Act Books, Vols. 1, 2, 3	30	0	0	40	0	0
PRINTING—						
W. Pollard & Co. Limited, Vol. 47	£60	14	2			
W. Barton & Co, Reports, 1904-5	4	10	0			
,, ,, Circulars	0	12	0	65	16	2
SUNDRIES—						
Mr. Mason, Rent of Stock-rooms, Dec. 1903 to Dec. 1904	£8	10	0			
Mr. Mason, taking care of Stock of Books, &c.	2	2	0			
Mr. Mason, Carriage, Brown paper, Packing, &c.	2	18	3			
Alliance Insurance Co., Fire Insurance of Stock of Books	0	12	0			
Hon. Treasurer and Hon. Secretary, Incidentals	20	0	0			
Bank Commission	0	10	7	34	12	10
Balance (Bank-book) 30th June 1905				270	0	3
				£410	**9**	**3**

Examined and found correct.
(Signed) R. D. RADCLIFFE, } Auditors.
         WILLIAM E. GREGSON,

(Signed)   J. PAUL RYLANDS,
                 Hon. Treasurer.

22nd July 1905.

LIST OF MEMBERS

Corrected to 26th October 1905.

AMHERST OF HACKNEY, The Lord, Didlington Hall, Brandon, Norfolk.
Antiquaries, The Society of, Burlington House, London, W.
Armytage, Sir George J., Bart., F.S.A., Kirklees Park, Brighouse.
Ashton, T. Gair, 36 Charlotte Street, Manchester.
Aspinall, Colonel R. J., Standen Hall, Clitheroe.
Assheton, Ralph, Downham Hall, Clitheroe.
Athill, Charles H., Richmond Herald, Heralds' College, London, E.C.

BAILEY, Sir W. H., Sale Hall, Cheshire.
Beazley, F. C., Fern Hill, Oxton, Birkenhead.
Bennett, John H. E., 66 Cambrian Crescent, Chester.
Bispham, William, 12 West 18th Street, New York.
Bostock, R. C., Beddgelert, Grove Road, Ramsgate.
Bramwell, W. H., Bow, Durham.
Brierley, Henry, Mab's Cross, Wigan.
Bromley, James, The Homestead, Lathom, Ormskirk.
Brooke, Sir Thomas, Bart., F.S.A., Armitage Bridge, Huddersfield.
Burke, H. Farnham, C.V.O., Somerset Herald, Heralds' College, London, E.C.

CARINGTON, H. H. Smith, Grangethorpe, Rusholme, Manchester.
Chippindall, Colonel W. H., 12 Oaklands Road, Bedford.
Chorlton, Thomas, 32 Brazenose Street, Manchester.
Cokayne, G. E., M.A., F.S.A., Clarenceux King of Arms, Heralds' College, London, E.C.
Crofton, H. T., Oldfield, Maidenhead, Berks.
Crompton, John, High Crompton, Oldham.
Cross, The Viscount, G.C.B., Eccle Riggs, Broughton-in-Furness.
Cross, James, Shirdley Hill, Ormskirk.
Crossley, E. W., Dean House, Triangle, Halifax.
Cunliffe, Walter F., 13 Arundel Gardens, Notting Hill, London, W.

DAMES, R. S. Longworth, 21 Herbert Street, Dublin.
Davenport, The Rev. G. H., M.A., Foxley, Hereford.

LIST OF MEMBERS

Davies-Colley, Thomas H., M.A., Newbold, near Chester.
Derby, The Earl of, K.G., G.C.B., Knowsley, Prescot.
De Trafford, Sir F. Humphrey, Bart., Hill Crest, Market Harborough.
Dixon, Colonel George, Astle Hall, Chelford, Cheshire.

EARLE, T. Algernon, 90 King Street, Manchester.
Edge, Sir John, Waverley Court, Camberley, Surrey.
Ellis, T. Ratcliffe, 18 King Street, Wigan.

FFARINGTON, Lieut.-Colonel, R.A., Mariebonne, Wigan.
Farrer, William, Hall Garth, Carnforth.
Fishwick, Lieut.-Col., F.S.A., The Heights, Rochdale.
Fletcher, J. S., Merlewood, Virginia Water, Surrey.
Frost, F. A., Grappenhall Hall, Warrington.

GLADSTONE, Robt., Jun., B.C.L., Woolton Vale, Liverpool.
Greenwood, W., Beaumaris, Spring Grove, Isleworth.
Gregson, W. E., 43 Moor Lane, Great Crosby, Liverpool.

HANKINSON, G. H., Woodlands Park, Altrincham.
Hargreaves, John, Ravenswood, Rock Ferry, Birkenhead.
Harrison, Commander M. J., R.N., King's Nympton Park, Chulmleigh, N. Devon.
Harrison, Henry, 16 The Grove, Wandsworth Common, London, S.W.
Healey, C. E. H., Chadwyck, 7 New Square, Lincoln's Inn, London.
Heape, Charles, Hartley, High Lane, Stockport.
Holland, Walter, Carnatic Hall, Mossley Hill, Liverpool.
Hovenden, R., F.S.A., Park Hill Road, Croydon, Surrey.
Hughes, H. R., Kinmel Park, Abergele.

IRVINE, Wm. Fergusson, F.S.A., 56 Park Road South, Birkenhead.

KELSALL, John, Hinxton House, East Sheen, London, S.W.

LEES, Samuel, Park Bridge, Ashton-under-Lyne.
Lever, W. H., Thornton Manor, Thornton Hough, Cheshire.
Library, Free Public, Accrington.
    ,,   Free Public, Ashton-under-Lyne.
    ,,   Free, Barrow-in-Furness.
    ,,   Free, Birkenhead.
    ,,   Central Free, Birmingham.
    ,,   Free Public, Blackburn.
    ,,   Public, Bolton-le-Moors.
    ,,   British Museum, care of Dulau & Co., 37 Soho Square, London, W.

Library, University, Cambridge.
,, Free Public, Chester.
,, Chapter, Chester.
,, Chester and North Wales Archæological Society, Grosvenor Museum, Chester.
,, Free Public, Chorley.
,, Free, Edinburgh.
,, Free Public, Heywood, Lancashire.
,, Leyland, Hindley, near Wigan.
,, The Storey Institute, Lancaster.
,, Public, Leeds.
,, Free, Leigh, Lancashire.
,, Historic Society of Lancashire and Cheshire, Royal Institution, Liverpool.
,, Athenæum, Liverpool.
,, Free Public, Liverpool.
,, College of Arms, London, E.C.
,, Guildhall, London.
,, Inner Temple, London.
,, Lincoln's Inn, London.
,, St. George's, Hanover Square, Buckingham Palace Road, London.
,, Sion College, Victoria Embankment, London, E.C.
,, Public Record Office, care of Eyre & Spottiswoode, 5 Middle New Street, London, E.C.
,, Chetham, Manchester.
,, Free Public, Manchester, C. W. Sutton, M.A., Chief Librarian.
,, Public, Moss Side, Manchester.
,, John Rylands, Manchester.
,, Lancashire College, Whalley Range, Manchester.
,, Cathedral, Manchester.
,, Incorporated Law Library Society, Kennedy Street, Manchester.
,, Owens College, Manchester.
,, Portico, Manchester.
,, Free, Nottingham.
,, Bodleian, Oxford.
,, Dr. Shepherd's, Preston.
,, Free Public, Rochdale.
,, Royal Free, Peel Park, Salford.
,, Central Free, Sheffield.
,, Free, Southport.
,, Free Public, St. Helens.
,, Museum and, Warrington.
,, Free, Wigan.
,, Melbourne Free, care of Agent-General of Victoria, 142 Queen Victoria Street, London, E.C.

LIST OF MEMBERS xi

Library, Bibliothèque, Nationale, Paris. ⎫
" Athenæum, Boston, U.S.A. ⎪ per Kegan Paul, Trench,
" Public, Boston, U.S.A. ⎬ Trübner & Co., Dryden
" Harvard College, U.S.A. ⎪ House, 43 Gerrard Street,
" Worcester Free, Mass., U.S.A. ⎭ Soho, London, W.

" New York State, Albany, New York, U.S.A. ⎫ per G. E. Stechert,
" Columbia University, New York City, U.S.A. ⎬ 2 Star Yard, Carey Street, London, W.C.

" Public, New York, U.S.A. ⎫
" Newberry, Chicago, Illinois, U.S.A. ⎪ per B. F. Stevens
" New York Historical Society. ⎬ and Brown, 4
" Public, Detroit, Michigan, U.S.A. ⎪ Trafalgar Square,
" Pennsylvanian Historical Society, Philadelphia, U.S.A. ⎭ London, W.C.

" Company, Philadelphia, U.S.A. ⎫
" Yale University, New Haven, Conn., U.S.A. ⎪ c/o E. G. Allen,
" Congress, U.S.A. ⎬ 28 Henrietta Street, Covent
" Cornell University, Ithaca, New York, U.S.A. ⎪ Garden, London, W.C.
" The Watkinson, Hartford, Conn., U.S.A. ⎭

" State Historical Society of Wisconsin, U.S.A., c/o H. Sotheran & Co., 140 Strand, London, W.C.
" New Hampshire State, Concord, New Hampshire, U.S.A.
Literary and Philosophical Society, Newcastle-upon-Tyne.
Longstaff, G. B., M.A., Highlands, Putney Heath, London, S.W.
Lockett, Richard Cyril, 34 Alexandra Drive, Liverpool.

MONK, R. B. M., Lingard-, Fulshaw Hall, Wilmslow, Cheshire.

NEWBIGGING, Thomas, C.E., Ardwell, Delahays Road, Hale, Cheshire.
New England Historic-Genealogical Society, 18 Somerset Street, Boston, U.S.A.
Nicholson, Major, 16 Pulteney Street, Bath.
North, Colonel Bordrigge N., Newton Hall, Kirkby Lonsdale.

PARKER, Colonel John, Browsholme Hall, Clitheroe.
Parr, J. Charlton, Grappenhall Heyes, Warrington.
Pemberton, Major-General, C.S.I., 13 Cresswell Gardens, South Kensington, London, S.W.
Philips, Herbert, Sutton Oaks, Macclesfield.
Pink, W. D., Winslade, Lowton, Newton-le-Willows.

RADCLIFFE, Sir David, Rosebank, Knowsley, near Prescot.

Radcliffe, R. D., M.A., F.S.A., Old Swan, Liverpool.
Ridgway, T. J., Wildersmoor House, Lymm, near Warrington.
Rigg, Henry, 49 Gordon Road, Ealing, London, W.
Roper, W. O., F.S.A., Yealand Conyers, Carnforth.
Roscoe, James, M.A., Oatlands, Harrogate.
Royden, E. B., Blyth Lodge, Bromborough, Birkenhead.
Rylands, John Paul, F.S.A., 2 Charlesville. Birkenhead.
Rylands, W. Harry, F.S.A., 1 Campden Hill Place, Notting Hill, London, W.

SANDERS, Rev. F., M.A., The Vicarage, Hoylake, Birkenhead.
Sephton, The Rev. J., M.A., 90 Huskisson Street, Liverpool.
Smith, J. C. C., F.S.A., Eastfield, Whitchurch, Reading.
Stanning, Rev. Canon, M.A., The Vicarage, Leigh, Lancashire.
Swettenham, Sir Alexander, K.C.M.G., The King's House, Jamaica.

TATTON, T. E., Wythenshawe, Northenden.
Taylor, Henry, 8 John Dalton Street, Manchester.
Tempest, Mrs., Broughton Hall, near Skipton.
Thornely, Samuel, Hatfield, Norton, near Worcester.
Threlfall, Henry S., 1 London Street, Southport.
Tonge, W. Asheton, Staneclyffe, Disley, Cheshire.
Toulmin, John, *Guardian* Office, Preston.
Tweedale, John, The Moorlands, Dewsbury.
Twemlow, Lieut.-Col. Francis R., D.S.O., Peatswood, Market Drayton.

WAGNER, Henry, M.A., F.S.A., 13 Half Moon Street, London, W.
Weldon, W. H., C.V.O., Norroy King of Arms, Heralds' College, London.
Wilkinson, William, M.A., Middlewood, Clitheroe.
Wilson, Colonel Edmund, F.S.A., Denison Hall, Leeds.
Woodcock, F. A., 8 St. James' Square, Manchester.
Worsley, P. J., Rodney Lodge, Clifton, Bristol.